SACRED ▌
of Bee, Butterfly, Earthworm, and Spider

"Please get this book and get back in touch with your mother—Nature. Reading about the sacredness of our earth creatures, the wild soul within you is ignited. Come to life! For anyone who wants to sustain themselves and the earth, this book is the medicine."

JAMES M. WANLESS, PH.D., AUTHOR OF
SUSTAINABLE LIFE AND *VOYAGER TAROT DECK*

"In this inspirational book bursting with ancient wisdom, we are reminded that some of the greatest examples of transformation occur in some of the smallest creatures upon the planet, such as the Honeybee, the Spider, the Worm, and the Butterfly. Together, like the medicine wheel, they remind us that life consists of continual cycles of creativity and change."

CHRISTINE R. PAGE, M.D., AUTHOR OF
THE HEALING POWER OF THE SACRED WOMAN

"The authors weave a fascinating tapestry of insight, arriving at the sacred consciousness of our interconnection with the innate wisdom, power, and love carried forward by early creation. A magical journey comes alive to the reader, quite an experiential book to read!"

PETER AMATO, AUTHOR OF *SOUL SILENCE*

"A refreshing dive into the living experience of Native American spirituality by two of the finest living translators of these traditions. How can one not love this book?"

ALLAN LESLIE COMBS, PH.D., DIRECTOR OF THE CENTER FOR
CONSCIOUSNESS STUDIES, CALIFORNIA INSTITUTE OF INTEGRAL
STUDIES, AND EDITOR OF *THOMAS BERRY, DREAMER OF THE EARTH*

"We live in a time where increasing numbers of people are turning once again toward the complex library of Nature, within which everything is true. The authors are to be commended for they have created sacred medicine to help us access those natural truths for guidance and wisdom."

HANK WESSELMAN, PH.D., ANTHROPOLOGIST AND AUTHOR OF *THE
BOWL OF LIGHT* AND COAUTHOR OF *AWAKENING TO THE SPIRIT WORLD*

"Sacred Medicine of Bee, Butterfly, Earthworm, and Spider illuminates the fascinating cycles, wisdom, and guidance of the insect realm. This beautiful, inspiring, and visionary text encourages us to walk the path of our soul's evolution with the support of the infinite depths of Nature's wisdom as our guide."

DANIELLE RAMA HOFFMAN, AUTHOR OF
THE TEMPLES OF LIGHT AND FOUNDER OF
DIVINE TRANSMISSIONS AND THOTH'S MAGIC ACADEMY

"The medicine wheel is a powerful and tangible path that has long been the basis for many people's spiritual walk. Star Wolf and Anna now offer a new dimension to these ancient teachings with the Instar Medicine Wheel. This is sure to be a great new tool in anyone's medicine bag."

REV. KATHRYN RAVENWOOD, AUTHOR OF
HOW TO CREATE SACRED WATER

"These insects teach us about renewal, strength, and illumination. As you journey through the pages of this wonderful book, may the shaman in all of you awaken to the beauty and power of the insect kingdom."

PANTHER WIND WOMAN (WIND DAUGHTER), MEDICINE CHIEF
OF THE PANTHER LODGE MEDICINE SOCIETY
AND KEEPER OF THE BETA STAR BUNDLE

"What a marvelous window this book provides into the magic, medicine, and mystery of the earth's smallest creatures and their connection not only to us but also to the stars. The visionary authors of *Sacred Medicine of Bee, Butterfly, Earthworm, and Spider* show us how these teachers are guiding us to our greater humanity."

THEA SUMMER DEER, AUTHOR OF *WISDOM OF THE PLANT DEVAS*
AND CLINICAL HERBALIST AND MEDICAL INTUITIVE

"All of life is interrelated and interconnected, and this amazing book shows how and why that will impact your life."

VON BRASCHLER, AUTHOR OF *SEVEN SECRETS OF TIME TRAVEL*

"Sacred Medicine of Bee, Butterfly, Earthworm, and Spider is a beautiful and significant book."

NITA GAGE, PH.D., DIRECTOR OF HEALER WITHIN RETREATS,
COFOUNDER OF NEUROIMAGINAL INSTITUTE,
AND AUTHOR OF *THE WOMEN IN STORAGE CLUB*

SACRED MEDICINE
of Bee, Butterfly, Earthworm, and Spider

Shamanic Teachers
of the Instar Medicine Wheel

Linda Star Wolf
and Anna Cariad-Barrett

Bear & Company
Rochester, Vermont • Toronto, Canada

Bear & Company
One Park Street
Rochester, Vermont 05767
www.BearandCompanyBooks.com

Text stock is SFI certified

Bear & Company is a division of Inner Traditions International

Library of Congress Cataloging-in-Publication Data
Wolf, Linda Star.
  Sacred medicine of bee, butterfly, earthworm, and spider : shamanic teachers of
the Instar medicine wheel / Linda Star Wolf and Anna Cariad-Barrett.
      p. cm.
  Summary: "Reveals spiritual lessons from insect archetypes of the Medicine
Wheel"—Provided by publisher.
  Includes bibliographical references (p.   ) and index.
  ISBN 978-1-59143-149-7 (pbk.) — ISBN 978-1-59143-806-9 (e-book)
  1. Shamanism. 2. Medicine wheels. 3. Spiritual life. I. Cariad-Barrett, Anna,
1983– II. Title.
  BF1621.W64 2013
  299'.93—dc23
                                                                2012016973

Printed and bound in the United States by Lake Book Manufacturing, Inc.
The text stock is SFI certified. The Sustainable Forestry Initiative® program
promotes sustainable forest management.

10   9   8   7   6   5   4   3   2   1

Text design and layout by Virginia Scott Bowman
This book was typeset in Garamond Premier Pro, Agenda, and Myriad Pro with
    J Roman and Italic used as display typefaces
Artwork by Francene Hart, based on designs by Anna Cariad-Barrett
Photo on page 18 by Ruth Anne Brown

To send correspondence to the authors of this book, mail a first-class letter to
the authors c/o Inner Traditions • Bear & Company, One Park Street, Rochester,
VT 05767, and we will forward the communication, or contact Linda Star Wolf
directly at **www.shamanicbreathwork.org** and Anna Cariad-Barrett at
www.instarmedicinewheel.com or **www.annacariadbarrett.com**.

We dedicate this book to the interconnected web of life, and the
unexpected wisdom teachers—great and small—
who illuminate its sacred mysteries.
This book is also dedicated to all those who are called to walk in
harmony with the natural world, remembering your true essence
along the way. As you open to the teachings of nature, your own
wisdom teacher emerges in sacred service.
Thank you for choosing to be all of who you are!

Contents

Foreword

When I first learned that Linda Star Wolf and Anna Cariad-Barrett were writing a book about the totemic power of insects, in particular Bee, Butterfly, Earthworm, and Spider, I secretly hoped that I would be asked to read the manuscript and perhaps write an endorsement. It is a great privilege for me to write the foreword for this book.

My first introduction to power animals and totems was given by initiation from my teacher Nadia Eagles in 1982. I was delighted. I felt a strong resonance with the concept of totemic relationships. My teacher, however, had strict rules—no insects and no creatures with fangs. She simply said they were dangerous, and I didn't give it much thought at the time; I was too interested in Elephants, Bears, Eagles, and Wooly Mammoths.

It was in the mid-1980s that I, quite unexpectedly, began receiving teachings about various power animals. Bee and Butterfly came quite naturally into the gathering of allies. It wasn't until Cobra showed up with a very intense journey to add to the work that was developing that I began to get nervous. Cobra offered a powerful journey of awakening kundalini that triggered my memory of Nadia's cautionary advice. I held back for about six months before I felt safe enough to give the teaching to a trusted friend and discovered its true potential. Cobra became one of the most important allies in my work, offering powerful gifts of healing and awakening consciousness. By the time Spider came to me, also in a very dramatic way, I already knew that whatever strictures Nadia had placed on the insect world were no longer necessary; the powers to heal often abide in the most dangerous and poisonous of creatures. Venoms that can kill are often the strongest medicines when given in appropriate doses.

Having coauthored two books with Star Wolf, and knowing what a deep and clear visionary seer she is, I was particularly interested in discovering what new and wondrous characteristics she had discovered in these four allies with whom I was already quite familiar (three of them appear in my book *Power Animal Meditations*). I was not disappointed! The collaboration between Star Wolf and Anna has brought forth a complex medicine wheel system that respectfully draws from a number of traditions. It maintains its own integrity as a unique expression of a transformative process that utilizes the power of these totems while empowering the reader to step up to the plate as co-creator in the interconnected web of life.

Anna's story of how she found herself in the midst of the insect world will resonate with all of us who have found ourselves dealing with magic that we don't initially understand. By staying the course, showing up, following her guidance, and doing her supportive research, she was richly rewarded—as will be her readers.

The purpose of the Instar Medicine Wheel is to replicate in our own life cycles the transformation that takes place for various insects during the period between molts. Caterpillars who become Monarch Butterflies go through five molts, or extreme changes, on their journey of metamorphosis. You will have the opportunity to go through many more on your journey through this Instar Medicine Wheel.

The cardinal directions of the Instar Medicine Wheel are portals held by the main characters. Cicada, Dragonfly, Cricket, and Katydid add to the multidimensional geometry of the structure of the wheel. Each insect has its specific pattern, which intersects and overlays to create an energetic matrix within which a multitude of possibilities for healing and transformation are available. This pathworking considers more than the essential gifts, teachings, and medicine of the individual species involved. The background information on the life cycles and behaviors of these allies are thoroughly covered and well researched. The journeys are deep and complex and will surely take you into a deeper understanding of your own potential to grow and change and ultimately find your sacred purpose in this life.

The ongoing relationships you make with these allies require only your attention. After you have completed the journey of the wheel, take time to further develop your new relationships and you will surely discover the many other teachings that are waiting to be discovered. This book is filled with gifts that keep on giving!

NICKI SCULLY

Nicki Scully has been a healer and teacher of shamanism since 1978. She lectures worldwide and specializes in spiritual tours to sacred sites in Egypt, Peru, and other countries. She is the author of *Power Animal Meditations* and *Alchemical Healing: A Guide to Spiritual, Physical, and Transformational Medicine.*

Preface
Anna's Journey

Birthing the Instar Medicine Wheel

Spider, Earthworm, Honeybee, and Butterfly have had a special presence in my life for many years. As an avid organic gardener, I have often stopped and marveled at the efforts of the Earthworm. As the majority of earth within which my plants grow has passed through the mouth of an Earthworm—like the Divine passing through a sacred channel—I often refer to them as "Priestesses of the Earth." I stop in my work when one of their pink, shining bodies emerges and place it in a safe location away from my spade, blessing it on its journey.

I close my eyes and listen to the golden hum of the Bees in my garden. They nuzzle into the center of flowers, pollinating and delighting in the glory of summer. I have always been fascinated by patterns and fractals in nature, and the perfect hexagonal forms of honeycomb delight me. Honeybee has buzzed its way into my creative dreaming and writing for many years.

Butterflies seem to me to have been touched by a painter's brush. They are living art that floats among us. More than that, Butterfly has illuminated the journey of metamorphosis, with all its travails and opportunities, when I have faced my own rebirthings of self.

I enjoy the Spiders in my home, knowing that they eat other bugs, and I have always loved the stories about Spider found in the indigenous cultures of the Southwest. When I visited Canyon de Chelly national monument and saw Spider Rock, the energy of this immense spire rising eight hundred feet in the air drew me to the edge of the cliff on which I stood. I opened my heart to the activational energy of Spider Woman and spread my arms like wings, as storm-filled clouds raced overhead. It was profoundly energizing and inspiring!

As I write this, a small striped Spider is hanging by a gossamer strand from my computer monitor. Last night I dreamed of webs pulsing and shimmering with light. It seems that these animal teachers have become my constant companions, especially Spider, reminding me to pay attention and illuminating the unfolding path of the Instar Medicine Wheel in my life.

In late winter 2011 the concept of an integrated medicine wheel made up of insects and related animal teachers entered my mind. These animal teachers, whether because they are small or because they are the subject of phobias and dislike, have sometimes been overlooked in sacred teachings. The integrative wisdom of insects certainly has never taken center stage. Having researched these animals extensively for this book, it has become clear to me that insects and small related animals—Spiders, Earthworms, and others—lead dramatic, profound, and surprising lives. We just need to learn to pay attention and begin to explore the small creatures that inhabit our world.

More importantly, it became clear to me that the integration of these animal teachers into one medicine wheel highlighted important shared teachings and medicine in the areas of sacred purpose and transformation. Just as each direction of the traditional medicine wheel is the keeper of certain elements, animals, and insights, each animal in the Instar Medicine Wheel brings a unique perspective on these teachings. In addition, the cardinal directions of the Instar Medicine Wheel create a progressive, developmental model for understanding the human life cycle and the evolution of human consciousness. The Instar Medicine Wheel offers us a special teaching, much needed in these times: how to fully embody our Divine potential, integrating higher frequencies of love and wisdom, while staying grounded and harmonious in our human bodies.

When I conceived the initial concept for this medicine wheel, I mentally filed it away, knowing that it was percolating for later expression. I finally understood why I had spent all those years daydreaming about Earthworms and Honeybees. I also began seeing Spiders in many new places in my life: in the shower and hanging in front of my face at odd moments—it was a startling experience!

Later that spring I traveled to Isis Cove, a retreat center in the magical Blue Ridge Mountains of North Carolina, home of Venus Rising Association for Transformation and Venus Rising University, for a monthlong intensive training. This was to be my final coursework for a doctoral program in shamanic psychospiritual studies. It was an incredible and transformational month, during which I connected with new soul friends, gained advanced facilitation skills to complement my background as a counselor and spiritual facilitator, and made new and transformational discoveries about my heart, soul, and psyche.

Throughout this course, Spider continued to show up with increasing frequency and intensity in my life. I had a powerful Shamanic Breathwork journey in which Spider came forward as a teacher, and the energy of my work as a medicine woman was revealed to me. My cojourneyer for that breathwork reported that physical Spiders attempted to climb onto my mat throughout this journey. In fact, it became a common occurrence for Spiders to catch a ride on me as I hiked in the mountains, or simply to come sit on me when I was journaling or reflecting.

Toward the end of the monthlong course, an image came to me of a Spider superimposed over a six-pointed star. I painted it with shimmering blues and purples. The next day, I hiked to the top of the mountain at Isis Cove to do yoga on the Spirit Temple deck and meditate. After yoga I sat down with my journal and asked, "Okay, what is going on here with Spider and star energies in my life? Is this somehow a part of my sacred medicine to share with the world?" Within ten minutes, three different Spiders had shown up. I would look up from writing, and there was another eight-legged arachnid! The first walked in front of me, tracing a path across the yoga mat. The next sat on my leg for a few minutes. The third crossed the mat to sit on my foot where my toe had been amputated, removed years earlier—due to cancer—and which I had taken to calling my "shaman's toe" as it was a live wire for energy in my body. "Okay," I said, "I'm listening!" Spider affirmed the truth I felt resonating in my soul.

I shared my experiences and the image I had seen with my mentor and doctoral advisor, Linda Star Wolf. She and I both processed this information and realized that a Spider-related medicine name was emerging for me: Blue Spider Woman. The next day I shared my calling to step in to this name with Star Wolf and a women's circle but expressed doubts about claiming a name whose energy I had only begun to understand. After I stopped speaking, Star Wolf turned to me and shared that while I had been talking a Spider had climbed from the earth to the Blue Star medicine bundle held in her arms and then turned around to begin its descent. I looked and saw the Spider floating on a gossamer strand back down to the grass, suspended from the medicine bundle. I couldn't believe my eyes! Star Wolf laughed and said, "This is getting a little ridiculous!" I smiled and agreed; Spider had been trying intensely for three months to share a message with me about my sacred work in the world and the essence of who I am. It was time to listen. Once again I opened my heart and my arms to the air and the mountains surrounding me and stepped forward to proclaim my new medicine name to Earth and sky!

Returning from the intensive monthlong course, I intended to relax and decompress. I had received Spider's message, which was a powerful experience, and thought that would be it for a while. To my surprise, Spirit called right away. I began to have dreams and visions about Spider, Earthworm, Honeybee, Butterfly, and the medicine wheel. I began to see images of sacred geometry related to each creature, which were clearly intended to activate consciousness, healing, and developmental transformation. I journaled and drew furiously, buying canvases and paintbrushes because these new images of the medicine wheel wanted to be manifested and expressed with urgency. The Instar Medicine Wheel was being born through my heart-mind into the world. The thought of a quiet spring melted away.

I contacted Star Wolf and shared the medicine wheel concept and the dreams I had been having for the first time. I asked her if I was crazy to be putting so much focus and fascination into a concept about "bugs." My ego had altogether different plans for my doctoral dissertation, but Spirit was signaling me, loud and clear. I learned long ago not to ignore divine symbols and messages in my life: they have opened new doors, insights, and adventures that have taken me exactly where I needed to be. Yet nothing has ever been so insistent and intense as the Instar Medicine Wheel. To my surprise, Star Wolf affirmed that my dissertation project had revealed itself and shared her own fascination and vision in this area, namely with Dragonfly and the Great Star Nations. She suggested incorporating Dragonfly, Cicada, and Cricket and partnered with me to fully develop the Instar Medicine Wheel. Our dialogue progressed, and we decided to collaborate together on the journey of this book. Over the following months, these animal teachers each began sharing their unique wisdom with us. We received additional initiations into the instar archetypal mystery school on the deepest levels of our beings. Both Star Wolf and I were separately hospitalized and experienced profound health journeys during the writing of this book that were directly related to being initiated to the deepest levels of its teachings. We were both also separately called to visit the Sacred Valley of the Peruvian Andes in the midst of writing this book. A number of sacred planetary locations and cultural frequencies appear to be connected to the transformative energies of the Instar Medicine Wheel, including the Quechua culture of Peru, the ancient Egyptian mysteries, and the islands and people of New Zealand. These mysterious connections are unfolding *now,* at this evolutionary time on the planet.

These animal teachers often show up in surprising ways in my life. Spider, the original creative weaver, still comes to sit with me when I write and visits me in my dreams. The day after I finished writing a chapter on Butterfly, a species of giant, luminous, green Caterpillar I had never seen before crossed my path. These and other animal teachers regularly surprise, teach, and delight me. I am filled with gratitude for the creative blessings that have filled my life, and for the guiding presence of the instar animal teachers and Great Spirit.

During the writing process, a powerful dream vision came to me. In the dream, I was gathered with Star Wolf and a circle of women. With a laser-clear energy that pierced the fabric of my being, Star Wolf said to the circle, "I would like *Neesa* to come forward and call in the directions of the medicine wheel." One woman in the circle questioned why I should come forward. Star Wolf again repeated her words, "I would like *Neesa* to come forward and call in the directions of the medicine wheel."

In the dream I knew with certainty that *Neesa* meant me, though I had never heard the name before. The next morning, when I woke up, I put my detective hat on and began an Internet search to see if I could shed some light on *Neesa*. At first nothing appeared. But then I put the words *Neesa* and *medicine wheel* together in the search engine. Something popped up that truly blew my circuits! "Neesa" means *Grandmother Moon* and is a song originated by and attributed to Grandmother Twylah Nitsch, the Wolf Clan Grandmother of the Seneca Tribe, who was the teacher and mentor of Linda Star Wolf. It is commonly sung in circles of women who have been taught by or honor the traditions of Grandmother Twylah. I had never heard of the song and couldn't believe that the big, wide Internet had led me right back to Grandmother Twylah and Star Wolf. When I e-mailed Star Wolf about the dream and the song, Star Wolf said as soon as she read the word *Neesa*, she felt that Grandmother Twylah had given me my true spirit name. Star Wolf said she had been singing that song for years.

I began to realize that I was being called on to share the wisdom that was coming through me about the medicine wheel. This triggered some of my deepest fears and wounds. I had come to Earth feeling different from everyone else, a sense I have had my entire life. Not better or worse, just wired with certain abilities and sensitivities. My shamanic path has helped me become the human being I am today, but in my early years it was at times a source of wounding and trauma. I experienced a difficult dichotomy between the soul knowing of my purpose in this lifetime and the limitations of being a child, at times powerless and overwhelmed in an adult world. My father's alcoholism and death had a profound effect on me, as did being the recurrent new kid in school where it wasn't cool to be bright and creative. I faced a number of traumatic life situations and was often overwhelmed by this sensory overload of my sensitive nature. I became used to feeling isolated and learned to shut down my heart and creative gifts in many situations to survive. In my teen years I vacillated between depression and feeling like an astronaut floating above my body. It didn't feel safe to be me and feel, so I stopped feeling.

I share this because, to this day, after so much personal journeying and growth, it still scares me to open my heart and share my authentic truth with others. It was only after I had a rare form of cancer at the age of twenty-two that I committed to being fully on the planet and began opening my heart. It has been a long road to self-love and acceptance.

When I had the dream about Neesa, I felt all my fears about being myself in the world again. I have always been scared, on a deep level, that if people knew the real me they would reject me. The wounds that I carried from childhood had created an internal belief that there was something defective about me. Yet I knew that I was called to service. I knew that if I did not stay in alignment with my soul purpose to share the teachings and creativity that were coming through me, I wouldn't stay sane in this life. I would get very depressed and shut down. While it was a choice, I know that "becoming Neesa," becoming the medicine woman I was meant to be, was the only choice to make. Just as Grandmother Moon orbits around Earth emanating her loving presence, this spirit name has given me greater insight and acceptance into my nature and purpose as a planetary guardian and advocate for all beings. I am passionate about honoring and creating safe space both for the new generations of children coming to this planet and the insect wisdom that sustains Earth's ecology. And I am called to assist others as they journey the transformative path of sacred purpose.

I share this story with you, because I believe it is essential for each of us to show up as our authentic selves, be centered in our hearts, and express our truths. When I work with children, I encourage them to be creative and work together, to BEE the change they wish to see, because this is how magic is created. It's that simple! Magic is just waiting to walk through the wise doorway of our hearts, when we each honor our sacred purpose and weave these creative tendrils into the collective web of life. This is how we will move through these times of transformation on the planet with grace, creativity, and innovation. We need all of us. I hope this book will provide an exciting new pathway that supports your own journey of sacred purpose and transformation. This is the shamanic medicine of my wounded heart, alchemically transformed, that I now share with others in service.

I know in my heart that these animal wisdom keepers are stepping forward to guide humanity, helping us to embody our soul's potential now, and changing our lives forever.

ANNA CARIAD-BARRETT
NEESA, BLUE SPIDER WOMAN

Acknowledgments

We would like to express our sincere gratitude to the incredible team at Inner Traditions • Bear & Company, especially Jon Graham, Jeanie Levitan, Ehud Sperling, John Hays, Manzanita Carpenter, Cynthia Fowles, Olatundji Akpo-Sani, Erica Robinson, Peri Swan, and Jamaica Burns Griffin. We would also like to thank visionary artist Francene Hart for creating the beautiful cover artwork and adapting the illustrations found throughout the book. Your artwork truly brings the instar medicine of this book to life! Special thanks to Jim Wilson, creator of the *Cricket Chorus Meditation* CD, for helping our readers to receive healing and inspiration from this amazing creature chorus!

A special thank-you to Casey Piscitelli, Dennis Corvin-Blackburn, and Brad Collins for the sacred crafting and building of the first Instar Medicine Wheel located in the Children's Peace Park at Isis Cove on Dove Mountain. And a big wolf hug and thank-you to all our shamanic grandchildren, especially Aidan, Cian, Ryland, Thomas, Madeline, Bliss, Anthony, Mikey, Katir, Harper, Lily, Nizzy, Aurora, Dahlby, Harlow, Bodhi, Olivia, Max, Maddy, Leilani, and Bella. It is these children who call us back to the magical world that resides within all the creatures who live in the sacred garden. Thank you for being the teachers you are and the visionary leaders we know you to be.

We also honor and send loving gratitude to the animal wisdom keepers of the Instar Medicine Wheel and the sacred natural world. You inspire us to look within and reconnect with our own essential natures!

May your wisdom inspire the world to weave unity into diversity with compassion and peace. We also send gratitude and love to Seneca Wolf Clan Grandmother Twylah Nitsch for sharing her wisdom so that the teachings may live on in our hearts and for serving as our guide throughout this instar journey.

Anna would like to thank her circle of family and soul friends who have loved, supported, and believed in both her and this work from the very beginning. In particular:

The generations of women who have come before me and those who continue to touch my life, most especially my mother, Carol Chase. You have taught me to honor and listen to the intuitive wisdom and visions that are part of my being. Your loving legacy is the foundation on which this book was written.

Charlei Chase (1945–2012), teacher, friend, and father of my heart, thank you for teaching me to believe in and reach for my potential, and for always encouraging my writing. I can feel your spirit soaring and your love expanding everywhere!

Star Wolf, my coauthor and mentor, thank you for joining me on this instar journey, for your tremendous shamanic heart, and for your dedication to the people and creatures of this planet.

Robert Barrett, my beloved husband and best friend, for believing in me and being my partner in every adventure. Your lion heart inspires me and brings such joy to my life.

Anyaa McAndrew, thank you for guiding me throughout the Shamanic Priestess Process and Magdalene Mysteries and inspiring me to discover, reclaim, and embody the Divine Feminine mysteries. Reclaiming our feminine wisdom is an essential aspect of journeying with the Instar Medicine Wheel.

Thank you to my Shamanic Priestess sister, Anne McQuinn, for your wonderful early support and editing skills with the Crystal Web Dance meditation journey. You are a kindred spirit and true advocate for all the instar animal teachers!

Star Wolf sends her gratitude to all her family members, soul friends, and Venus Rising students, for your commitment to your healing transformation for yourselves and the world. In addition, Star Wolf would like to thank:

Great Mystery, I offer a heart filled with infinite gratitude to the Blue Star mysteries that continue to inspire and inform my life and path daily, and to Dragonfly, guardian of the Blue Star Mystery School.

Thank you to Grandmother Twylah Nitsch and my own Mammy Jones for teaching me how to humbly listen, love, and learn from all of Earth's creature teachers, both large and small.

Also a special thanks to past medicine wheel teachers Sun Bear, Karen Kelley, Wind Daughter, Daniel Giamario, Erick Gonzalez, and all those who have shared their sacred medicine wheel teachings with me over the years.

Thank you to my beloved husband and soul mate, Brad Collins, for your steadfast love and support on the ever-changing spiral path of life.

A special wolf hug to my son Casey Piscitelli, for your assistance in capturing some of the downloads around the creatures and your editing skills and great sense of humor!

Blessings and gratitude to Anna Neesa, my coauthor for this book, who is truly a magical creature herself, part human, part star being, part fairy/elf!

Long live the Garden and may we all show our gratitude to Pachamama–Mother Earth by becoming the pollinators and ambassadors for all creatures great and small!

Introduction

Illuminating the
Instar Medicine Wheel

Eagle soars above us in the sky. Wolf howls to the moon from a mountain precipice. Mother Grizzly Bear protects her cubs with maternal ferocity. These animal archetypes are majestic and familiar to many of us. Yet, beneath the tree roots of the cedar, hanging on tendrils suspended in the misty air, a presence exists that, while minute and intricate, has grand implications for human consciousness.

The insect world and its related organisms are often overlooked, batted away, or eradicated by people. Indeed, though often ignored, these creatures are a daily presence in our lives and exist in astounding numbers all around us. We step on thousands of insects while walking on the earth. More than 425 million insects, arthropods, and related organisms can be found in one acre of forest soil, or 9,759 per square foot. A cubic mile of air contains 25 million insects and related animals. For each human being, there are 1 million of these diminutive creatures. Insects comprise approximately half of all named species; more than half when related organisms, such as Earthworms and Spiders, are added to the count.[1]

As human beings, how are we to understand and relate to these animal members of the web of life? It is easy to relate to the medicine of Raven, winging his way past, or shiver at the mystery of Coyote's unnerving cry. Yet how do we relate to the subtle presence of this

1

multitude of insects and their ilk? How can they be teachers in our lives, and what can we learn from them? Do they have a significant message for humanity at this time in our collective journey?

The Instar Medicine Wheel explores the sacred teachings of nine animals: Spider, Honeybee, Earthworm, Butterfly, Cicada, Dragonfly, Grasshopper, Cricket, and Katydid. Each of these animal beings is the bearer of consciousness. Each scuttles, glides, and flies a distinctive archetypal life path that serves the unfolding of human consciousness, if only we were to listen.

Historically, a number of indigenous cultures around the world have honored and followed the spiritual paths of these animal teachers. The Hopi, Pueblo, and Navajo/Dineh peoples of the American Southwest, as well as the Teotihuacan civilization of Mexico, have long venerated Spider Woman as a creator deity and a liaison between Divinity and humanity. In ancient times the Honeybee was celebrated and honored by Mediterranean Minoan-Mycenaean, Central American Mayan, Indian Hindu, and Egyptian cultures. In Minoan and other traditions, priestesses who followed the sacred path of the Honeybee were called the "Melissae." Similarly, the Delphic oracle priestesses were often referred to as "the Bees."[2]

Cardinal direction holders of the Instar Medicine Wheel, the Spider, Earthworm, Honeybee, and Butterfly, are all creators of sacred patterns, whose geometric structures are highly archetypal and activational to human consciousness. Spider weaves a glistening web. Earthworm is a vessel for new earth as it moves through her. Honeybee nurtures her children and offers us sweet honey from hexagonal honeycombs. Caterpillar transforms himself within the chrysalis and emerges at an evolved octave of being—the Butterfly. These sacred patterns have the potential to act as portals for transformation and manifestation between Spirit and Matter, which this text will cover in depth. These four beings have much to teach us. Most important, to paraphrase Teilhard de Chardin, they are teaching us how to be spiritual beings having a human experience; how to be fully embodied and fully divine as we walk our human life paths. It is often the smallest or most unexpected teachers who offer us our most profound lessons.

The medicine wheel holds diverse elements in balance and highlights their sacred relationship to one another. No direction or element is more important than another, and truly, without the community of all on the sacred wheel, life would not exist for any. The medicine wheel is a celebration and teaching about the gifts of life and how they can enrich human experience. Accordingly, as we begin to journey with the medicine of each individual animal on the wheel, we also begin to understand that—in their integrated relationship with one another—a synergy exists. The Instar Medicine Wheel offers us a sacred medicine that is larger than the sum of its parts and that can bless and inform our sacred purpose and soul expression as "human beings doing" on Planet Earth.

Imagine living your life fully embodied and centered in divine knowing as you express your sacred purpose in the world. What would this feel like, and how can you step in to this whole sense of being and purpose? The Instar Medicine Wheel is ready to teach you. At this time of transformation on Planet Earth and within human consciousness, it is essential that each of us embody our sacred purpose for the health of our world. We each have beneficial gifts and wisdom to contribute to the collective. We are truly the ones we have been waiting for, and the time is now.

To fully express our sacred purpose, we must first explore how to be in harmonic, authentic relationship with our human bodies and understand how we relate to sacred purpose in each phase of our lives. Each of the four cardinal direction animal wisdom keepers expresses a distinctive way of being in relationship to the Earth and sacred purpose through the dance and journey of their bodies. They seek sinuous paths in the darkness, enriching the earth. They practice the sacred rite of going within, letting go, and dissolving to all that was once known in service to their higher selves. They dance and weave the web of life, teaching us about receptive creativity and interrelationship. They emerge from honey-kissed golden portals to fly a sacred union dance with the flowers. Insects and related creatures have the power to teach us how to transform ourselves and express our soul's purpose through the dynamism of activating our bodies in the present moment.

Each animal wisdom keeper in this book goes through significant transformational and developmental changes in its life cycle. They break through the limitations of smaller skins, emerging as new, more complex creatures. These teachers climb up from under the Earth after years underground, to exist in the expansive Air. They take flight, where before they had no wings. These animals also transform Earth's ecosystems with their presence, and transform the elements to create new substances, such as honey, soil, and silken webs. In scientific language, the word *instar* refers to the developmental stage between each molt (the shedding of form) that insects go through before reaching maturity. The very essence of the medicine wheel discussed in this book is the transformational journey we undertake on the path of sacred purpose. This is the shamanic wisdom that these animal teachers have come forward to share with us. Accordingly, the sacred medicine wheel of Dragonfly, Honeybee, and their kin is called the Instar Medicine Wheel.

As we emerge from childhood into adulthood, we take our first step on the path of exploring, expressing, and contributing our sacred purpose for the collective highest good. Each insect on the wheel represents a life-cycle phase and a particular archetype of sacred purpose and transformation. As we walk our human paths, we journey through each of the doorways of these animal wisdom keepers. At certain points in our journey, we emerge through their transformational portals, utilizing their sacred patterns as maps in our consciousness. Each archetype has its own dance of manifestation and transformation, its own song of bringing Spirit into Matter. Each animal teacher has a distinctive way of relating to the elements: Earth, Air, Water, Fire, and Spirit.

Perhaps, at certain points in your life, you have found yourself in the darkness, breaking down the old. Through this, you may have discovered a gift for transforming whatever no longer serves you into new forms, fertile with potential for the future. You may have found yourself withdrawing from the outside world, needing to turn within—

to dissolve into yourself, emerging sometime later more radiant than before. At these times, in the darkness, in the unknown, you may have asked yourself these questions: Why am I here? What is the purpose of this time in my life? What is the big picture, and am I alone? During this period, you were embodying the archetypal vessel of transformation and connection to the Divine through lived, human experience. Know that you were not alone and are not alone today as you continue to grow into your sacred purpose and power. Your life is the synergic center of the medicine wheel.

Perhaps you have experienced your creative body as a sweet liquid center, generating or sustaining life with your nurturing attention. Bringing children or new ideas into the world, loving and guiding them. Finding sacred union with a divine consort as you co-created future generations and new wisdom—tasting the sweetness of life together. You may be finding new expressions of your divinity in this sacred work.

You may find yourself sovereign, once again, spinning your web of dreams and waiting. Having faith that, as you ride the tendrils of your own creation in the swirling air, you are in the perfect place to receive the visions and understanding that will sustain and bless the next seven generations. (For many indigenous cultures, the impact on the next seven generations is considered when evaluating a course of action or worthiness of a cause.) If you build it, grace will come.

In this time of transformation, we all yearn for this grace. We need our wise elders and weavers to vision the future and plant the seeds for that which will sustain the next generations. We need our pollen-spangled midwives tending the hives and sweet lovers meeting in sacred union, nurturing new co-creations. We need to remain humble, close to earth, as we learn how to bring the Divine through our heart-mind-bodies in collective service. We need to find new winged expressions of ourselves. We need those who sustain life as an energetic conduit, connecting unity and diversity through the heart. We need shamanic journeyers who delve into the depths of initiation, and soaring flyers into the highest dimensions of consciousness. It is time to step in to the Instar Medicine Wheel and become a synergic embodiment of these unexpected animal wisdom keepers. The time is now.

In this book we will explore nine instar animal wisdom keepers: Earthworm, Honeybee, Butterfly, Spider, Cicada, Dragonfly, and the Grasshopper/Cricket/Katydid family. Because they are mentors and keepers of the sacred directions offering insights to the reader, the names of these animal teachers are capitalized in this book. (Out of respect for the natural world, all animals, directions, and elements will also be capitalized.)

Each animal teacher will be given a rich context in which to understand its multifaceted nature. All these creatures are capable of extraordinary physical feats and creations. They also face daunting challenges in the face of human ecological stresses. Our exploration will include biological and ecological discussions, with specific attention paid to current environmental themes and how humans can relate to these wise animals in mutually enriching ways. The instar wisdom keepers also have a rich history of mythological and spiritual interpretation and celebration in diverse cultures around the world. This heritage and how it informs contemporary partnership with these animals will also be explored.

As we discover the contextual foundation of each creature—so that we can be grounded in our understanding of their medicine—we will begin to plumb the depths of their teachings on transformation and sacred purpose. You will have the opportunity to journey directly with all the instar animal wisdom keepers, delving into the portals of their sacred patterns and unlocking hidden aspects of who you are along the way. You will be able to create a foundation for sacred purpose and self-understanding at each stage of your life cycle. New meaning, perspective, and structure will be found that illuminates the dark and challenging points of transformation through which we emerge as more authentic, whole human beings. We will offer experiential practices—such as archetypal dances, Shamanic Breathwork journeys, and visioning exercises—that you can carry into your daily life to enhance transformation and manifestation. You will come to know, on a deep level, how profoundly connected you are to myriad life-forms—a network of grace and illumination.

After we have finished exploring the cardinal directions of the sacred medicine wheel, we will introduce new animal teachers in a discussion of the Great Above, Below, and Center/Within. We will dance with the Great Star Nations and their teachings, including Blue Star frequencies of higher love and wisdom, the Earth dimensions below our planet's surface, and the heart path of unity located in the center of each cell, being, and the entire universe.

Finally, we will discuss the sacred synergy that occurs when the animal archetypes are integrated into one energy being and one multi-dimensional initiatory sacred purpose path. In this time of planetary transformation, this synergy is an incredible opportunity for expansion and evolution of human consciousness. As you embody the integrated Instar Medicine Wheel, you will become one more cell in the universal body, enlivening this collective unfolding with your sacred purpose. As the collective human psyche embodies this new form of integrated sacred purpose, our relationship to Mother Earth, her creatures, one another, and our own sense of collective human purpose will shift to a more harmonic, balanced frequency.

What would it feel like to dance with the eight legs of Spider; to fly with Butterfly's wings; to experience the infinite cycle of death and rebirth with Earthworm's fluid form; to fly, gold-and-black-banded, carrying the sweet essences of life back to your hive? What would it feel like to sing a shamanic medicine song that pierces your very soul with its truth, to fly through all the dimensions as a visionary messenger, and to infuse the web of life with your sacred purpose? What would it feel like to integrate these energies into your being and be able to access all of them at the same time? The animals of the Instar Medicine Wheel are beckoning to you. It is time. Many blessings to you on your journey with this sacred medicine wheel.

1
The Medicine Wheel
Ancient and Contemporary

The traditions of the medicine wheel are as varied as they are ancient. With no definitive written records of their purpose to the most ancient tribes, we are left with remnants of forgotten ceremony and mysticism— a heritage of oral tradition embraced by shamans and seekers to this day.

However, the power and significance of the medicine wheel as a spiritual tool is as strong today as evidence shows it was for the ancients. Remnants of age-old wheels show that their construction was invariably aligned to the four (or more) directions and the rising of various stars and constellations. Indeed, similar attention to cosmological alignments can be seen in the ruins of other lost civilizations all over the world. While in more recent times medicine wheels have been brought to the attention of the Western world through the Native American tradition, their similarity to the spiritual tools of other cultures cannot be ignored. Consider the concentric circles of Stonehenge, the Indian mandala, and the Mayan calendar.

What is clear is that the circular shape, the directional alignment, and the connection to nature are programmed into human consciousness as a means of bringing about spiritual alchemy. Modern wheels share these alignments—a testament to our enduring fascination with and reverence for nature and the heavenly bodies. Some wheels contain specific numbers of stones, indicating attention to a form of prehistoric numerology. Tradition holds that medicine wheels not only served as a type of lunar calendar but were symbols of peace and harmony, a means of communion with the spirits, and venues for ritual and ceremony and perhaps celebration and dance.

This universal appeal has translated into a resurgence of the medicine wheel not only in the native cultures that have kept this tradition alive but also in modern-day mysticism, as native rituals and the esoteric teachings of ancient wise ones enjoy a new popularity with the shamans, mystics, seekers, and soul-journeyers of today. It is worth remembering as well that these monuments were of great practical use to the ancients.

The science of keeping track of the equinoxes would have told farmers when to plant and when to harvest, when the rains would come and when the dry season would begin, when the river would flood and when it would recede. The very survival of some cultures would have depended on this knowledge. While modern science makes it unnecessary to consult medicine wheels for these purposes, we can still find practical value in the spiritual connections and personal growth we derive from spiritual practices. As our spiritual teacher Grandmother Twylah Nitsch used to say, "True spirituality grows corn on the earth." In her signature simple but eloquent way, she explained that the way to tell if something is of true spiritual merit is if it is truly life-giving—if it fits into the cycle of life in the way of all true spiritual traditions.

THE MEDICINE WHEEL LINEAGE OF STAR WOLF

Just as medicine wheels have served important purposes for various tribes in history, my personal connection with them has evolved through the years. My understanding of the wheel is a collection of my experiences with many different teachers. Therefore, when describing it, it is impossible to simply say, "The teachings of the medicine wheel are . . ." Just as one might stumble across myriad explanations for the meaning and significance of Stonehenge, so is the medicine wheel experience a subjective, personal experience.

For example, one of the most popular medicine wheel teachers of the twentieth century was Sun Bear.[1] Sun Bear was a medicine man of Ojibwa descent who, in the 1960s and 1970s, had a vision of bringing the medicine wheel tradition back into the forefront of Native American spirituality. Sun Bear believed strongly that the resurrection of his people's teachings would include the passing of these traditions on to those of both Native and non-Native descent. For this he encountered resistance. Non-Natives considered the wheel, along with all other Native rituals and ceremonies, pagan or satanic. Many Native Americans resisted his teachings because of a general distrust for outsiders and because it drew attention to their ceremonies, many of which were banned by the United States government through the early 1970s.

However, Sun Bear's vision proved to be wise. His medicine wheel ceremonies and his books on spirituality, Earth astrology, and the medicine wheel became very popular, and his following grew to include spiritual seekers from all walks of life. Some controversy continues to this day among more traditional Native American teachers who believe these teachings should remain the sole heritage of Native peoples.

A sacred medicine wheel, in the tradition of Sun Bear's teachings and vision, resides at our Isis Cove Retreat Center in the mountains of western North Carolina. The stones were placed in the winter of 2009 and brought to life with ceremony, ritual, and dance in the summer of 2010 by Sun Bear's student and adopted granddaughter, Wind Daughter. The wheel is now part of Venus Rising University's Earth Temple and consists of thirty-seven stones (thirty-six traditional stones plus a Star Stone), each weighing between 1,500 and 2,000 pounds and placed in the pattern envisioned by Sun Bear as a young man.

Another cultural example of the medicine wheel comes from a recent trip I took to Machu Picchu, Peru, with a group of students. I remarked on the remains of what seemed to be a sundial that looked like a kind of medicine wheel. Despite the obvious similarities, I was quickly corrected by a guide who stated that it would not have been called by that name—that it was merely an instrument to measure the procession of the equinoxes. What is clear is that for thousands of years we have understood that there is a connection between us and the Heavens—as Above, so Below. We have created sundials, temples, pyramid calendars, standing stones, medicine wheels, and all manner of ceremonial tools to mirror the Heavens on this Earth and to reinforce our connection to the Great Star Nations—to ground the energy of the stars and of the elementals. The evidence for this can be found in the ruins of indigenous peoples from all over the world.

So we use the term *medicine wheel* to describe a living temple while acknowledging that it has been called many, many different names and continues to be an evolving tradition. We must move away from the tunnel vision, New Age concept of what the medicine wheel is and accept a wider vision of this subjective, practical, and mystical tradition. As such, we neither claim to be authorities on the medicine wheel nor contend that one specific wheel tradition has more value or relevance than the others. Rather, we want to introduce a new medicine wheel that honors an overlooked steward of powerful medicine on this planet.

We call forth a new wheel in this time of transition for the planet that honors the recyclers, the weavers, the transformers, and the pollinators. Mostly persecuted and rarely revered, they significantly outnumber us, and we could not exist without their vital contributions to our ecosystem. Humanity has moved away from a nurturing mind-set when it comes to nature, which is widely viewed as a resource for us to use up rather than protect and honor. The Instar Medicine Wheel is an additional step in integrating this lost wisdom furthering our reconciliation with nature.

My first encounter with the medicine wheel was from a teacher who followed a couple of Native American teachers and traditions: one of them was the Sun Bear medicine wheel teachings as well as the Lakota medicine wheel traditions. From these teachings I learned that the East direction was the direction of emerging life, associated with the

Air elementals, the color yellow, the rising sun, and the winged ones. With that, there is the expansion of consciousness, new thought, birth, new beginnings, and inspiration, moving from dreamtime into this dimension.

Moving clockwise to the South, we see the noonday sun, the heat of the day, and Fire. South is associated with the color red, youth, passion, fertility and sexuality, lessons learned (both positive and negative), the Coyote (trickster), and the Mouse.[2] We learn how to be human in the South.

In the West, the sun begins to set. Associated with the color black, Water, the dark night of the soul, dissolution, the chrysalis, and the Bear, we enter a place of maturity and adulthood.[3] As the Bear slumbers, much is happening—visioning, dreaming, and gaining wisdom. In this place of embracing your shadow, there is acceptance of a need to redesign yourself and to step in to your soul purpose.

In the North, the place of the midnight sun, we stand in the snow, illuminated by the full moon. Associated with illumination, the Earth, and the color white, this is the place where we stand on the shoulders of our ancestors and the wisdom they have acquired through all their successes and failures. It is home to the Great White Buffalo (gratitude), the Wolf (teacher), and the Owl (wisdom). This is the time when your experience, and the wisdom gained from it, allows you to step in to the role of teacher.

As you can see, the wheel is not static but, rather, a cyclical path. Some traditional teachers believe that the wheel represents one complete lifetime. In other words, you begin in the East at birth and end in the North as an elder. However, a new way of interpreting the wheel holds that you may walk this cycle many times in your lifetime. So, in my teaching, the wheel can be envisioned as a spiral path—we all go around the wheel many times and end up in the North as we learn from our experiences. Then, it is time to dissolve and become the fool again—the trusting innocent in the East where it is okay to "not know." Building on what we have learned, we enter a place where we are teachable once again. The spiral continues. Some may become stuck for a time in one of the stations. The wheel offers us introspection and guidance to move through it with integrity.

While the wheel honors the four directions, in many traditions, such as the teachings of Grandmother Twylah, there is much more to be considered: the Above, the Below, the Within, and the Left and Right sides of your physical self. The Above world consists of the Great Star Nations, your spiritual allies and guides, and your relationship to the Creator. Some associate the Above with the color blue.

The Below, or Mother Earth (not to be confused with Earth as an element), is the relationship between all living things and how we nurture each other through symbiotic coexistence. For us it is gratitude for our humanity and for our place in the cycle of living beings on the planet. Below is associated with the colors green and brown.

The Within is your core, essential self. Gram called it your vibral core. This is the part of us that is connected to the Source. It can never be lost and it exists beyond our physical body, our mind, or our emotions. It lives in the heart-mind of the Creator, and it is eternal. It is most often associated with the color gold.

Your physical left and right sides correspond to your feminine and masculine attributes—receptivity and directivity, respectively. While these attributes may be used in many different ways, the point is that they illustrate my heritage of medicine wheel wisdom: a combination of wisdom from Sun Bear, Lakota teachings, Grandmother Twylah, and my own direct experience.

INSTAR EVOLUTIONARY MEDICINE
A Transformative Guide for Humanity

The Instar Medicine Wheel has emerged at this time to guide humanity. We are currently experiencing the transformative energies of an unfolding evolutionary dance of collective consciousness. Inherent within this dance are the energies of death and rebirth. Both personally and collectively, we are watching the structures, beliefs, and paradigms that no longer serve us fall away. In the midst of this dissolution, new harmonic forms of higher consciousness are emerging and expressing themselves throughout the web of life.

The Instar Medicine Wheel recognizes the birthing contractions of transformation that we are experiencing internally and externally. While some medicine wheel models have a broad, explanatory focus, seeking to articulate all the facets and archetypes of creation, the Instar Medicine Wheel has emerged with a targeted focus to support the soulful evolution of humanity. It has two primary purposes.

The purposes of the Instar Medicine Wheel are taught and expressed through the directions, animal wisdom keepers, elements, sacred geometry, and patterns of the natural world. The Mystery School of the Instar Medicine Wheel provides a framework that guides and empowers humanity through the transformation and evolution of soul consciousness. As we have shared, the word *instar* is a scientific term that describes the developmental stages insects and related animals pass through to attain maturity during their life-cycle journey. This is the perfect word to describe the soulful developmental journey each of us experiences as we step in to our potential and navigate the cycles of change inherent in being human.

In harmony with this developmental journey, the Instar Medicine Wheel also shows how each of us can step fully into our sacred purpose and express it as the divine co-creative beings we are. The wisdom of the instar animal teachers has shown up right on time, partnering with humanity as we step in to our birthright and potential to become fully actualized and mature, divine, co-creative beings.

We are entering a time in which it is essential for each of us to tap directly in to the divine creative matrix, to express our sacred purpose in the world, and co-create as fully embodied, soulful human beings. This may appear to be a tall order, but our potential is written into the DNA codes of humanity—just as the blueprint of a majestic oak tree is embedded within the acorn.

It is the least of us, the smallest, the often overlooked who have emerged as beacons of the incredible potential that exists within all of us. It is the insects and related animals who have stepped forward, turning all our assumptions on their heads, as they challenge us to look Below, Within, Above, and all around us. Insects are among Earth's most ancient inhabitants. They have bathed in the wisdom of the stars and listened to the voice of the wind since the mountains were young on the Earth. They remind us that minute, intricate lives hold vast mysteries that astound us with their beauty, magic, and relevance for the more than human journey. Through these ancient archetypal teachers, the essential wisdom to journey through every instar of embodied soul consciousness is emerging. The Instar Medicine Wheel teaches us how to pass through the eye of the needle—and become who we are meant to be.

MAPPING THE INSTAR MEDICINE WHEEL

The Instar Medicine Wheel is made up of nine directions and embodies an interconnected network of natural elements, patterns, and animals. Larger than the sum of their individual parts, the aspects of the Instar Medicine Wheel work together synergistically to illuminate an evolutionary path of soul purpose and expression. This will be explored in great detail throughout the chapters of this book. We now present a foundational map to orient you for our upcoming instar journey together.

Beginning in the East direction and the season of spring, we will meet Earthworm. Earthworm resides within the layers of soil and decomposing matter beneath our feet. Earthworm acts as a channel for the Divine and transforms matter within its body so that this new composted material may fertilize future creations. Earthworm teaches us about the necessary death and dissolution inherent in every new beginning, our empowerment as sacred change makers, and the role of the apprentice on the soul purpose path. This is the life-cycle stage of the young adult. Earthworm teaches the importance of building a foundation for the future, and provides us with the skills to create this new earth through the composting of the outdated structures of our psyches.

The Honeybee is the wisdom keeper of the South direction and the season of summer. Honeybee embodies the roles of the sacred consort and midwife in the dance of creation. As a sacred parent and community holder, Honeybee brings new dreams and creations into form, teaching us how to manifest and nurture our own soulful creations. Honeybee alchemizes the element of Fire (from the sun) into the sweetness of life, reminding us how to ecstatically embody our experience of life in every moment.

Butterfly is found in the West direction and the season of autumn. Having passed through the first creative season of our lives, leaves begin to fall from the trees and we reassess our sacred purpose. Butterfly teaches us how to transform ourselves into a higher octave of being and soul expression, moving from the earthly existence of Caterpillar through the alchemical fire of the chrysalis, into the winged element of Air as we embody our new Butterfly forms. At midlife Butterfly teaches us how to embody and express our authentic soul truth in greater alignment with our divine intuition and purpose.

Spider is the elder found at the end of the human life cycle, in the season of winter and the North direction. Having integrated and embodied all the wisdom and medicine of its life, Spider lives between the veils of the human and Spirit worlds. From this place, Spider teaches us how to build and embody a web portal of creative expression that brings through new visions and dreams in sacred service to the next seven generations. Spider dances through all the elements of the natural world as it connects us with the realm of Spirit.

Earthworm, Honeybee, Butterfly, and Spider are the four cardinal direction holders of the Instar Medicine Wheel. They hold the four circular points that create the wheel on which the drum of life is played. Their relationship to one another is essential in forming the cycle of life through which humanity journeys.

Cicada and Dragonfly can be understood as the drum head that energizes the music of the four-directional drum. Cicada is the wisdom keeper of the Great Below direction and Dragonfly is the keeper of the Great Above direction. Both these animal teachers help us to embody the resolution of opposites through the path of shamanic initiation. Cicada spends many years burrowed beneath the Earth's surface, learning from the Great Earth Mother. Dragonfly spends all its formative life beneath the Water's surface, learning how to travel through mystic veils. Both these animals emerge into the Air element after reaching soulful maturity. Cicada teaches us to sing our piercing shamanic medicine song of authentic truth as we climb the World Tree. Dragonfly teaches us how to fly through the dimensions, receiving wisdom from the Great Star Nations, and returning as an awakened messenger to Earth.

The Great Within or Center is held by an archetypal family of related creatures: Grasshopper, Cricket, and Katydid. These animal teachers hold the center of the drum, on which the drum head plays, and exist in dynamic relation to all the other directions and elements. Grasshopper, Cricket, and Katydid are the great connectors of life, teaching us how to transform energy through our beings so that it may flow throughout the network of creation. Cricket and Katydid show us how diversity emerges from the Center of creation, into masculine and feminine, right and left. Masculine and feminine are the musical notes that resonate from the head of the drum into the music of life. These wisdom keepers teach us the lessons of how to sustain life, how to create sacred union between unity and diversity, and how to center our lives in the path of the heart. Through this, the music of our lives is manifested and sustained in harmony.

Running through all these directions and teachings is the energy of sacred union. This is the path—creating union within the self and outward into the world—that spins the wheel of transformation. Sacred union is the medicine of the instar wheel through which we are transformed into the highest octaves of our potential: integrating human and soul awareness and fully embodying our unique sacred purpose expression.

EXPERIENTIAL PRACTICE

Creating an Instar Medicine Wheel

Medicine wheels come in all shapes and sizes. They can be built on a large scale such as the Instar Medicine Wheel at Isis Cove Retreat Center in North Carolina. This nontraditional medicine wheel has been built in the form of a multidimensional star tetrahedron. Each point of the star honors an instar wisdom keeper, as well as the direction and elements it represents. This star structure takes the form of a merkaba (see page 185) and is so large that a person can climb into its center to sit on a platform and commune with the sacred energies of the Instar Medicine Wheel and the web of life. This wheel was envisioned by Neesa and built by sacred carpenter Casey Piscitelli, Dennis Corvin-Blackburn, and an incredible team of people in the summer of 2012. Star Wolf envisioned the Children's Peace Park in which the wheel lives, and Brad Collins contributed his Green Man energy to the gardens that surround it. Casey

Instar Medicine Wheel at Isis Cove Retreat Center in North Carolina

shared that a hawk sat in a tree and called to him repeatedly during each day of the building process, acting as a sacred guardian for the instar energies coming into form. A hawk also acted as guardian for the building of a Blue Star Wheel nearby at Isis Cove a few years earlier. We also discovered that during the month the Instar Medicine Wheel merkaba was being constructed, a merkaba crop circle was created in the United Kingdom. The energies of higher love and wisdom are being expressed on Planet Earth more than ever before and are emanating through the sacred mysteries of the Instar Medicine Wheel.

Medicine wheels can also be built on a smaller and less permanent scale, such as a grouping of stones that can be held in your hands or displayed on an altar. As the bodies of the instar animal teachers are delicate and ephemeral, stones offer us the opportunity to weave their energies into our lives through prayer, healing, and ceremony.

Stones, gems, and crystals are known to have diverse properties and uses. The instar wisdom keepers have revealed a kinship to certain stones that can be laid as a medicine wheel. These stones can be carried in a medicine bundle or bag and utilized whenever you would like to call the love and wisdom of the Instar Medicine Wheel in to your life.

In sacred space, begin to create your Instar Medicine Wheel. Each of these stones also activates a chakra energetic center in the body. In the center, place the green stone of Amazonite for Grasshopper, Cricket, and Katydid. This stone is the heart of the Instar Medicine Wheel, representing the Center or Great Within direction, home of the heart path of unity in diversity. From this central point, the entire wheel radiates outward into creation. Amazonite activates the fourth, heart chakra of the body, home of compassion, love, and harmony.

Next, in the East direction, lay a stone made of Jasper for Earthworm. Jasper carries a strong resonance with Earth energies. There are many varieties; we enjoy one called Mook Jasper from Australia, which echoes the aubergine and umber tones of Earthworm. This stone activates the third, solar plexus chakra of the energy body, home of right action, responsibility, and use of power.

In the South, lay a piece of golden Citrine for Honeybee. If possible, find an untreated crystal formation of Citrine. This crystal has six sides, reminding us of the hexagonal honeycomb. This stone activates the second, sacral chakra, home of sexual and creative energies.

In the West, place a piece of Labradorite for Butterfly. Evoking the transformational energies of Butterfly, Labradorite is a mysterious stone that shimmers with colors as you move it. Often this stone reveals the brilliant blue color of the Morpho Butterfly. This stone activates the fifth, throat chakra, home of creative expression and communication.

In the North, lay a Kyanite stone. A blue, threadlike crystal, Kyanite reveals the gossamer strands with which Spider weaves its dreams. This stone activates the sixth, brow or third-eye chakra, home of intuition and visionary abilities.

Next, honor the Great Below and Cicada by placing a Bloodstone at the base of the wheel, or just below the Center stone. Bloodstone is a highly grounded stone, deep green in color with red flecks, echoing the green body and red eyes of Cicada. While Earthworm and Jasper honor the element of Earth, Bloodstone is aligned with the energy of the telluric realms, the Underworld, and the darkness and density beneath the Earth's surface. Bloodstone activates the first, root chakra. This chakra connects us to life, our home planet, and our sense of security, safety, and groundedness.

Finally, place a stone of Lapis Lazuli at the top of the wheel or just above the Center stone to evoke Dragonfly, the Great Above, and the Great Star Nations. Lapis Lazuli is deep blue and flecked with gold, just as the blue Dragonfly is keeper of the Blue Star mysteries. This stone activates the seventh, crown chakra, home to our connection with higher dimensions of consciousness, Divine Presence, the greater universe, and our spirit/higher self.

These stones can create a wheel for ceremony and prayer or be placed on the energy centers of the body for healing and transformation. Hold each stone in your hand and ask the instar wisdom keepers to infuse them with their love, wisdom, and archetypal energies. When not in use, place your stones within your medicine bundle or the altar of your home. Treat your medicine wheel stones with honor and reverence so that they will continue to transmit their energies throughout your life.

2
The Shaman's Path

Linking Nature and Soul

In the past animals were seen as teachers and symbolic omens that had the power to impact individual and collective experience. Coyote was the expansive trickster. Raven accompanied you into the dark places of your soul. Snake invited you into the feminine and sexual mysteries. In fact, much of nature was seen as having a deep impact on human experience. In the past, and for many indigenous cultures today, human beings viewed themselves as part of the web of life. We understood ourselves as part of a living system that could dance with winged feathers and hoofbeats, who cried out with the Lion's roar, who keened with the sighing of the wind.

When humanity lived closer to the Earth, the seasons, elements, and animals were a more immediate part of our experience. We ate because we studiously tracked their migration patterns and habits, and we foraged for subtle vegetation growing in the wild. We were, in fact, more wild ourselves, more in tune with the primal dance of nature. We saw ourselves reflected in nature, and saw nature reflected in ourselves. We were more sensitive to the living organism of nature, and more open to its inherent wisdom. *Becoming Animal* and *The Spell of the Sensuous*, two books by David Abram, are excellent explorations of our inner wildness.

Throughout history many societies have moved away from nature-based living patterns and feminine aspects of spirituality. In many matriarchal and goddess-based societies, feminine aspects of the Divine encouraged us to fully experience the sacred through our bodies, our senses, our sexuality, and our direct lived experience. In these nature-based societies, direct experience was found in the phases of the moon, the deep quiet of winter solstice, or the archetypes of animal teachers.

There are a number of reasons for this rejection of the feminine and nature. As the pendulum swings, in prehistory (or, more correctly, "pre-herstory"), matriarchal societies expressed the origin of our evolutionary consciousness. In the past millennia the intuitive and body/Earth-based wisdom of the feminine and nature have been rejected and persecuted by patriarchal consciousness, industrialization, and scientific reductionism. Western organized religions taught that the body was sinful and not to be trusted, woman (the feminine) was the origin of sin, sexuality was purely for procreation, and nature was simply a resource to be mined and cross to bear in the testing of souls for later ascension to Heaven.

In the past thousand years many Westerners who shared this religious worldview set out to conquer new lands and "save" their peoples. Nature-based, indigenous peoples were called "savages" by foreign colonizers. *Savage* is commonly thought to mean "vicious" or "violent" in behavior, but its true definition actually means "wild" or "undomesticated." In the Americas, and other places around the globe, nature-based wisdom and societies were systematically stamped out or forcibly evangelized by colonial invaders.

Having swung to the other extreme—that of patriarchy—many people fear their own wild natures and seek to repress them. It's not "civilized" to be wild, free, and instinctive. Many free spirits who have chosen to live authentically, relinquishing the dominant worldview of civilization for their own primal experience and the wisdom of nature, have been persecuted. Examples of this are etched throughout history, whether it is the women's holocaust (more commonly called the witch burnings), the genocide of indigenous peoples, or the treatment of avant-garde artists.

Consider an example drawn from contemporary, suburban society: it is fascinating to witness the intensity with which people cultivate turf lawns in the United States. The goal is to create a uniform green space, made up of one species. Biological diversity and uniqueness are denigrated and actively eradicated. Many homeowners also recoil at the reality that the wildness of nature is just beneath the surface of their awareness in the teeming biological organisms and plant life of their yards, such as insects and other related animals. Many television commercials advocate spraying turf with insecticides and herbicides to kill these organisms. Yet, these animals and plants actively contribute to a healthy, balanced ecosystem.

From a psychological perspective, a uniform and controlled lawn represents the repression and fear of the wild that lives within our psyches. Just as these suburban turf ecosystems are out of balance— requiring fertilizers to maintain them (because pollinators and fertile diversity have been eliminated)—so too this highly polarized industrial, patriarchal worldview is not sustainable or balanced.

Running parallel to patriarchy, industrialization has consumed most societies around the planet. Industrialized society has introduced concepts that "bigger is better" and that materialism can offset the internal psychological schism and struggle we experience because of our disconnect from nature. This is far from the case. Materialism and attitudes toward consumption have led to high rates of addictive behaviors in humanity. Industrialization has ravaged our ecosystems, throwing the entire web of life out of balance on this planet at all levels.

Neither masculine nor feminine principles are superior to the other. Instead, we must collectively find balance between the masculine and feminine principles within ourselves and our societies. As the consciousness of this planet evolves, we move in a spiral, taking the lessons of the matriarchy (symbolized by the circle) and patriarchy (symbolized by the line) into our beings and transforming old paradigms into fertile ground for new harmonic creations. The spiral path alchemizes circle and line into the sacred union of masculine and feminine.

It is also time for many of us to wake up and face our fears of the primal, instinctive aspects of our own psyches and nature. To do this we may need to confront our internalized belief systems, fears, body issues, and areas in which we have forcibly shut down our experience. For many, creeping, crawling, and flying insects evoke fear and prejudice. This book—and the fields of deep ecology, ecofeminism, and ecopsychology—promote the process of healing the split between self and nature. Highly charged or repressed animal archetypes, such as the instar teachers of this book, also have particularly strong potential to act as healing and inspirational sources for our psyches.

As Clarissa Pinkola-Estes advises us in her book *Women Who Run with the Wolves,* it is time for us to run wildly with the wolves of our own psyches and to journey through the forests, prairies, and mountains outside our doors. It is time for us to remember who we are and reclaim our relationships with the wisdom teachers of nature.

THE CURRENT DIRECTION OF HUMAN ENVIRONMENTAL CHOICES

In the early twenty-first century, animals and ecosystems are being decimated and destroyed by industrialized, consumer-driven, and militaristic societies. The sources of insect endangerment include loss of habitat, fires, floods, animal predation, competing organisms, introduction of exotic species, pesticides, and pollutants. Insects act as canaries in the mine for humans, alerting us to dangerous situations and choices.

We stand on the brink of irrevocable actions that could drive many species beyond the point of no return, including our own. Humanity's actions have moved past the boundaries of our homes and cities and are now threatening entire ecosystems and Planet Earth as a whole.

Honeybee offers us a stark example of this, which cannot be ignored. As has been documented in the news media in recent years, Bee populations around the planet have suddenly begun dropping at an alarmingly fast rate.[1] This has been termed *colony collapse disorder.* Honeybees—

known for their organization and interdependency—are experiencing increasing disunification within the hive. They have left their hives and not returned home. Their behavior patterns have become erratic, affecting the life of the entire hive. Whether due to a particular fungus, chemical sprays, cell phone use, disruptive forced migration by industrial agriculture, or another cause, the Honeybees are facing possible extinction and are experiencing destabilizing chaos.

This has an immediate impact on human survival as well. Bees are the most significant pollinator of ecosystems and our agricultural system. Four out of ten bites of food come directly from the work of Bees. Two-thirds of all plant life would disappear without Bees. Currently, industrial agriculture transports truckloads of Bees to different fields. As most crops are farmed in monocultures by industrial agriculture— which holds that efficiency is king—there are not enough diverse plant species blooming at different times to sustain a local population of Bees. Instead, when the almond trees of central California come into bloom, the Bees are trucked in for a few short weeks to pollinate them.[2] In addition to the deplorable ethics of animal treatment inherent in this, this farming practice starkly illustrates the drastic situation in which the Bees and we humans find ourselves. In order to eat, human beings must relearn to collectively respect the needs and interests of Bees.

Colony collapse disorder also symbolizes themes found in human society. Up until now, collective human behavior has often resulted in disconnection, isolation, and conflict. Many people live each day unconscious of their divinity and unique gifts. Instead of co-creating a world that honors collaboration and sees each person as a manifestation of divine love, we have emphasized competition, fear, and scarcity consciousness. Just as we have experienced fragmentation and its destructive consequences, so have our teachers, the Bees.

The world we have created reflects the consequences of unconscious, fearful, and disconnected choices. Yet, thankfully, this has already begun to change. We are in a time of great possibility, and yet our conscious intention is absolutely essential for the unfolding potential of Earth.

Ours is a time of transformation. Planet Earth, humanity, and the Bees are experiencing immense changes that have a higher purpose when it comes to the unfolding story of the universe. The current upheaval in the Bee population signifies the essential remembering of our own divinity, the importance of mirroring the Bees' interconnected collaboration in our own actions, and the elevation of human collective consciousness to a harmonious expression of divine love and sacred union.

In addition to the physical food these pollinators provide for us, we can be psychically and spiritually nourished by Honeybee's wisdom. It is time for humanity to rebuild our community hive (the nurturing Earth home that we co-create), embrace the wisdom of the natural world, and incorporate this into a new expression of sustainable consciousness.

PERSONAL AND COLLECTIVE TRANSFORMATION

Exploring the Link between Ecology and Shamanic Spirituality

As we noted, humanity and Planet Earth stand at a crucial point: the current worldview and collective industrial and patriarchal choices are no longer sustainable and threaten our continued survival as a species and planet. As Earthworm will teach us in chapter 3, it is time for us to look directly at the choices of our matriarchal and patriarchal histories. In order to transform the present so we can create a harmonic new expression of the future, we must acknowledge the role that these worldviews have played in the unfolding and development of human consciousness. It is time to honor their lessons and ask these worldviews to journey with us into transformation, to be composted and recycled, to lay a fertile foundation of new earth in which the seeds of the future can be planted.

Mirroring the cyclical patterns of nature, shamanic spirituality frames human experience as a spiraling developmental life path that incorporates cycles of death and rebirth within the human psyche.

Our consciousness follows this spiral path throughout our lifetime, as does the unfolding collective consciousness of humanity. As we move around the spiral we have the opportunity to revisit higher octaves of familiar themes, but at a new point in our development and awareness. For example, we can revisit the positive and constructive qualities of matriarchal and patriarchal worldviews, understanding and then releasing whatever does not serve us, so that we may more fully embody our current place on the spiral of life.

In the opening decades of the twenty-first century, we stand at a pivotal time in which new directions must be taken, new innovations seeded, and new perspectives evolved. This book posits, as do others in the field of deep ecology, that there is a link between human experience and nature-based experience. Our bodies are microcosms of Mother Earth. As her atmosphere is poisoned by pollution and toxins, so too do Earth's human inhabitants find themselves with skyrocketing rates of asthma, cancer, and other disorders. Genocide, a pervasive "us versus them" mentality, and widescale pollution are better understood when we consider and explore the unprecedented rates of autoimmune disorders; that is, when a body's immune system attacks itself. Our experiences are intimately linked and inform one another. In this way a path of solution and an opportunity for transformation are illuminated. As individual human beings, each embracing our own healing and transformation of consciousness, we light up like harmonic cells in the universal body. As each Honeybee remembers its wisdom and the dance of its life purpose, the hive is renewed for the greatest good.

When we look to nature once again for wisdom and symbolic teachings—renewing our relationship with the web of life—the natural world will share its incredible abundance of wisdom, teachings, and guidance with us. As we heal and transform ourselves, the Earth evolves with us. And nature itself can be our guide in this symbiotic path of discovery, recovery, and transformation. Nature's wisdom and activational energies have always been with us; we simply need to develop our capacity to listen and fully inhabit the wildness that surrounds and is within us.

Yet nature is a subtle teacher. The softly emotive rains on the prairie have quiet stories to tell. The lyrics in birdsong are not readily apparent. The muddied footprints of migration make for intricate and subtle art. And none more so than the insects and related animal teachers. Theirs is a wisdom that is both minute and immense at the same time. You will find them in hidden webs and crevices, beneath the Earth, and in the center of honeyed hives and chrysalises. Yet they are exquisite and powerful teachers for humanity in this time of transformation. They have come together in a medicine wheel of sacred wisdom for the activation and evolutionary growth of humanity.

INSTAR PERSPECTIVES OF SACRED PURPOSE AND TRANSFORMATION

There is an astounding number of insects and related animals on Planet Earth, many with surprising abilities and fascinating behaviors. They can lift many times their own weight, jump many times their own height, migrate thousands of miles, and lay vast numbers of eggs. Insects assist humans in growing our food and play essential roles in Earth's ecosystems, such as feeding animals, protecting plant species, and recycling dead animals and other natural matter.[3] Insects and related animals (such as Spiders and Earthworms) are found around the world and have an incredible spectrum of abilities, colors, and habits. With this richness of diversity, how did the animal wisdom–based Instar Medicine Wheel explored in this book come to be?

First, it is important to note that all living beings and elements are citizens of the web of life and have sacred wisdom to share. Readers are encouraged to notice which animal teachers and natural patterns cross their path in daily life and invite shared meaning to emerge. Readers are also encouraged to notice which animal teachers resonate with their own experience and develop individualized relationships with the teachers to whom they are called. That said, the animal teachers in this book have a history of archetypal resonance with human collective consciousness that spans thousands of years. The animals that make up the Instar Medicine Wheel have caught the collective imagination across cultures, centuries, and traditions.

The specific behaviors of the instar animal teachers are in alignment with principles and elements traditionally attributed to the directions of the medicine wheel. The four cardinal directions of the medicine wheel—North, East, South, and West—are each held by an animal teacher who is the maker of a sacred pattern found in nature; for example, Spider and its web or Butterfly and its chrysalis. In addition, the animal teachers or keepers of the directions of the Instar Medicine Wheel have come together at this time because they offer distinctive perspectives on shared shamanic medicine teachings.

The Instar Medicine Wheel

The sacred medicine wheel in this book focuses specifically on the development of sacred purpose and the journey of transformation. Let's take some time to discuss each of these areas.

Sacred Purpose

Each being comes to this planet because it is an excellent opportunity to expand and evolve consciousness. Third-dimensional reality—being in human bodies experiencing time and space—offers us the chance to practice opening our hearts fully to love, connect with the web of life, and share our authentic creativity within this web. As individual cells in the universal body, we each come into living form with specific gifts, talents, and abilities. We are able to develop these abilities through our path of life experience. As we live into our full potential as divine human beings, we bless and harmonize all life with the gift of our truth. In this lifetime we have the opportunity to practice and develop our sacred purpose, to benefit collective reality, and to evolve into more complex and intricate universal beings.

The animal teachers of the Instar Medicine Wheel will help increase your awareness of your sacred purpose, release the blockages that have held you back from expressing it, learn to manifest and co-create with Spirit, transform yourself as a shamanic being, and receive and share cosmic visions that benefit all. In terms of sacred purpose, this medicine wheel offers insights into specific life-cycle and developmental phases, as well as an evolutionary model for stepping fully into the birthright of your gifts and abilities as a divine being.

Transformation

Metamorphosis is defined as "a profound change in form from one stage to the next in the life history of an organism, as from the caterpillar to the pupa and from the pupa to the adult butterfly." Instar animal teachers morph from one form to another and manifest energy in distinctive and profound ways. Whether it is recycling and composting as the sacred channel (Earthworm), or transforming the self to a higher octave of being (Butterfly), each of these teachers will help you explore and discover new ways of transforming yourself, bringing forth new creations, or changing reality for future generations.

Transformation is nothing less than an alchemy of consciousness, one that these weavers, recyclers, pollinators, and transformers of Spirit actively co-create as part of their daily lives. From the perspective of physics, all life is made of energy. Spinning a web, composting new earth, making sweet honey from flowers, or changing oneself within a chrysalis are specific ways of transforming energy into new forms, new creations, higher octaves of purpose. These small beings are exquisite examples and masters of transformative reality right here on Earth.

In summary, the animal teachers of the Instar Medicine Wheel can be seen as a particular constellation in the night sky, resonant and familiar to human viewers here on Earth. While the stars may be light-years apart in distance, their relationship to one another offers a shared wisdom, filled with archetypal stories that teach, activate, and inspire. In the next chapter we will begin our journey around the medicine wheel, beginning in the East with Earthworm.

3
Earthworm

*Transforming the Past into
a Foundation for New Creations*

> *It is a wholesome and necessary thing for us to turn again
> to the earth and in the contemplation of her beauties to
> know of wonder and humility.*
>
> RACHEL CARSON, *THE SENSE OF WONDER*

Earthworm may seem like an unexpected teacher on the medicine wheel. Certainly, it does not have the popularity of Butterfly or Spider. In fact, Earthworm is often seen in a displeasing light, a representative of the teeming Underworld, just beneath the surface. But, just as Earthworm emerges to drink in the thunderous rain of a summer storm, so too does Earthworm emerge in our psyches as a teacher and true master of transformation.

Earthworm is a compassionate guide into the realms of self-love, teaching us to find balance and right relationship within ourselves. Earthworm assists us in opening the way to access our sacred purpose and begin to communicate with the Sacred in our lives.

In this chapter we will explore Earthworm's identity as an organism embedded within an ecosystem, as well as its archetypal nature and sacred teachings. Earthworm is truly an extraordinary being, capable of great feats and service to the Earth's community.

Up until very recently, in the past two hundred years or so, very little was known about Earthworm. Its behaviors and impact on the ecosystem were either ignored or misunderstood. Before Charles Darwin championed the Earthworm in the nineteenth century, Worms were thought to harm plants and soil.

Today, many still perceive the composting behaviors and dark sinuous nature of the Earthworm as negative or unsavory. Just as we have repressed the shadow of our psyches, so too have the dark earth and Earthworms beneath our feet been relegated into mystery. Cleopatra and the ancient Egyptians viewed the Earthworm as sacred, perhaps connecting this animal teacher to the viability of agriculture along the Nile. The term *wyrm* in older forms of the English language referred to one's fate or a great Dragon. Beyond this, little is known about Earthworm's role, if any, in mythology or cultural lore.

Charles Darwin was a pioneer in the study of Earthworms. He wrote one of his first scientific papers on the topic and dedicated his final book, *The Formation of Vegetable Mould, Through the Actions of Worms, with Observations on Their Habits,* to the behaviors and ecological contributions of the Earthworm. Many of his contemporaries dismissed his assertions as exaggerations, but science has borne out Darwin's conclusions that Earthworms play a vital role in nature, and they have an extraordinary impact on the ecology, evolution, and transformation of Earth's landscape.

Contemporary science estimates that one million Earthworms can be found in one acre of soil. Earthworm scientists, or oligochaetologists, have proved that Earthworms, "through their actions, substantially change the earth. They alter its composition, increase its capacity to absorb and hold water, and bring about an increase in nutrients and microorganisms. . . . They move the earth, a remarkable accomplishment for a creature that weighs only a fraction of an ounce."[1] Gardening journalist Amy Stewart notes that "the Earthworm's shape allows it to be an extraordinary vessel for soil—the perfect container for holding, transporting, and transforming earth."[2] It does all this while holding less than a teaspoonful of soil at a time.

In its travels through the earth, the Earthworm seeks out decaying organic matter, ingesting it along with sand or clay, as it builds a permanent home. At night, the Earthworm excretes what it has eaten at the surface of its home: aerating, recycling, and contributing new earth with its Worm castings. It then transports organic matter from the surface back down into deeper layers of soil, thus diversifying soil content and redistributing fertility throughout. A single Earthworm can eat a third of its body weight in soil per day and, as a collective population, Earthworms move almost twenty tons of earth per acre in one year.

The castings of Earthworms amend the soil with nutrients that assist plant growth. In addition, even the movement, or dance, of the Earthworm enhances fertility within the soil ecosystem. Its mucus and castings promote the growth of helpful bacteria and fungi. Earthworms have few natural enemies or predators.

In fact, they provide a fascinating glimpse into living in dynamic harmony with one's surroundings. Soil is made of a complex mixture of ingredients from single-cell bacteria, protozoa, nematodes, and fungi to organic components such as mineral particles, decomposing plant matter, roots, and the like. If one were to add bleach to a cup of soil, it would decrease dramatically in size as the organisms that dwelled therein were destroyed. Living organisms make up such a large percentage of the soil community, that the earth itself is truly alive. Earthworms are much larger beings relative to most members of the soil community. Stewart compares Earthworms to giant whales in the ocean.[3] Earthworms live among bacteria and other tiny beings in the soil, and these organisms also live within Earthworm's body as it ingests soil particles. Earthworm lives in the earth, creates the earth, ingests the earth, and contributes to the life and death of a vast array of organisms within a complex ecological web that is the very structure of earth itself.

There are three main types of Earthworms: Endogeic Worms, which live among plant roots; Anecic Worms, or Night Crawlers, which live in deeper layers of earth; and Epigeic Worms, which prefer to reside in and recycle rapidly decomposing matter.

Earthworms are blind and breathe by absorbing oxygen through their skin. Earthworm species have between one and five sets of hearts. They exist in a fascinating state of multiplicity and balance, both within and without. They are hermaphroditic, possessing both masculine and feminine sexual pores. Procreation between two Earthworms usually lasts for multiple hours, as their sinuous shapes twine together, head to tail, so that their opposite sex organs can line up. At the end, each partner has been gifted with the procreative materials—sperm and egg—to form cocoons. Not yet fertilized, these cocoons can exist in the soil for months before fertilization conditions are ideal.

The life spans of Earthworms vary. Night Crawlers can live up to six years, while other varieties have a life span that is decades long. Indeed, Earthworms, as a species, have incredible longevity. They survived two mass extinctions that wiped out many other life-forms and originated hundreds of millions of years ago on the ancient unified Pangaea landmass.

EXPLORING EARTHWORM'S PLACE ON THE MEDICINE WHEEL

The East Direction and New Beginnings

Earthworm is the keeper of the East cardinal direction of the Instar Medicine Wheel. East is the direction of new beginnings, the golden rays of the sunrise, the season of spring, and the aspiring climb of the morning star. Earthworm is a master of new beginnings, because it understands that every beginning is a child of darker endings. Embodying the infinite circle of life, Earthworm teaches that every ending in our lives—that which no longer serves us—becomes the rich compost within which new dreams and possibilities are planted and fertilized.

It is commonly believed that if we "stay positive" and keep our focus fixed on what we want to happen next, that this will manifest something we yearn for. Keeping our eye on the sun makes for parched earth and barren ground. Instead, we must delve down into the rich darkness of our psyche, acknowledging the old creations that no longer serve and that we still carry. These are last year's leaves, broken down minerals from mountains, remnants of minute life-forms. As organisms, Earthworms continuously bring matter from the surface into the dark earth beneath; inviting us to do the same within our own psyches. In the darkness of earth, Earthworm finds many things in her sinuous travels. Some experiences and objects are her own; some belong to the collective and seasons past. In acknowledgment, Earthworm communicates, "I see you. I honor you. I ask you to journey with me that you may be transmuted and recycled for a higher divine purpose."

For Earthworm does not simply see the littered remnants of the past but instead honors them as collaborative, co-creative partners in her life's mission. She asks them to dance with and, more importantly, *through* her. Earthworm embodies the purpose pathway of the sacred vessel, or channel, inviting divine creation to move through her being. As we learned in the preface, the majority of soil on Planet Earth has passed through the body of an Earthworm. Earthworm embodies the path of the priestess, opening to receive potent universal energies through her form that they may be manifested on Earth as they are in Heaven. To Earthworm the mystical path of the channel is not all sunshine and rainbows. Instead, she knows that it is essential for the situations and objects that no longer serve us to be broken down, dismembered, and reconstituted. In the churning chasm of her being, the minerals, leaves, and old relics of the ecosystem are recycled into their base elements, reconfigured, and given new life as a rich, fecund foundation for new creations. Earthworm is the midwife for death, honoring the past for its value and final contribution to the future.

For those of us who wish to bring new creations and opportunities through our beings, we must first prepare the ground. We must build a foundation on which to firmly plant our feet, and plant the seeds of our dreams. Darkness is the fertile companion of the light. It is here, within Mother Earth, in collaboration with all that has come before, that we find the materials and alchemical magic to create authentic, new beginnings.

SACRED PURPOSE

Recycling and Channeling as the Sacred Vessel

For those who are called to a path of sacred service, Earthworm indicates where each of us must begin. We must first learn to listen, to hear the call of Spirit, both within ourselves and from the universe. Through listening, a dialogue is born between self and Spirit. The root of the word *humility* means "close to the earth" and is related to *humus,* another term for soil. To truly hear Spirit's call, and be able to answer it, we must first explore, acknowledge, and transmute the old creations that clutter our lives and stifle our spiritual energy. As Earthworm teaches, this does not mean throwing our junk out in the street for the garbage man to haul away. Instead, we are called to get our own hands dirty, to be our own recycling sanitation official, and get to work.

We must acknowledge, honor, and integrate the past within our beings. In this way the past is transformed, informing and fertilizing our connection with the Divine. Our human life experience is the rich compost for our soul expression. Finding right relationship between the two is essential. Moving from clutter or repressed trauma within the psyche, we then choose to consciously face these aspects of our experience. We can honor them and ask them to be conscious collaborators instead of cutting off challenges as "uncomfortable." We acknowledge the old structures within, alchemizing them into a new, higher form that is more in alignment with our soul's truth. In this way we build the sacred vessel of our beings, which becomes the communication tool we can use to hear and talk to Spirit.

Our soil is teeming with Earthworms living out their purpose recycling humus. And though some of us have forgotten, each of us too has a sacred purpose. We each have a right to a direct relationship with the Divine, formed through personal healing and development. The democratization of a direct, personal relationship with the Divine also offers fertile blessings for our planet. As each of us taps in to our own nature as a sacred vessel for Spirit, higher wisdom, peaceful soul-utions, and innovative ideas can move through the channel of our being for the highest good of society and the planet. By doing our personal work we make way and create a structure for the Divine to move through us. Through the teachings of Earthworm we each become the sacred vessel of transformation and divine communication.

EARTHWORM AND THE HUMAN LIFE CYCLE

Apprenticeship

East is the direction of new beginnings. Accordingly, Earthworm's place in understanding the human life cycle is that of apprenticeship. Through the process of recycling and integrating within our psyches— doing our personal work—we make room for the first beginnings of a lifetime dialogue and connected relationship with Spirit. Transforming the old structures within our psyches and bodies is often the first step on the path to sacred purpose. This process of transformation creates our personal shamanic medicine, which we can share in service with others, while opening an authentic dialogue with Great Spirit in our lives.

Building the sacred channel within ourselves is the first opening into spiritual adulthood. Instead of depending on others to define our world for us, or listening to an external truth, we learn to journey internally, creating alchemical gold inside our beings and listening to the voice of Spirit within. Walking the path of the sacred channel or vessel is the first step in a rich life of sacred purpose. We learn to truly look at and listen to ourselves and, through this process, hear the call of Spirit.

Apprenticeship is a learning path, and there are many lessons to be learned at this stage of the life cycle. Chief among these is learning to walk with integrity as we express our gifts. It is easy to become distracted by ego, and as we begin to access and use our gifts, it is easy to be seduced into an ego-based self-definition of sacred work. It may be tempting to skip this step in sacred purpose development. If this occurs, we lose the opportunity to learn the craft of our sacred work, which provides a strong foundation for ethical service and alignment with Spirit.

Many public figures have been "brought low" after they centered their lives in ego and external definitions of self. Earthworm teaches us that we can unconsciously be brought back to humility, often through lessons that are painful to the ego. Or we can choose to center our lives in humility, honoring our abilities and gifts, but holding them in humble service to humanity, Planet Earth, and the Divine. When we listen to Earthworm and remember to orient our sense of self in a grounded, centered relationship of service, we can truly open ourselves as a wide, co-creative channel for divine expression.

Earthworms are not usually seen as glamorous. Instead, they may more routinely be defined as "lowly." Yet these humble creatures create the new earth every day, in sacred service to all. When we are grounded in the truth of who we are, and in service to Spirit, we are each capable of truly extraordinary things. This is the lesson of Earthworm.

TRANSFORMATION

Cycles of Death and Rebirth through the Self

Many of the animal teachers of the Instar Medicine Wheel can be said to walk a shamanic path, perhaps none more so than Earthworm. Much of Western society can be seen as light-polarized, focusing on positivity while ignoring its growing collective shadow. Challenges and hardship are seen as negative. Vulnerability and ambiguity are shunned. Death is a terrifying thought for many, except as an ascendance beyond the travails of the Earthly body into the light. This has been reinforced by many religions, which have taught that the body is sinful, the Earth is here only as a resource for humanity, and that this material world is simply a test for those "lucky enough" to move beyond the body.

The Latin root of the word *material* is *mater,* which means "mother." Shamanic traditions teach that our Mother Earth is a home for our human selves, nurturing us and offering humanity a special opportunity. As human beings we have been given the opportunity to enter time and space—third-dimensional reality—because it offers us a dynamic framework within which to learn and grow as divine beings. As philosopher, priest, and scientist Teilhard de Chardin has said, "We are not human beings having a spiritual experience. We are spiritual beings having a human experience." Earthworm gently reminds us that to be close to our Mother Earth, to be in material human bodies, is a blessing. When we renew our relationship with the Earth, the fertility of our dreams is seeded and enriched.

Yet many fear to open into a direct, authentic relationship with the material Earth experience. This is often because, as we become more honest with ourselves and embrace the reality that surrounds us, we open ourselves to directly experiencing the emotional impact of challenges and past traumas we may have been avoiding. This may be anxiety provoking, uncomfortable, and sometimes overwhelming. Is it any wonder that many have sanctified a light-polarized path as more "holy"?

Orienting our beliefs so that we consider love and light as sacred, while the challenges and ambiguity of Earthly life are viewed as bad or evil, is not only untrue, it robs us of the fertile components we need to fully live into our soul purpose. Instead, Earthworm teaches us "the light, the dark, no difference." We need both to be fully creative and to be wholly ourselves. For we each embody both dark and light. They are not separate teams competing for victory; rather, light and darkness are in dynamic relationship with each other. How can the light shine and sparkle in the Heavens if not bordered by the darkness of space? A flower receives a high degree of its energy from sunlight and air, yet it must first be seeded in the earth and grow from the darkness of its life-giving foundation. Earthworm teaches us that when we deny the darkness in our beings, we become two-dimensional, cluttered psychologically, and incapable of communing openly with Spirit or creating our dreams.

We must travel into the darkness of earth, travel within ourselves to bring our light and dark—the rich potential of our past creations and experiences—into right relationship with our Spirit. This is the alchemy of Earthworm's path of sacred purpose.

Earthworm teaches us that the darkness—the hidden paths through the earth and through ourselves—are not to be feared. Instead, they are to be embraced for the rich opportunities they offer us. In meeting its shadow, Earthworm says, "I see you. I honor you. I ask you to journey with me that you may be transmuted and recycled for a higher divine purpose." In actuality, this is an aware opening of the psyche to move into a conscious death so that fertile rebirth may occur. Again, this asks us to be willing to go into our uncomfortable feelings, to touch our fears, to be open and vulnerable to the inevitable surrender of death. What we find, as we let go, is that death and rebirth flow in a never-ending spiral of evolution.

As we allow our past creations and experiences to consciously die, they begin to break down and compost, reassembling their elements into a rich, fecund humus that supports and nourishes a vibrant rebirth. As we learn to live in conscious, healthy relationship with our shadow, it becomes the foundation and food for future dreams and new possibilities.

Earthworm's spiraling form, delving into the darkness in sacred service to all life, teaches us that we too can spiral. We too can evolve our consciousness, that we may fully embody our sacred purpose in this lifetime. Our bodies begin to move in a sinuous dance, surrendering and opening to transformation in our lives. The foundation for transformation is always to be found in the direct experience of our bodies and an authentic relationship between light and shadow. Through this we hear Spirit's call and can embody our birthright as sacred channels of divine wisdom.

LESSONS AND SHADOW

Close to the Earth—Exploring Humility, Shame, and Rejection

As we noted earlier, Earthworm helps us remember to practice humility, staying "close to the Earth" by being grounded and placing authentic service at the center of our sacred purpose. From this humble sense of self, we honor and offer our soul's creative gifts in sacred service to all life. In this way, each of us has the capacity to make a meaningful contribution to the web of life, for the highest good. And, as the "lowly" Earthworm reminds us, all life-forms—big and small—deserve respect for the essential collective contributions that each makes with its own life.

At the same time, this humility is not about denying our gifts or "playing smaller" than we really are. The shadow of humility—what Earthworm teaches us to transmute and recycle—is a repressed sense of shame and fear of rejection. As an apprentice, learning to practice and share our sacred gifts for the first time, a common fear is this: "If I share my unique gifts or personal expression of sacred purpose, will I be rejected by others?" When we are giving voice to the Spirit moving through us, or sharing our own creative genius for the first time, we do not know how it will be received by society. This can be daunting, especially as we learn to honor the subtle voice within ourselves. It can be tempting to water down or censor our internal creative channel, yet Earthworm assures us to practice courage.

Imagine being deep within the Earth, its density pushing in on your delicate form on all sides. This place is dark and unknown. You are the only one who can carve a path forward. Yet you feel a yearning, a hunger, to open yourself fully to something larger than yourself, to offer the sanctity of your being, to nourish yourself and the world around you by acting as a sacred vessel; transforming the past that it may nurture the future. Deep inside, you can also begin to hear Spirit calling to you, co-creating the transformation of alchemical gold within your being. And so, through your yearning, collective service has been offered, and fertile new earth created. What if the smallest of us did not offer our own contributions? The world would be a much different place, devoid of much of its vibrant life. Where would the plants and flowers grow that feed us and create habitats were it not for Earthworm? If you are living small, you are denying the world the treasure of your human being-ness.

Earthworm counsels us to practice courage. The root of the word *courage* is *cor,* which comes from the Latin, meaning "heart." The French word for *heart* is *coeur.* Courage is not about having no fear. It is about acknowledging our fear and transmuting it, recycling it, moving sinuously through it, and coming into our hearts because we hear the call of our sacred purpose. When we feel the call of our sacred purpose, this yearning opens us into a fuller expression of ourselves. This is an initiatory process, through which Earthworm can be our guide. As the Caribbean American writer-activist Audre Lorde shares, "When I dare to be powerful, to use my strength in the service of my vision, then it becomes less and less important whether I am afraid."[4]

For some of us, past wounds—especially from our family of origin— can create a belief framework that is grounded in shame and rejection. Perhaps we were rejected for being our authentic selves. Perhaps we experienced childhood abandonment. For others, shame was used as a teaching or behavioral tool to control us, so that we would color between the lines and meet others' expectations. We may have experienced forms of abuse and were taught that we were lowly as a Worm, that we were dirty, that we were wrong in some way because of who we were.

Earthworm is here as a compassionate teacher who understands and can help us heal these wounds. Past abuse or life experiences that created a belief system focused on shame and rejection are perfect examples of old creations that do not serve us and clutter our psyches. If this is something you are ready to transform within yourself, ask Earthworm to be your guide as you acknowledge and honor these life experiences as past lessons in your evolving human experience.

Ask these beliefs to journey with you, as you consciously transform and recycle them. Encourage these beliefs to serve a new purpose by breaking down and acting as fertile ground for your new creations of self-esteem, poised to grow and blossom: courage, determination, belief in yourself, self-acceptance, self-honoring, and love. Earthworm teaches us that humility is not the absence of a "big head" but is instead practicing right relationship between honoring our birthright of sacred purpose expression and establishing a firm grounding in heart-centered truth and service.

Activist and author Marianne Williamson offers us exceptional words on this matter.

Our deepest fear is not that we are inadequate. Our deepest fear is that we are powerful beyond measure. It is our light, not our darkness, that most frightens us. We ask ourselves, Who am I to be brilliant, gorgeous, talented, fabulous? Actually, who are you not to be? You are a child of God. Your playing small does not serve the world. There is nothing enlightened about shrinking so that other people won't feel insecure around you. We are all meant to shine, as children do. We were born to make manifest the glory of God that is within us. It's not just in some of us; it's in everyone. And as we let our own light shine, we unconsciously give other people permission to do the same. As we are liberated from our own fear, our presence automatically liberates others.[5]

PORTAL OF TRANSFORMATION AND SACRED GEOMETRY
The Earth and Self as Vessels

Earthworm, Honeybee, Butterfly, and Spider are each the keepers of one of the cardinal directions of the Instar Medicine Wheel: East, South, West, and North. We can recognize these animal teachers as such, because they each contribute an archetypal sacred pattern to collective consciousness. It is easy to recognize and resonate with Butterfly's chrysalis or Spider's web, but what about Earthworm? As you might have guessed, though more subtle, Earthworm's sacred patterns may have the grandest scale of all. The first is the new earth that Earthworm creates through its body. This forms a large component of the soil structure on Planet Earth. Indeed, Earthworm makes and remakes our planet every day of its life, just as humans constantly re-form their body's cells. As humans, we benefit especially from Earthworm through the fertile growing humus from which we harvest much of our food.

From the perspective of Earthworm medicine, this new earth is the transmuted and recycled old forms and creations that no longer serve us. They are given new life in death as compost for the next generations of evolutionary consciousness. Each of the sacred patterns explored in this book is also a portal through which transformation occurs and sacred purpose is manifested. The sacred pattern of the new earth is created through the transformational portal of Earthworm's body itself. Accordingly, the second sacred pattern or portal to be found through Earthworm medicine is the sacred vessel of the body, through which we can experience the Divine within ourselves.

Earthworm teaches us to delight in our bodies, relishing and honoring them as multisensory organisms through which we can fully experience and learn from life on Planet Earth, as well as bring forth our soul purpose creations.

The image on the following page shows Earthworm dancing in an infinite spiral of death and rebirth, recycling and transforming both self and world. The infinity symbol is also in the shape of the number eight, which is the number of *Ma'at,* or the Egyptian principle of divine order and balance. In this case, divine order is expressed by right, balanced relationship between light and dark, death and rebirth, old and new, humility and self-honoring. Ma'at supports us in learning to love the truth about ourselves and striving to create balance in our lives. Earthworm's expression of Ma'at teaches us that as we embody this divine order within ourselves, our capacity to manifest and express our soul purpose creations deepens and expands.

Finally, as Earthworm forms the symbol for infinity, its mouth and

Earthworm transformational portal image,
which incorporates the sacred geometry of the hexagon,
the spiral, the infinity symbol, and the ouroboros

tail meet in the center, paralleling another ancient symbol, the ouroboros. The ouroboros is traditionally expressed as a snake eating its own tail, and as a symbol it connotes an endless process of re-creating the self, as well as cycles of death and rebirth. The ouroboros is also one of the main symbols of historical alchemy. Jungian psychologist Carl Jung connects the two, noting:

> The alchemists, who in their own way knew more about the nature of the individuation process than we moderns do, expressed this paradox through the symbol of the Ouroboros, the snake that eats its own tail. The Ouroboros has been said to have a meaning of infinity or wholeness. In the age-old image of the Ouroboros lies the thought of devouring oneself and turning oneself into a circulatory process, for it was clear to the more astute alchemists that the prima materia of the art was man himself. The Ouroboros is a dramatic symbol for the integration and assimilation of the opposite, i.e., of the shadow.

This "feed-back" process is at the same time a symbol of immortality, since it is said of the Ouroboros that he slays himself and brings himself to life, fertilizes himself and gives birth to himself. He symbolizes the One, who proceeds from the clash of opposites. . . .[6]

And so, we can see that through the infinite cycle of the ouroboros, Earthworm resolves the duality of light and shadow, transmuting the old and, through this process, renewing the self. Earthworm helps us to understand that we are in an evolutionary cycle of death and rebirth as living beings, through which we support the growth and development of our consciousness, expand our ability to listen to and channel the Divine within our beings, and fertilize our psyches for future creations.

EXPERIENTIAL PRACTICE

Earthworm Guided Meditation Journey and Dance

Earthworm teaches us to ecstatically embody the divine channel, opening the way to sacred communication and transforming our past creations for the highest good. After having experienced Earthworm's guided meditation journey, a new pathway of practice is opened to you. In addition to the compost created by Earthworm, its primary sacred pattern is the body itself. As a living channel, your body, through its exquisite experiential sensitivity, grants you the opportunity to practice alchemical transformation and commune with the divine universe. If you so choose, you are invited to weave this guided meditation journey and your own intuitive body movements together into a dynamic activational process.

As you prepare for Earthworm's Guided Meditation Journey, please be sure to set a sacred space for yourself. This can be as simple as creating privacy, lighting a candle, cleansing with sage smoke, or arranging a simple altar. In addition, it is highly recommended that you call in the sacred medicine wheel prior to any activities listed in this book. The medicine wheel and its teachers will help to orient, guide, and inspire you in your practice. All you need to do is bring your conscious attention and open yourself to the directions of the wheel and these animal teachers. They are already there, ready to dance with you.

Dance and intuitive movement enliven and activate the body's physiological systems, as well as stored cellular memory and connection to Spirit. You do not have to be a dancer, just as you do not have to be an artist to express the birthright of your creative energies. Simply open to your instinctive, internal knowing and allow your body to flow where its energies take you. Consider also bringing conscious awareness to the breath as you move: this further heightens visionary capacities as the body becomes oxygenated.

Select music for the meditative journey that does not have English lyrics, or is solely instrumental, and that is long enough for you to comfortably complete your dance and integrate your experience (fifteen to thirty minutes). There are no rules regarding music selection; pick something that resonates with you at the time of your dance. You may find inspiration in Earth-based or heart-centered music with drum rhythms, chanting, or resonant toning.

You can choose to read the journey to yourself with a soft gaze, record these words yourself and play them back, or ask a partner to read the words to you, slowly and thoughtfully, so you can concentrate on them with your eyes closed. The experiential journeys in this book are also facilitated in person to circles around the country. Journeying with a group with facilitator support offers a dynamic and supportive container for transformation. Learn more about these events at www .instarmedicinewheel.com.

When you are ready, breathe in and allow your body to settle into full relaxation. Breathe out, and release anything in your energy field that is not in alignment with your highest good in this moment. Continuing to breathe evenly and deeply, invite your gaze to soften, releasing your immediate environment.

With your next breath, allow your awareness to drop down into your heart. Feel the oxygen of your rhythmic breath, thrumming in the walls of muscle around you and throughout your energetic heart center. Within the center of your being, light and shadow mix in liquid currents. Notice the colors of your body and blood: ochre, dark red, Earthen hues, tumbling down into darkness. Breathe more deeply into this sacred space. Invite yourself to let out a sound, a sighing "ahh" as you come more fully into this Earthen chamber of your being. Notice how you have become a small witness inside this heart space.

If you are willing, within the chamber allow your arms to reach above your head with your fingertips touching, elongating yourself into a cylindrical tube that ends in a point at your fingertips. Between your brows sits a glowing star of intuitive wisdom. Use your intention and will to send energy from this sixth chakra up through your body, along your arms, until it meets your fingertips, creating a point of intense blue light. Reach with all your being, turning your focus within, and dive, dive headlong down into the darkness at the seat of your heart center.

You are traveling down into the Earth, away from the steady beam of sunlight that brightens the day. As you move downward, underneath the everyday world, notice that your body has become sensitive and supple. It has lengthened, internalizing your limbs into a delicate cylinder of being-ness.

Notice the way the earth feels around your body. Does it feel cool, or perhaps warm? Does the soil seem claylike, with heavy and smooth contours, or rough and granular? Your Earthworm body has exquisite sensitivity to seek out all facets of your surroundings. Travel through the Earth, examining the soil around you until you find a place that feels familiar and calls you to stay for a while.

Settle into this new space. Feel it holding your body, encasing you in density, yet supporting you. It is time to bring your attention to the energies you found resonant in this place. What does this space look like? What does the energy of the Earth feel like all around you? What colors do you see, shimmering in the darkness? This is a space made up of your creations, the bones of your past—your ancestors who have settled into this place, forming the bones of the Earth. You may also sense relics of your psyche that are ready to transform. Begin to notice that tiny minerals are resonating and shimmering softly within the Earthen structure that surrounds you. Begin to call these minerals to you. Call them from their dark confines. As if your body were a magnet, beseech these minerals with your yearning. Allow this yearning to engulf you, to keen and sing and cry. Feel your call rippling throughout your being and see these minerals drawing closer and closer until they stretch out in a plane before you.

Allow your yearning to open you, from your crown down through your entire being. It is time to transform that which no longer serves you. Your yearning becomes a hunger. You long to satisfy the higher truth of your being, to draw these glistening minerals into your body. To feed yourself, to sustain yourself from the truth, to call the past into right relationship with the future through your being. Your body ripples with this yearning call, this whole-body urge.

When you are ready, begin to move, undulating the sensitive cylinder of your body. Rock to the rhythms of your yearning, your hunger for change. Allow this hunger to intensify and expand into a knowing that, through you, transformation is manifested. Through your birthing dance, call yourself forward, open the mouth of your crown, and draw the earth into your body: minerals, old structures, past creations, whatever has served its purpose. Call it into the channel of your being. Moving forward, strong and yet delicate, open and sensitive, absorb this substrate of matter. Feel it moving through you, earth on the outside, earth on the inside, and you—a delicate ring of conscious flesh encircling all.

As the earth reaches the center of your being, call the transformative energies of the universe to you. Call Ma'at, bringer of divine order and balance. Call your ancestor, the self-eating ouroboros. Call the universal matrix of transformation, that which honors the wisdom of death and rebirth. Call your inner shamanic alchemist. Within your center, a golden light begins to glow. Call these energies to your center, and ask them to assist you in transmuting the old, so that it may die to feed the new.

As their time of dying draws near, the old creations, beliefs, and structures within your being begin to unspool as a shining film: the life they had, flashing before your awareness. Allow the images to wash over you; see them and let them go. Tell these earth structures within you, "I see you. I honor the lessons you have taught me, and the purpose you have served. I ask you, now, to live out your final purpose. I ask you to die, that you may be transformed: fertilize and cradle the new forms that yearn to be born."

The images rush past you with greater frequency, running into a single band of light. The golden light within your being now shines, lighting up the darkness. With a deep breath, call the universal matrix of transformation into your being and surrender to the dance of its process. Notice the images that come to you, as your form is taken over by this cosmic dance.

As the past creations of earth release into death, notice that a surge of energy has begun in your tail. It is a rainbow column of light—radiant life-force energy—spiraling up and through you. The intensity mounts ecstatically within you. You are a cylindrical fountain of light! Your cry for change, your hunger, your passionate surrender have acted as a lightning rod, drawing divine awareness into your flesh, marrying the two in ecstatic union.

Invite the rainbow energy of your vessel being to pour forth, both receiving and giving to the earth around you. As you do so, the remnants within your midsection pass through you. To your eyes, they are changed, rearranged into a new form. They have broken down; in their dying they have merged into something new. They have become fertile grounds through the ecstatic dance of your being.

Release them, with a sigh, into the earth behind you. Notice how the frequency of the earth around you has changed. Your dance of transformation has changed not only your past but also your entire energetic being and the collective earth of our Mother Planet. You have created new earth, fresh compost for new beginnings, by living into the truth of who you are. At this time, ask the divine energies you have called into yourself if they have any messages for you. Take some time to receive and commune with the universal matrix.

When you are ready, slowly begin to move closer to the surface of the Earth. Notice how the sun of creation reaches down into the topmost layers of soil. Feel its warmth on your face, and emerge into the sunlit morning of your conscious awareness. Taking a few deep breaths, gather the significant images and experiences of this journey within your conscious mind, and come back fully into everyday reality.

Earthworm Invocation

Blessed Creature of Shamanic Realms, containing both light and dark, reconciler of opposite energies, you who understand and teach us of the depths that we each must travel in order to reemerge into a bright new beginning . . . Show us the way. It is your sacred wisdom that teaches us that nothing is truly ever lost or wasted when we learn the great lesson of recycling our past experiences of hurt and disappointment into gifts for the future. . . . Show us the way. May we learn, by your simple humility, how to bow low to the Earth Mother and open our hearts so that we may hear her spirit sing her song of eternal creation. . . . Show us the way, we pray.

4
Honeybee

Embodying the Bliss of Sacred Union,
Service, and Creativity

As we become purer channels for God's light, we develop
an appetite for the sweetness that is possible in this world.
A miracle worker is not geared toward fighting the world
that is, but toward creating the world that could be.

MARIANNE WILLIAMSON, *A RETURN TO LOVE*

Honeybees have captured the imagination and curiosity of humanity since ancient times. Whether it is because of their fascinating relationships with flowers, their ability to transform nectar into honey, or the geometrically precise structures they build, humans have avidly studied, celebrated, and worked with Bees throughout our history.

During the Ice Age, approximately ten thousand to twenty thousand years ago, prehistoric cave paintings depicting honey hunting were made in Spain. Others, possibly much older, have also been found in South Africa. During this time, wild honey was hunted as a sweet and sometimes protein-filled treat (as many combs contained larvae). At some point humans transitioned to keeping their own Bees; perhaps after discovering hives that had moved into abandoned human-made containers.[1]

The ancient Egyptians were beekeepers, and Egyptian culture had a deeply intertwined relationship with Bees. The earliest archaeological record of beekeeping in Egypt is found in the sun temple of King Ne-user-re at Abu Ghorab dating from 2400 BCE. This decorative frieze illustrates the Egyptian honeymaking process, beginning with the beehive and proceeding to its storage in containers.

The Egyptians believed that Bees originated as tears of the sun god, Ra. Honey was used as a sacred offering to the gods and was left as food for the afterlife in the tombs of the dead. Many believed that the soul took on the form of a Bee after death. For four thousand years the symbol of Lower Egypt was the Bee. In Greek mythology many divine infants were said to be nursed on milk and honey, including Zeus and Aristaeus. Aristaeus was tended to by the nymph Melissa, Chiron the Centaur, and the Hours. In Greek mythology the nymph Melissa educated others on the uses of honey. The name *Melissa* means "honeybee." The priestesses of the oracle at Delphi were known as the "Delphic Bees" and drank mead, a fermented honey beverage mixed with hallucinogens to evoke visions. Throughout the ages, there have been various Melissae, or Bee priestesses, who have connected to divine energies through the path of the Honeybee.

Both Virgil and Aristotle wrote extensively on the behaviors and products of Honeybees. Pliny is said to have wondered if honey was the saliva of the stars or the sweat of the sky. In India the gods Krishna, Vishnu, and Indra were known as the "nectar-born" and were symbolized by the Bee. In Central America the Wasp and the Bee were important figures in Mayan cosmology. To the Maya, who practiced beekeeping, the Bee was an aspect of the Planet Venus and was connected to the sacrificial Diving God. The Honeybee is found throughout indigenous North American mythology and culture, with many stories describing the industrious and highly ethical nature of the Bee.

Symbolically, Bees have been traditionally connected to the regeneration or resurrection of life. Swarms are most commonly seen in the spring, the season of regeneration. Some traditions hold that Bees surrounded or emanated from Christ during his crucifixion. Bulgarian folktales base the creation of their mountains and valleys in a conversation between God and the Bees. Bees have also been connected to diligence, ethics, organization, purity, creativity, and other virtues.

Honeybees are part of the order Hymenoptera, or the membrane-wing order of insects. Their evolutionary history highlights an intimate relationship with flowering plants. Bees and flowers developed on Planet Earth at approximately the same point in time, 140 million to 160 million years ago, between the Cretaceous and Jurassic periods. They coevolved in a symbiotic dance, changing their forms to entice and meet the needs of the other.

Today the highest concentration of Bee species is in tropical areas, but Bees range all over the world, from the arctic tundra to the Himalayas. Two species of Honeybees developed the capacity to form an "inert cluster." An inert cluster is a technology used by the Bees to regulate the temperature of the hive. In essence, Bees cluster closer together to preserve and create warmth and space themselves out, fanning their wings to create cool temperatures. This ability to regulate temperature allowed the Honeybee to migrate beyond temperate zones.

There are between 16,000 and 22,000 named species of Bees, but only 7 of those species produce honey. The famed Honeybee is *Apis mellifera,* which means "carrier of sweetness." *Apis mellifera* is not indigenous to North America but has spread throughout the continent after having been introduced by Spaniards and early settlers in the seventeenth century. Before this, other species of honeymaking Bees existed in North and Central America and were cultivated by pre-Columbian beekeeping cultures, such as the Maya.

Bees are amazingly complex creatures. Honeybee genetics is closer to that of vertebrates than that of other insects. Interestingly, Honeybees have circadian rhythms, like mammals. In twenty-one days a Bee morphs from egg to adult within a hexagonal wax cell, experiencing five form-changing molts before emerging. The larvae are fed honey, royal jelly, and pollen. The specific types of food and ratios given depend on the type of role the new Bee will play in the hive.

As a Bee flies past you in the garden, its wings are beating two hundred times per second, which creates its well-known buzz. Bees have the ability to see ultraviolet light, and they use these frequencies (in addition to other sensory inputs) to seek out flowers. When a Bee lands on a flower, she is gathering nectar and spreading pollen. A Bee can remember if a flower has a good nectar yield for approximately twelve days. Bees have a strong sense of time and visit certain flowers at certain times of the day, depending on when it produces nectar.

Nectar and pollen are taken back to the hive to be used as food. Honey is a concentrated form of nectar. A single hive can produce 150 pounds of honey in one year, yet a single Honeybee will only produce less than half a teaspoon of honey in its lifetime.

Bees communicate by dancing. The dancing of Bees communicates incredible detail about nectar locations. Through these dances, other Bees are able to find specific locations and plant types miles away. When a foraging Bee returns to the hive and begins to communicate, other Bees always join in on the dancing, mimicking it to help pass on information to other Bees nearby. The vigor and intensity of the dance indicates how good a nectar source is. A Bee's dance includes multisensory components, including movement, buzzing, nectar scent, intensity, and the angle/orientation of the dance. Through this, the community learns the direction, distance, plant type, and how many Bees are needed for the collection task.

Honeybee hives are usually made up of 60,000 to 100,000 community members. If a hive becomes too large, a second queen is made and she migrates with many of the existing hive members to a new location, which she instinctively chooses. This migration is called a swarm, which, while it may have historically inspired fear in human viewers, is a largely peaceful group of Bees intent on finding a new home.

EXPLORING HONEYBEE'S PLACE
ON THE MEDICINE WHEEL

The South Direction and the Sacred Family

Honeybee is the keeper of the South direction of the Instar Medicine Wheel. The South direction is the place of life's abundance, the verdant growing months, the sweet blessings of lived experience, and the sacred family. Honeybee expresses all these aspects of the South direction.

The Honeybee is one of Earth's most intensely communal and interdependent creatures. The hive is the densely interconnected and multifaceted center of Bee civilization. Its structure brings forth new generations of life and stores the golden nourishment of honey. The hive is a waxen structure, but it is also the Bees themselves. In their community, the Honeybees become a superorganism. As many as 60,000 Honeybees can live in a hive, and each has a sacred purpose. The primary focus of the hive is to bring forth new life and sustain it with myriad practices. Accordingly, the hive can be understood both as a community of individuals and as a unified superorganism, which parallels the cellular community of both the human body and our planet as a whole.

Earthworm teaches us to access and learn the craft of our sacred purpose. Honeybee builds on that Earthen foundation, teaching us how to express our fertility in the world, generating new life and co-creations, while learning the dance of sacred union. The sacred family is an expression of this. Co-creation and manifestation are achieved through the resolution or union of differing principles, such as masculine and feminine, dark and light, human and divine. Through the sacred union of the two, the synergistic co-creative child is brought forth.

Honeybee offers us the archetypal teaching of how to bring forth co-creation in our families, communities, and within ourselves. Honeybee embodies the divine consort, the midwife, and the sacred child—a golden trinity of generative co-creation. As human beings, each of these sacred family roles is within us. They are each facets essential for the alchemical process of fertile co-creation—be the goal an innovative idea, an art project, a new business, or a beloved child. To be co-creators in this life, we must fully embody each aspect of the golden trinity, or sacred family.

SACRED PURPOSE

Co-creation through
the Sweetness of Sacred Union

There are approximately six thousand Honeybees in the hive. This population is composed of three types of Bee: the female "worker" Bee, the male "drone," and the female "queen." The vast majority of Bees are female worker Bees, with a few hundred male drones, and only one queen Bee.

It is easy to presume a hierarchical framework within the hive and to draw extensive meaning from the common names given to the different Bees. As part of the Instar Medicine Wheel, however, these three types of Bees make up a collaborative, golden trinity of co-creation. Each has an essential purpose. The Honeybee is an excellent teacher of sacred purpose because each Bee type plays a highly specialized role. Human beings need not go into the specialized extremes of Bee life, because we embody all the facets of the golden trinity within ourselves. It is in their relationship that our sacred purpose is illuminated and expressed.

The Divine Consorts, the Queen, and the Male Drone
The queen Honeybee begins her life in the same manner as any typical female worker Bee. Within the hexagonal waxen chamber, her egg is identical to a worker Bee egg. The queen's very existence is based on the hive's decision that a new queen is needed to take the place of the old queen. At this point a future queen's larva is initiated into new dimensions of self and purpose. The larva is fed royal jelly, a milky substance

secreted by a midwife Bee. This triggers morphological changes—enhancing the queen's size and structure—so that she may become the single fertile egg layer for future generations of the hive.

Once she has emerged from her cell and confirmed her supremacy as the only queen, the queen Honeybee is ready for her virgin or nuptial flight. As she begins the only flight of her life (save for relocating her hive, if necessary), the queen is joined in the air by many male drones.

The male drone is fed and nurtured by the hive until the queen is ready to mate. To the hive, this is the moment for the expression of the drone's primary purpose, to inseminate the queen as the divine consort. The male drones race along currents of air in pursuit of the queen. She mates with many of the drones, though not all, during her nuptial flight. This mating ceremony inseminates the queen with a lifetime of sperm. After this flight, the remaining drones are not allowed back into the hive. The queen then turns her attention to a new focus, one that will dominate the rest of her existence: laying eggs. She moves from hexagonal cell to cell, depositing an egg in each chamber. A queen Bee may lay up to one million eggs in her lifetime—as many as two thousand a day. She lives for approximately two years; cared for, fed, and cleaned by her daughters, the worker Bees.

The divine consorts—the queen and the drones—are the seeders and conceivers of new life. In their courtship and coupling future generations are conceived for the continuation of the hive. Both these Bee types experience a laser-sharp focus of purpose, yet this focus highlights the ceremonial importance of sacred union in our lives. Whether it is a union of masculine and feminine principles, darkness and light, or human and divine, sacred union is the alchemical, transformative moment in which the sacred child or co-creation is conceived and brought forth from other dimensions.

The nuptial flight is the moment of inspiration—the eureka!—experienced by inventors, artists, and mystic muses throughout the ages. This co-creative union occurs within the self, after we have opened to the divine or the co-creative process (supported by Earthworm's fertile foundation). Once opened to our dance of purpose, we can offer all of ourselves into a single moment. In this moment we invite the sacred other into the depths of our being, into our heart. The sacred other invites us within itself. In this merging of Spirit, a transformative, alchemical miracle occurs. Inspiration is drawn through the dimensions to reside within our beings. As a seed is planted, an egg is fertilized.

The divine consorts initiate us into the willing, vulnerable dance of sacred union, in which we lay all of ourselves on the altar of experience. Through this vulnerable merging with the sacred other, we experience bliss. We experience the blinding, prismatic light of new life and also death. Both are present in the conceptual moment. We must be willing to lay it all on the table in service to our own evolution, transformation, and union. Whether sacred union occurs within the self or with another, we must be willing to die, metaphorically, to breach the boundaries of isolation and self-containment. We must be willing to live into merging, knowing that our selfhood is transformed in the union—even as we retain our autonomy. Through this, new life, new dreams, and new creations are conceived.

Midwives of the Hive, the Worker Bees

Worker Bees comprise the vast majority of Honeybees within the hive. If you spy a Honeybee on the wing or visiting a flower, she is a worker Bee. Through her energy and actions, the worker Bee enlivens and sustains the entire hive community. Bees are acclaimed for their busy-ness, but while they have a strong sense of purpose and contribution to the hive, in actuality Honeybees spend as much as two-thirds of their lives waiting and conserving energy. The Honeybees wait until their energy can serve an effective purpose, such as when a load of nectar and pollen arrive back at the hive. At that point, Bees spring into action!

According to British food writer Hattie Ellis:

The worker bee is the ultimate multitasker. From the moment she is born to the moment she dies, she performs a series of widely different tasks: cleaning cells, tending and feeding the larvae and pupae, building and repairing the honeycomb and nest in general, receiving nectar from foraging bees and processing it into honey, receiving and packing pollen into the cells, ventilating the hive to keep it at the right temperature by flapping her wings, guarding the entrance to the hive, and then, about halfway through her life, going out to forage flowers, bringing back nectar and pollen, reporting back good finds to the hive making honey, eating some honey herself, and going out again to forage some more. A worker bee in summer may live six weeks before dying, eventually, of exhaustion. In her life, she may have collected enough nectar to make just a quarter ounce of honey, less than half a teaspoonful.[2]

As stated previously, a worker Bee spends the first half of her life—about three weeks—within the hive. She has just recently left her own hexagonal birthing chamber; turning immediately to assist the cycles of birth and caring for the young and the hive, which were just recently bestowed on her. In this golden and shadowed internal world, the hive hums with life, energy, and work.

In this stage of her life, the worker Bee experiences the initiation of stepping in to the role of midwife. While the children she nurtures and feeds are not her direct offspring, within the collaborative weaving of community co-creation, she is both midwife and parent through the larvae's developmental stages.

As midwife, the worker Bee cares for all aspects of the creative process, which brings forth new generations into the hive. She cleans and cares for the hive structure and honeycomb, she cleans and feeds the queen and drones, and she directly assists the new Bees with all their needs.

This is an internal initiation in which the worker Bee learns to embody collective service and purpose through her own actions, focusing on bringing forth new life within the hive. The midwife worker Bee teaches us how to nurture our creations and inspirations through direct care and consistent, dedicated work. Earthworm prepares the fertile ground for new creations, while the Honeybee divine consorts seed and conceive the creation. The Honeybee midwife is the one who assists in the gestational process of bringing forth the pregnant ideas and creations of our souls.

This time of internal initiation within the hive can be seen as nurturing a pregnancy, whether one's own or in service as a midwife. To bring the co-creative sacred child forward—whether an idea, an action, or a literal child—we must nurture both this new being as well as our own sacred vessel, with dedication and consistency. For we are the portal through which divine inspiration enters the world. As we gestate, we must remember to imbibe the sweetness of life, so that we can bring forth the next generation of innovation, creativity, and human beings.

The midwife Honeybee teaches us how to fully embody this essential component of the sacred alchemy process. We can have the most exciting, creative idea in the world as individuals or a society, but until we learn how to midwife ourselves through the gestational process of transformation, many creations may be miscarried or terminated before birth into the world can occur.

In the second half of life, worker Bees are ready to expand beyond the hive into the fragrant air currents of the pollen flight. As they make their way from flower to flower and back to the hive, their average speed is fifteen miles per hour, with an average pollen load distance of thirty-seven miles, and an average daily flight distance of sixty miles!

Worker Bees leave their primary role as midwife behind and fly into the air, seeking out the tantalizing fragrances of flowering plants. They entice her with seductive colors, scents, textures, and ultraviolet frequencies. Imagine yourself—the minute size of a Bee—visiting a flower for the first time. You notice a gorgeous, nectar-filled scent and are pulled toward the limpid petals of the flower. You alight and step softly on its velvety texture. Soon you notice a darker opening, through which the pollen-spangled pistil and stamen emerge. You enter this dark depth, the sweet intoxicating musk growing stronger. The folds of the flower grow closer around you, and pollen attaches itself to your body. In the very center, you come upon a font of elixir—nectar! You dive into it, sipping, tasting, imbibing! Your entire being is wrapped in sweetness and softness, perfume and nectar emanating from the core into which you have dived, nuzzling and wriggling in delight.

Once you are filled to capacity with the sweetness of life, you return to the hive. There, you deposit your treasure trove of nectar and pollen. These will be taken into the hive by other worker Bees. At the opening of the hive, in the community of other Bees, you feel called to express your story through dance. You wriggle, wave, and flex your body with intensity to communicate where others can find the abundance of nectar you just savored. In this way, both the nectar and the pollen you brought back—and the information of your journey—are offered to better the hive. Your lived experience feeds the hive on multiple levels and in many ways.

While a female worker Bee's life is intense, short, and at times exhausting, it is also a grace-filled weaving of all aspects of hive life. A worker Honeybee's life may be seen as an ecstatic embodiment of purpose. The existence and sustainment of the hive is danced through all aspects of her being, connecting her to every facet of the community—whether it is nourishing and caring for the young, building a honeyed cathedral of light, flying aloft on perfumed air, or delving into the orgasmic heart of a flower. Her life is a service to the collective, and through the sweet richness of her experiences, both she and the hive are transformed.

Though she is not a divine consort, the worker Bee's lived experience fully embodies the ecstasy of sacred union—a union of self and purpose. This is the initiation of the foraging worker Bee: learning how to create sacred union of self and purpose, and through this tasting the sweet joys of living. As we learn to follow Honeybee's example, unifying the actions of our work with ecstatic bliss, we too can experience the excitement of flight and the sweet ecstasy of the flower in every moment.

This may seem like a tall order, especially when we are waiting in line or changing a flat tire, yet Honeybee challenges us to make embodying the sweet union of self and purpose a sacred practice. As we meet the challenges and opportunities of life, how can we more fully synthesize our lived experience and work into soulful living? How can each moment more fully embody the sweet bliss found at the center of a flower? How can we experience both the freedom and purpose of the pollen flight, while buying groceries or weeding the garden? Honeybee encourages us and illuminates this process.

HONEYBEE AND
THE HUMAN LIFE CYCLE
The Sacred Family

As we have learned, Honeybee embodies the Golden Trinity of co-creation: divine consort, midwife, and sacred child. Each of these roles is within every human psyche, ready to dance creatively with inspiration. This trinity is the sacred family.

After we have journeyed in our apprentice years with Earthworm—learning to first access and practice the craft of sacred purpose and divine communication—we are ready to move into a new phase of life. Each phase of life on the Instar Medicine Wheel has two important themes in common: sacred purpose and transformation. Each place on the wheel expresses the themes differently. For Honeybee, sacred purpose is focused on conceiving, bringing forth, and sustaining the co-creative child (or creative idea). The preservation and enhancement of the unfolding hive community is paramount. Accordingly, personal purpose is connected to sacred collective service.

As we each conceive, bring forth, and sustain our own creative gifts and purpose, the collective is enriched and enlivened—encouraging collective evolution and transformation. Our unique contribution may be less than half a teaspoon of honey, but the magic of its concentrated essence is immeasurable to the collective.

Within the human life cycle, the sacred family represents the life phase of householder, lover, parent, and midwife. As partners and parents, or as midwife to a collective goal, we hold safe nurturing space and provide for dreams and creations to unfold and develop. These dreams may be a child, but they may also be a soul purpose career, a nurturing family nest, an innovative idea, or the developmental experiences of life. In this time, we bring our first creations forward, learning how to nurture them as they gestate, so they may come into the light of the world. We learn how to bring Spirit into Matter, creating the sacred cathedral of the hive in our own lives or for the collective in our work. In this way, we learn to embody and practice the craft of manifestation through the alchemical union of self, purpose, and the sacred other.

This phase of the Instar Medicine Wheel is more highly collaborative than any other, though there is co-creation in every phase. We learn to open to the vulnerability of sacred union for the first time, laying ourselves bare and merging with the sacred other so that co-creations and bliss may spring forth. We move from singularity into the synthesis of union, while learning to retain our autonomy. This is no small task and will be discussed in depth in a later section.

Finally, we also learn to become ecstatic lovers of life. We experience the sweet joys of abundance, like Honeybee visiting a field of flowers. We learn to more fully embody pleasure, to taste the sweetness of human experience. We learn to balance the challenges of parenthood, midwifery, and relationship with the blessings and joy of purpose inherent in these roles and relationships. More deeply, we learn to marry sacred purpose to our experience of each moment, that it may become a soulful opportunity for bliss and union with the Divine.

All these teachings are part of the sacred family phase of life. Whether we find ourselves in a relationship or parenting a family, or whether we are on our own, our sacred purpose is always connected to the collective hive. Because we are beings capable of divine co-creation, present within us are the facets of the golden trinity. As living beings, our every moment is relational: with the elements, with the sweet moments of life, with our loved ones, with our own creative inspiration, and with the Divine.

Honeybee teaches us how to nurture our relational selves, and to open our hearts to sacred union. Through this, the sacred co-creations of our dreams come into the golden light of the world.

PORTAL OF TRANSFORMATION AND SACRED GEOMETRY

Sacred Union and the Golden Trinity

Each animal teacher of the Instar Medicine Wheel offers a sacred pattern that acts as an initiatory portal for transformation of consciousness. The sacred purpose of Honeybee is expressed through the initiatory life phase of sacred union and midwifery of the co-creative child. Through these acts we learn to fully embody and express the birthright of our co-creative natures. In the image below, Honeybee is at the center of a six-pointed star. In the middle of the star is a hexagon, and within that

Honeybee transformational portal image utilizing the sacred geometry symbols of the hexagon, the honeycomb, the six-pointed star, sacred union, and the flower of life

hexagon are smaller hexagons. These hexagons illustrate the hive and honeycomb, through which new life and the sweet essences of Spirit spring forth. The Honeybee both comes from the hexagonal portal of new life and tends to the next generations of life that come after her, as midwife. The hexagonal comb is a portal within a portal. As Honeybee steps into these initiatory life phases, she experiences sacred union.

Revered by many cultures and spiritual traditions, including a strong resonance in Judaism, the six-pointed star is the symbol of sacred union. It is the marriage of two triangles, one pointing up and the other down. In yogic tradition the seven chakras of the body are illustrated as triangles. The three lower chakras have their apexes at the top, moving upward toward the crown chakra. Meanwhile, the three upper chakras have their apexes at the bottom and are moving directionally downward. The upper three and lower three chakras (six in all) meet as a six-pointed star of union in the heart chakra. The heart chakra is the center in which sacred union, co-creation, and sweet bliss occur. Within the large six-pointed star, there is always a honeycombed hexagon, representing union in the heart. At the center of this hexagon is another six-pointed star, and within that, we find Honeybee.

Honeybee brings a new expression of co-creation to the six-pointed star through the golden trinity. The golden trinity is made of all partners in the co-creative process: the divine consorts who conceive the child, the midwife who nurtures the child and helps bring it into the world, and the sacred co-creative child itself. It is important to remember that each point of this triangle is part of our human psyche, and they work in tandem. In this way, a six-pointed star is created when the sacred family of the golden trinity comes together within us; this is one triangle. The other triangle represents the merging of our soul with our purpose, with the Divine, with the sacred other.

As the two triangles come together in sacred union, new creations are conceived and brought forth into the world. The new creations are illustrated as the seed or flower of life symbol at the tip of each star point. The flower of life symbol is an ancient, cross-cultural symbol of sacred geometry. According to Drunvalo Melchizedek, an expert on the flower of life, in the Judeo-Christian tradition the seed of life represents the six days of creation, during which *Elohim* (God) created life. Within the seed or flower of life is also the vesica piscis—a symbol of sacred union—as illustrated by two overlapping circles (with a third almond shape in their space of union). In addition, the intertwining Borromean rings (which represent the Holy Trinity from a Christian perspective) can be found.[3]

It is interesting to note that the Honeybee has 6,900 hexagonal plates on each eye lens. Within the threes and sixes of the Honeybee's sacred geometry, the number of lens plates and their hexagonal shape is a surprising synchronicity and affirmation of sacred union. We can bring forth new co-creations through the lens of our being, in sacred relationship with ourselves and the Divine.

TRANSFORMATION

Alchemy of the Hive

As has already been discussed, the hexagonal cells of the hive are a portal through which new life emerges. Remember also that the hive acts as a cellular superorganism, paralleling the human body and our world as a whole. This parallel underlines our ability to co-create with divine energy through our beings, personally and collectively. The conception and birth of new life is an alchemical process in which life-force energy is transformed into new forms (whether a child or a creative idea) through the living ceremony of sacred union. Accordingly, generating the next generations of Bees is a main subject of alchemy within the hive. Bees also act as sacred alchemists in a variety of other ways. This will be explored in the following sections.

From Flower to Fruit

Because of their essential work in the cross-pollination of plants, Bees are the alchemists who assist plants in the vital transformation from flower to fruit. This service allows plants to reproduce, sustains ecosystems, and feeds the world with its bounty. Honeybee and its golden trinity offer wisdom about each stage of the creative cycle. Yet Honeybee's central teaching for human understanding highlights a critical stage in the creative process: when the blossoming of our ideas is manifested into the fruit of reality. Through its willingness to open into sacred union, consistent dedicated action, and nurturing midwifery, Honeybee assists us in bridging this precarious phase of creativity. Bee offers itself as a midwife and guide on our human creative journeys as we seek to bring forth new ideas, projects, children, and purpose. If you find yourself in this critical stage, ask Bee to infuse your project with the golden light and honeyed sweetness of its nurturing guidance. And at this critical juncture, as we seek to bridge the past, present, and future in healing transformation as a planet, let us invite the love and wisdom of the Bee to be our guide.

Honeybee creates a variety of other sacred and symbolic medicines through the co-creation of the hive. Many of these sacred medicines can be used for health and healing on physical and other levels of experience. The American Apitherapy Society (www.apitherapy.org) is an excellent resource for additional information on this topic. Please contact a health professional before using any of the substances that are discussed in this book medicinally.

Honey

Honey is the essence of its surrounding environment. It is the alchemical treasure of clover, orange blossom, lavender, thyme, and myriad other flowers. Specific to the region, time of year, and a Bee's flight path, a unique honey is born. Honey can range from dark and musky to light and ethereal, with a range of flavors as vast as the number of flowering plants.

Honey begins as the nectar found in flowers. Flowers use nectar to entice Honeybees into their perfumed and pollen-spangled centers. In this way Bees carry pollen from blossom to blossom, aiding plants in a mutually beneficial dance of cross-pollination. When a Bee has reached its nectar-carrying capacity, she returns to the hive and deposits her load with another worker Bee. The nectar is passed Bee to Bee within the hive, condensing it with each transfer. Within the hive, nectar is concentrated through evaporation until it takes on the recognizable form of honey. Along the way the Bees add preservative enzymes. Pure honey never spoils. Honey represents the alchemy of the Honeybee, a transformative blessing in which the sweetness of life becomes nourishing food for the entire community.

Aristotle did not believe that Bees made honey. Instead, he believed that honey was the precipitation of rainbows, which Bees gathered as dew from leaves. It is a lovely thought to see honey as the alchemical product of rainbows, but from an energetic perspective this is a fertile concept to explore. Rainbows are made when light and shadowed, moisture-filled vapor meet in sacred union in the atmosphere. Flowers take the energy of the sun into their bodies through photosynthesis and drink water from the rain through their roots. Flowering plants perform their own sacred union of these opposing principles, which is manifested as sweet nectar and pollen. Honeybees collect these floral products, and through their own transformative process distill nectar to its essence. Light and water, through the prisms of flower and Bee, create a luminescent sacred child: honey. Energetically, partaking of honey is truly ingesting a rainbow of sacred union!

Honey is the food of the Bees. Honey is truly golden energy in motion. A Honeybee's flight and its actions caring for the hive are fueled by this sweet substance. In this way honey creates more honey by fueling the future flights of Bees to flowers. Honey's energy maintains the bodies of worker Bees caring for new bees, feeds the young and old alike, and assists in building the substance of the hive. In short, the sweet alchemical beauty of lived experience nourishes, sustains, and builds a blessed present and future. And this present and future go on to create more honey through the dance of life.

Honey has been used medicinally for thousands of years. It is a broad-spectrum antibiotic and is a painless antiseptic. Honey can be applied to the skin as a healing treatment for a variety of ailments, including rashes, wounds, scarring, fungal infections, and burns. It is soothing to the nerves, assists sleep, and heals gastrointestinal issues and a number of eye issues. It is also an easily digestible sweetener.

Beeswax

Beeswax is made from digested honey within the Bee, which is excreted for a new purpose. In the hive, beeswax takes the form of honeycombed walls, in which Bee eggs hatch and form into adults, and in which honey is stored. The hexagonal-celled structure of the honeycomb is the lightest way to store the maximum amount of honey, using the least amount of wax. As we've learned, the lens of a Honeybee's eye is made up of 6,900 hexagonal plates. So, in a sense, how Honeybees see the world is the form that their creations take.

According to the American Apitherapy Society, beeswax is formed and used in the following manner.

> Young bees in the hive, after feeding the young brood with royal jelly, in their third week of life, take part in the construction of the hive. Engorged with honey and resting suspended for 24 hours together with many other bees in the same position, 8 wax glands on the underside of the abdomens of the young bees secrete small wax plate-lets. These are scraped off by the bee, chewed and masticated into pliable pieces with the addition of saliva and a variety of enzymes. Once chewed, attached to the comb and re-chewed several times, they finally form part of this architectural masterpiece, a comb of hexagonal cells, a 20 g structure which can support 1000 g of honey. Wax is used to cap the ripened honey and when mixed with some propolis, also protects the brood from infections and desiccation.[4]

Beeswax forms the structure that surrounds and nurtures the Bee community. Wax is used in protective and containing service to the co-creations of the hive, namely as growth containers for young Bees and as a storage system for honey. It is essential for our sweet creations— be they children, inspired ideas, or new projects—to have a supportive structure to house them as they gestate, or when they return from flight into the world. This structure may take the form of a healthy, harmonic body, a safe and loving family, a nurturing home or work setting, or even a healthy psychological space within the mind. The sweet liquid of honey in our lives needs the grounded, Earthen structure of beeswax to flourish.

Royal Jelly

Royal Jelly is a protein-rich food derived from eating pollen. A milky substance, it is fed to all Bee larvae, but royal jelly is given in a high concentration only when it is time for a new queen to emerge. Honeybee queens are made, not born. They begin life as the same type of egg as female worker Bees. When a hive decides that a new queen is needed for the welfare of the hive, a small number of worker Bee larvae are given a high concentration of royal jelly as their primary food source. Royal jelly incites morphological changes in a Bee, increasing her size and characteristics, so that she may step into a new purpose as the soul egg layer for the entire hive.

Symbolically, royal jelly is a Divine-infused substance that inspires development, evolution, and radiant well-being. In this case *morphology* refers to the energetic blueprint of our bodies and soul in this lifetime. As children, some of us were lucky to have parents and living situations that fed us "royal jelly," a substance of love and inspired belief in our talents, abilities, and soul expression. In addition, many young children retain a connection with Spirit or the universe, through which they receive the royal jelly of insights and loving wisdom from higher dimensions of consciousness. If we received this royal jelly as children, our soul purpose and creative development were given a rapid growth path in which to fully manifest and share our soul's expression with the world.

From a shamanic perspective, human beings can also receive the evolutionary support of royal jelly by embracing the wisdom inherent in lived experiences, be they challenging, heartbreaking, or full of delight. In fact, it is the sometimes harrowing flight to the flower of life through which we bring back the food and sweet riches of our fullest selves. You may have experienced a taste of royal jelly in your life at points of rapid growth, development, or transformation.

As adults, we also have the opportunity to feed ourselves the royal jelly we did not receive as children. This takes the form of developing a strong internal sense of self-love, self-acceptance, and self-worth. As we begin to believe in and advocate for our needs—learning to embrace our authentic selves—we automatically begin to reach out for developmental growth opportunities, such as therapeutic support, spiritually based workshops, or breathwork. These developmental opportunities enhance the blossoming of our fullest self and soul purpose. The royal jelly of adulthood can also take the form of reclaiming our direct relationship with the universe and Great Spirit. Through this we can feed ourselves on all levels of being.

In addition, royal jelly can be ingested as a health supplement. It can be found at many cooperatives and natural health food stores. For human health purposes, royal jelly offers the following benefits.

Royal jelly, which is high in B vitamins, has a metabolic stimulating action, which aids in the processing of proteins, carbohydrates, and lipids. It also increases oxygen consumption, improving endurance and decreasing fatigue. As a powerful antioxidant, royal jelly decreases levels of free radicals which are thought to cause aging. Royal jelly has a direct effect on the adrenal glands leading to an increased secretion of adrenaline which can be cardioprotective. With its protective effects on the cardiovascular, pulmonary, and immune systems, it is no wonder royal jelly is a prized commodity in many cultures.[5]

Bee Pollen and Bee Bread

Bee pollen is the male seed of a plant. The hairs on a Bee's body create an electromagnetic charge that draws pollen to it when it visits a flower. Bee pollen is high in protein and amino acids, and it is the Honeybee's primary source of protein. Bee pollen can also be mixed with honey and enzymes that inhibit germination, making Bee bread.

According to the American Apitherapy Society, Bee pollen "has become a popular energy-enhancing nutritional supplement because it is about 25% protein and contains all the essential amino acids and vitamins and minerals needed by humans, except vitamin B_{12}."[6]

Propolis

Propolis is a sticky, gluelike substance that Bees create from plant resins. Propolis is well known for its antiseptic, detoxifying, and antimicrobial properties. Bees coat the inside of their hives with propolis to inhibit the spread of bacteria and fungi.

In human health, propolis has flavonoid compounds that contribute to anti-inflammatory and antioxidant activity. These flavonoids appear to have tissue-strengthening and regenerative effects. In addition:

> Used as an antiseptic wash or salve, propolis is able to prevent the growth of bacteria in cuts and burns and it can also promote the healing process in lesions of the skin that have not healed. Used as a mouthwash, propolis is able to prevent bad breath, gingivitis, tooth decay and gum disease and it is commonly taken as a remedy for sore throats. Propolis is capable of acting as an anti-inflammatory as well. It can help with symptoms of arthritis, boils, acne, asthma, dermatitis, ulcers, and inflammatory bowel diseases. Propolis has also been found to have antimutagenic effects, which may aid in the prevention of cancer. In conjunction with royal jelly it can ameliorate the side effects of chemo and radiation therapies.[7]

Symbolically, propolis may be seen as the development and use of healthy and appropriate interpersonal boundaries. As we develop a sense of self-love and self-worth, we begin to see that we have the right to create a safe space for ourselves and our families. This safe space may be physical, leaving a dangerous location or social situation; emotional and psychological, naming our truths and not accepting anyone else's beliefs or ideas as our own; or spiritual/energetic, keeping our energy fields clear of others' energies and empowering ourselves to connect directly to the Divine Universal Source, which feeds and blesses our lives.

LESSONS AND SHADOW
Sacred Union and the Self

Through the initiations of the Honeybee, we learn how to fully embody sacred union, so that we can manifest the divine children and creations of our lives. Learning to create on this level is a tremendous and powerful path of experience. As we step onto the path of authenticity and soul expression, anything that stands in the way of this goal often comes up to be processed, transformed, and released.

Common themes may be experienced during the initiation of the Honeybee. The core theme of Honeybee medicine is sacred union. Sacred union occurs when two opposing or differing principles come together, creating synergy. Synergy is defined as a state in which a result is more than the sum of its parts. This is the divine third, or child, co-created through sacred union. Sacred union can occur between masculine and feminine principles, light and shadow, human and Divine. There are infinite types of sacred union and co-creations. Because this union takes place in the merging of self and other, selfhood is an important developmental theme during the Honeybee initiatory process.

First, in order to co-create and merge in union with the sacred other, we must be willing to be vulnerable and open. Many of us have experienced wounds or have beliefs/frameworks about self that inhibit, protect, or defend against openness and vulnerability. To meet another in sacred union we must first be willing to trust, not only the other but also ourselves. Trust is an essential ingredient that allows us to open ourselves fully to another and to this sacred co-creative process.

If we believe that the person or situation we cherish or are attracted to may hurt us when we reveal our authentic self, we cannot open fully to the sacred moment. If we do not trust ourselves to hold our own autonomous space, even as we merge within another, we cannot open up safely. Just as propolis can be seen as healthy boundaries, beeswax symbolizes the essential trust needed to form a safe cell in which sacred union can take place. This can be seen in the image on page 66. At the core of the six-pointed sacred union star is the beeswax hexagonal cell. Through this central place, the co-creative child emerges.

Propolis, or healthy boundaries, is a state of dynamic balance. Healthy boundaries do not mean an extreme of militant self-defense or, conversely, to lose oneself in another. In union we must be able to retain a sense of who we are. We cannot lose our truth or sense of self to our divine consort or the sacred child we are creating. Yet, at the same time, we must open to allowing our reality and self-definition to shift, so that it can inhabit the new energetic matrix of sacred union.

True partnership, and the ability to parent/midwife without losing ourselves to our co-creations, must have a grounding in autonomy, trust, and healthy boundaries. Mutual respect, tenderness, compassion, and communication are important foundational elements for creative partnerships of any kind. Whether the sacred other is a collaborative work partner, lover, family member, friend, or child, investing in the exploration of our personal beliefs regarding sacred union is essential to creating healthy relationships and vibrant creations.

EXPERIENTIAL PRACTICE

Honeybee Guided Meditation Journey

The following guided meditation journey can support you in exploring the fears, wounds, and beliefs that inhibit you from fully experiencing sacred union and co-creation. Your role and identity as a participant in sacred union will be illuminated and affirmed. This journey is a healing and harmonizing opportunity that can enhance future co-creations, authentic truth, and the blissful experience of union.

In this moment, all possibilities exist, both within you and within the ever-unfolding universe—for they are the same. Inside your cells lives a starry night of infinite universal presence. Let your breath begin to flow, activating your conscious awareness as a creative being. Come into the spark of the present moment and know that you have the ability to create galaxies and oceans, smiles and laughter, health and harmony. Breathe in . . . and release your breath out. Breathe the infinite universe into your cells . . . and breathe out, sending your soul's unique song to touch all life with its beauty. Fully present in this moment, begin to open yourself to the journey of the Honeybee.

Find yourself floating slowly through warm currents of air. There is a wild garden of flowers growing all around you. You can see emerald greens . . . a jeweled rainbow of colors . . . soft textures. Take the time to notice one flower in particular. This flower calls out to you in a silent song. Notice its particular color and shape. Allow yourself to be carried to this flower and alight on its petals. Notice what it feels like to be encircled by this crown of petals.

Will you go deeper? If you sense that this flower is your resting place, then stay and enjoy its blessings. If you are called to go deeper, begin to gather the flower's pollen. Roll, nuzzle, and delight in the flower's scent, its sacred passion. Move your body intuitively and collect golden nodules of pollen into the hairs of your body. You will need it for your journey.

When you feel you have collected enough pollen and have completed your flower dance, express your gratitude to this flower. Send love from your heart, the center of your being, radiating out to all that is.

This flower is a portal. If you are called to go deeper, approach the center of the flower. There you will notice a central opening. Yes, there it is! This opening is the perfect shape for your body. With ease, move through this central chamber into a dark void. This place is the center of all creations. You can recognize it by its no-thingness.

Are there any fears coming up for you? Allow them to rise to the surface of your consciousness and then let them go. This is the dark womb of the feminine, and you have carried with you the masculine pollen-seed.

Allow a sense of right timing and right action to settle into your being. It is no accident that you arrived here in this moment of co-creation. Become familiar with this dark creative womb of the feminine . . . it is a place of all possibilities.

As you are ready, feel the creative impulse that runs along your spine begin to move and wriggle. Allow this electroenergetic light to move you into a slow spiral dance. Keeping your body moving at a slow, safe, rhythmic pace, allow the rate of your spiral energy to speed up and out. Notice as the golden nodules of pollen you are carrying fly off on the spiral currents your dance is generating. They meet the darkness and lodge themselves in perfect points of space surrounding you.

With a gentle, flowing outbreath, allow your spiral energies to slow and come to a resting point near your body, ahhh . . . Your dance has created a space of divine union. Your masculine pollen-seeds have united with the dark fertility of the feminine. They begin to emit a golden glow . . . points of light in the darkness.

The points are spread out, far and near. Some points glow faintly in the distance, here and there in the darkness. Some points are closer to you, emitting a brighter glow of golden light. These close points of light come into focus as a six-pointed hexagon. Lie down in the center of this hexagon temple. You are softly supported from below by velvety cushions. Rest here for a moment, surrounded by a six-pointed golden glow. Let its radiance seep into your body structure. Ahhh . . . allow it to balance and harmonize any places of imbalance. Allow this thick honey light to ease any brittleness in your bones and make them supple.

This is a gift from the Bees. Bees carry star energy on Earth. They embody the high frequency of the Divine and the diamond. They are the diamond carriers of light.

Allow the vibration of their buzzing to enter your awareness. The Bees are a vast, interconnected network unified by sacred purpose. Notice what emotions or thoughts come into your awareness as their buzzing comes closer.

Social messages have created fear about Bees, especially fear of their sting. If we are living our lives unconsciously, the intensity of Bees' frequency may evoke fear in us. We may be afraid of the sting of something that feels too big or overwhelming. Our fear for survival may have been triggered. The birthright of our divinity may be something for which we feel unprepared.

The Bees' message is that we are by birthright divine beings of light and universal love. This is the highest frequency of Unity. With conscious intention, allow any fear of the Bee sting to release. It no longer serves you. Instead, allow it to be replaced with a glow of awareness. This is the message of the Bees. They hold the highest frequency of Divinity for all life.

Notice now what the vibration of the Bees' buzzing feels like as it touches your body system . . . The Bees encircle you in a wide arc. A choice point begins to glow in your awareness. If you choose, in this moment, you can consciously co-create a journey to the heart of your divinity.

If it feels right for you to stay here, held in golden light with the divine message of the Bees, then stay and rest as long as you like. You can always return.

Do you choose to move deeper, into greater expansion of the truth of who you are? You are in a space of infinite love and possibility. You are already divine. There is nothing you have to do to become divine; divinity is being-ness and knowing-ness. This moment is an opportunity to journey to the heart of yourself—to really know yourself, to expand your sense of who you are. You may notice that your cells have begun to whisper, "Yes . . . Yes . . ." Listen and trust. Relax and trust.

Notice now as the sacred energy of the Bees manifests in your awareness. They may appear as twenty-four diamonds of light encircling you. They hold a ring of light on the perimeter of your experience. Their purpose is to hold the frequency of Divinity throughout your journey.

Return your awareness to the center. Each of the facets of the golden hexagon have become mirrored by other hexagons. Six hexagons have joined in a honeycomb of light. And you are in its center, in the seventh central hexagon. Within each of these six hexagons is an angelic being of light. In this space of divine union, you are on a journey as soul within body. The honeycomb is the Earth matrix holding your body system in connection to your human experience and providing safe structure for your journey.

Feeling this support and your connection to your home planet, if you so choose, speak your affirmation of this process to the universe and the six beings of light who are here to hold space for your journey.

At this time, you may become aware of what these light beings feel or look like . . . What are your senses telling you? These beings are universal love in motion, offering supreme strength, caring, and integrity. Take this opportunity to receive any messages they may have for you . . .

With your affirmation, a new overlay of energy suffuses the honeycomb. You may recognize it as the flower of life. It is a multidimensional form of interconnected circles, forming flowers within flowers of energy. You may notice that the widest circle arcs and meets with the twenty-four Bees of diamond intensity. Notice also that the circles of light interconnect perfectly with all points of the honeycomb.

Take a breath, and notice further that all circles intersect in the center of the honeycomb, in the heart-center of your body system. Breathe all this into your heart, opening and embracing it. . . This is the sacred geometry of divine order. It is the sacred pattern of nature, the very web of life. This energetic overlay is the celestial component of divine union with the Earth matrix.

Yes . . . allow your breath to flow into an affirmation of this union. Ahhh . . . and so it is. You are at the center of all life, at the point of intersection between Heaven and Earth.

At the center, begin to breathe . . . With your breath, the great wheels of the flower of life begin to turn. Great wheels revolving around you. Arcs of moving opalescent light. With this turning, the Bees begin to increase the frequency of their diamond glow. Their brilliant crystal light moves through you, harmonizing with your cells.

Its intensity builds and builds . . . A glowing music of song begins to resonate within your cells and flow outward. It is a harmonic convergence of brilliant energy, brilliant love. The wheels revolve ever faster around you, and you are held in their still point, at the sacred center of all things.

The six beings of light send you greater love. Expanding, warming love. You are suffused with golden honeycomb light, soft angelic light of the six beings, the opalescent light of the revolving wheels, and the diamond light of Divinity.

There is a great merging, merging . . . All of who you are, all of this moment, becomes a single point of diamond light! Behold its vast radiance for a moment . . .

Then with a peeling musical tone, it unfolds into an infinite rainbow spectrum of divine presence. Simply float in this stillness and allow your divine light to radiate out, fully expressing itself in the grace of divine presence.

Notice now your divine presence.

Deep in the center of who you are, allow a phrase to come forth: I AM . . . I AM . . . allow your I AM self to glow and express itself. What does it feel like? There is a musical song in the air, and it is uniquely yours. What does it sound like? You are a radiant vision of light. What do you look like?

You have an infinite story that precedes and goes forth beyond you. Is there a particular part of the story that is important for you to know at this time? Listen . . . and trust what comes to you.

Ahhh . . . receive. Receive all of who you are as a divine being. Do you have a greater sense of your purpose as an embodied soul for this lifetime? Allow your sacred purpose to expand in your awareness and being.

Notice now your infinite connection with all of life, every aspect of the cosmos. Feel this sense of deep relationship with the entirety of the universe. Softly realize that you *are* the universe. Separation is a myth; any limitations are a myth. You are universal love, the life-force energy that forms the sacred pattern. We express ourselves in ever-expanding complexity as part of the unfolding universal story. In its essence we are unified as grace: the ever-flowing love of the universe, returning to itself in increasing brilliance and harmony.

You can take this glow of divine awareness with you always. Your cells and light body hold information more vast than your conscious mind can comprehend. Take this moment to fully embrace your divine presence. Let it synthesize with every aspect of your being. I AM . . . I AM . . .

This experience has become a part of you and will travel back as a part of you to inform your Earth journey. Are there any themes that want to be a part of your conscious awareness? Notice what these themes are and trust that you will remember what is significant. Simply trust and be one with this experience.

Know now the gift of your humanity: you are conscious intention manifested. Your human story is essential to the unfolding of the universe. If you choose, you can live every moment of your life in conscious awareness that you are divine union in a dance of expression. You are the unfolding universe. You can bring this presence to every moment of your life. Every interaction. Every opportunity for right action and right presence.

You can anchor and express the energy of Divinity on Earth as it is in this moment, in Heaven. You can *be* Heaven on Earth. And so it is. And so you are.

In this moment feel all the blessings of divine love and the divine beings enfolding you. You can always return. We are always with you. Affirm to yourself your divine truth in this moment.

And now let the six beings of light come into your awareness. Let them encircle you in the honeycomb. Arcs of light flow out from this center point, ray upon ray. Let go of any attachments you may have to this experience. Simply allow it to be.

More arcs of light radiate out like ripples in a lake. Bring more of yourself back to this moment, here on Earth. Ripples of water, ribbons of light. Softy, bring your awareness to this day, this Heaven on Earth.

Thank you for being here. Your universal song is a blessing to all of life. Thank you for your divine presence, ever unfolding here on Earth. Take a moment now to feel your divine presence settle more deeply into your light body. Take this time to integrate your interdimensional experience fully into time and space.

Bring yourself slowly back to the present moment. Send yourself radiant love and self-acceptance. Be gentle with yourself. Live each moment in the light you are and in the light of the divine presence of all life. We are precious and essential to the unfolding Universe. And so it is. And so you are . . .

Dance of the Honeybee: Embodying Sacred Union and Purpose through Movement

Honeybee is an ecstatic dancer of life. Movement can be used as an expansive developmental practice to open into new aspects of self, release emotions, have cathartic breakthroughs, and dance your way into beauty and bliss. Honeybee offers myriad dance and movement patterns that may help you explore sacred union, co-creation, community, and the sweetness of life.

The Pollen Flight

As we have learned, a foraging Bee may fly many miles in a day, visiting flowers, collecting nectar and pollen, and returning to the hive to deliver this abundance. Select music that evokes the spirit of summer, abundance, and the heady perfume of flowering blossoms.

Begin your dance in flight: imagine floating and buzzing your small body with the frequency of the Honeybee. Feel the sun on your skin and notice the eddies of air in which you are flying. Allow your focus to center on a field of flowers below you. Notice which flowers call your attention. Go to them, and allow your movement to become an ecstatic dance of the senses. Land on a flower, feeling its texture, smelling its sweet perfume. Wriggle your body and notice tiny nodules of pollen fly to your form, as your electromagnetism calls them. Crawl deeper into the flower, experiencing the exquisite sensual closeness of this canal. Dance your way into the center and begin to lap at the sweet nectar within. Draw this sweetness of life into your body, sending it wherever your body-mind-heart-spirit needs it most. When you are ready, continue to revel in the delights of this blossom as you leave it, saying farewell, and expressing your gratitude. You are now laden with gifts to bring back to your community. Notice what they are, and begin your flight home in gratitude.

The Nuptial Flight

In this dance, if you dance alone, you are encouraged to play the parts of both the queen and the male drone Honeybees. Or you may choose to co-create this dance with a safe and supportive partner. This is the dance of the divine consorts, who are drawn to one another, mating in the air as an expression of sacred union.

As the queen, begin your flight, leaving the hive. Allow a sense of purpose and a longing for intimate connection to fill you. Energetically, begin to breathe into the kundalini life-force energy at the base of your spine. In your dance, float in the air and then begin to fly with increasing intensity.

Now, bring your attention to the role of the male drones. A chorus of them has left the hive. Send yourself into their bodies. Feel their urgency and their longing. They pursue the queen as the great golden goddess of life and fertility, each hoping to have the chance to join with her and add their essence to future generations of community.

As you are intuitively led, allow your awareness to float between the queen and the drones. She leads and they pursue, flying ever farther into the heights and reaches of the sky. Continue to breathe the kundalini life-force energy of your body up your spine, activating and enlivening each of your chakras.

As the queen, call the male drones to you. As the drones, reach forward, drawing closer in urgency to the queen. As the queen, when your kundalini reaches your heart center, open this energy center in radiant joy and express your fertile beauty for all to experience. As the drone, dance for the queen, showing her the masculine expression of your energy and the intensity of your passion. Open all of your being to her.

As both queen and drone, as you feel led, call yourself into union. Open yourselves to one another, merging and delighting in this ecstatic flight. Feel the intensity, the bliss, the surging joy. Experience your essences merging and uniting in synergy. Allow your kundalini to emerge in a fountain of ecstasy and bliss through the crown of your head. Open to that which needs to die within you—so that you may fully embody the sacred union of experience. Release this to the winds.

Begin to bring the seeds of life into your being—knowing that you will carry them with you for your entire life—fertilizing all your creations. When you are ready, bring your attention back into your individual reality, and notice the visions that have come to you through this dance.

The Alchemy of Honey

Honey begins its life as nectar from the flowers. The honey within you is the gift of prismatic union of the self with the Divine and the sacred other. It is the rainbow bliss of Unity. This dance allows you to concentrate the sacred unity of your being into its essence. In the hive, this is accomplished by passing nectar from Bee to Bee, each fanning it with wings so the excess moisture evaporates.

In your dance, music evoking the golden shadows and hum of the hive is helpful. This may take the form of music with drumming, toning, or a choir of voices.

Bring yourself into the hive, and call your Honeybee sisters to join you. This is a safe circle of beings who love and support you just as you are. Open your heart to them and take a sweet node of nectar from this energy center. Share the nectar of your heart with your sisters, asking them to bring it into their own hearts, adding their unique essence to it. Dance with them as they pass this nectar among themselves, adding the nectar of their own experiences to it. As the nectar is passed, it becomes more concentrated. Place the nectar concentration in the center of the circle, and fan it and bless it with your wings.

When you're ready, join hands with your priestess sisters—you who are the alchemical Melissae of the honey! Breathe onto the honey and send the divine energy that moves through you into its crystalline structure. When you feel that the honey has reached its most concentrated form, dance with it for a few moments. Celebrate and honor the beauty of this sacred union essence. Finally, join your sisters and taste the sweet bliss of this alchemical magic. Feel it nourishing and enlivening you. Offer this sacred honey of the heart to the world in service.

Dance as Communication

If you feel the need to enhance the effectiveness of communication in your life, let Honeybee inspire you. If you are grappling with an issue in your life for which you need additional support before you feel comfortable giving voice to it, take the opportunity to practice dance as a communication tool.

Bring the theme into the center of your awareness, ground your body using the breath, and open your heart to the present moment. Then use all parts of your body to express the meaning of your theme. How can your hands, arms, torso, and legs express what you need to say? How can the movements of your body indicate tone, emotion, and significance? Notice what type of music you are drawn to dance to, and explore how this musical energy can assist you in speaking effectively with others. As you dance, allow Honeybee's buzzing to resonate in your throat chakra. This will assist in activating your creative expression. Don't forget to breathe, and allow the breath to guide and enhance your process.

If you have significant emotions within you that are blocking you from communicating effectively from a place of centered openheartedness, you can use dance as an expressive catharsis and processing tool to move through and transform these emotions. Dance brings us fully into our bodies, and when we are centered in the truth of who we are, it is much easier to effectively share our authentic truth with others.

🐝 Honeybee Invocation

Holy Trinity Dancer and God's Pure Channel of Divine Light, when at last we meet you upon the path, may we follow your holy dance patterns in midair, with great joy and passion, to our sacred destiny. . . . Show us the way. Keeper of the faith, mystery teacher of manifestation and sacred union, one who brings abundance to the whole tribe . . . Show us the way. Golden orb of alchemical energy, may we taste the sweet fruits of our labor with appreciation and gratitude. . . . Show us the way. And when our final task is done, may we gently land on some fragrant bloom, resting in the glow of all that we have accomplished, watching with humble satisfaction as the next generation begins their dance of creation. . . . Show us the way.

5
Butterfly

*Transforming Ourselves to
a Higher Octave of Purpose*

Be the change you wish to see in the world.

MAHATMA GANDHI

Butterflies are a beloved and celebrated member of the insect tribe of creatures. They appear as physical rainbows and vibrant patterns, flashing in the sun as they take wing. Yet they also hold a deeper symbolism that illuminates profound transformations of the psyche and soul.

The Butterfly is significant to many cultures around the world and throughout history. Tribes from Sumatra, Madagascar, and India believe they descended from Butterflies.[1]

Almost universally, Butterflies have symbolized the soul, death, rebirth, transformation, and immortality. The Latin word for *Butterfly* is *papilionis,* which describes the idea that a person's soul returns as a Butterfly after death. After World War II, those liberating Polish concentration camps found images of hundreds of Butterflies carved into the walls by their prisoners, often children, expressing a belief in the freedom of the soul, both in life and in death.

Butterflies decorated Egyptian tombs, jewelry, and amulets. In

Hindu culture, the god Brahma is said to have developed the concept of reincarnation from observing the transformation process of a Caterpillar evolving into a Butterfly. Hindus viewed this transformation as a rebirth leading to perfection, or nirvana, as part of the process of reincarnation.

Many Butterfly and Moth species take their names from Greek and Roman myths, such as the Hercules, Atlas, and Promethea moths. In Greek and Roman myth Eros, the god of love and the son of Aphrodite, falls in love with a mortal woman, Psyche. Because of their different statuses, one human and the other divine, they are initially separated by Aphrodite after Psyche discovers that Eros is a god. When it becomes clear that her son's happiness is at stake, Aphrodite conceives a plan in which three seemingly impossible tasks are set before Psyche. If Psyche could complete these tasks, then she would become immortal and divine, like her love, Eros. In each of the tasks, when stymied by their impossibility, Psyche's profound yearning and love for Eros draws helpers to her aid, and the tasks are completed. Eventually, Eros and Psyche are reunited, and Psyche is elevated to divine immortality.

This myth teaches us that the yearning for sacred union with the divine can open portals into learning (seemingly impossible tasks), through which humanity can transform its mortal nature into divinity. Psyche evolves into a new octave of sacred being. Eros and Psyche represent the union of human and divine. As we have already learned, Butterflies are traditionally associated with death, rebirth, and transformation. Is it surprising then, that the Greek word for *Butterfly* and *soul* is *psyche*?

Aztec and Toltec traditions are filled with Butterfly symbolism and deities. It is said that Quetzalcoatl first entered the world through a chrysalis, illustrated on a palace wall frieze in Teotihuacan, Mexico. He came into the world in perfection through this process, like the Butterfly. The mother of Quetzalcoatl, Xochiquetzal, is said to have held a Butterfly between her lips as she made love to soldiers on the field of battle. Xochiquetzal's kiss symbolized the assurance of rebirth after death. Itzpapalotl is the obsidian Butterfly and deity of the Aztec calendar.

The Butterfly is also found in many North American indigenous folktales and symbols. To the Blackfoot people Butterflies are the symbol of sleep and dreams. The Hopi people have a Butterfly clan, dance, and sacred kachina figure.

Butterflies are part of the Lepidoptera order of insects. *Lepidoptera* means "scale-wing." *Scale* refers to what is often mistaken as powder on a Butterfly's wing. In fact, Butterflies are covered in scales, which easily come loose from their bodies, aiding in potential escapes, for example, from a Spider's web.[2]

There are 165,000 Lepidoptera species in the world, made up of both Butterflies and Moths. This is second only to beetles in terms of population. There are ten times as many Butterflies as there are mammals and birds combined!

Insects are thought to have appeared 380 million to 400 million years ago in the Devonian period of the Paleozoic era. Insects were the first creatures to take to the air and fly on Planet Earth, predating reptile-birds. Butterflies and Moths went through many evolutionary changes and adaptations before emerging in their contemporary forms.

The oldest "true" Butterfly to be found in fossil records is a swallowtail from forty-eight million years ago. Modern Butterfly families developed and differentiated from one another by the beginning of the Cenozoic era, approximately sixty-six million years ago. This differentiation of Butterfly families aligns with the emergence of flowering plants, which are the primary food source of adult Butterflies. The ideal Butterfly flower has a deep corolla (into which a Butterfly can extend its proboscis for gathering nectar), a flat surface for Butterflies to land, and nectar with a high percentage of sugar.

Butterflies are ectothermic, or cold-blooded, meaning they regulate their temperature from external sources of warmth. For this reason, Butterflies can often be seen sunbathing. In fact, Butterflies often begin the warming process by shivering, which builds up enough heat in the thorax so that a Butterfly can move to a warmer location.

Some species of Butterflies, including the Monarch Butterfly, migrate for thousands of miles and gather in colonies. Butterflies use the sun and an internal electromagnetic compass to navigate. Each year, though they have never visited before, Monarchs fly from Canada to Mexico. Wintering in Mexico allows Monarch Butterflies to enter a state of semihibernation but continue necessary behaviors to survive. As temperatures rise in the spring, the Monarchs become energized and mate. Butterflies begin as eggs, hatch as larval Caterpillars, and pupate into the chrysalis before emerging as adult Butterflies. As they fly northward, successive generations of Butterflies are laid as eggs on plant hosts. These new Monarchs may live far more briefly than their Mexico-wintering parents, yet they too feel the urge to fly north, mating and laying eggs. This process continues until that year's Butterflies reach Canada—and the northernmost habitat of their favorite host plant, the milkweed.[3] It is essential that we allow wild spaces that are not sprayed with chemicals along roadways and in fields, parks, and backyards so that native plant species are available for Butterfly habitat. Many Butterflies are particular about laying eggs only on certain plant species. If no suitable host plants are allowed to grow in a geographic area, the migration chain of the Butterfly is broken.

Butterflies journey to new destinations in their geographical location, in their place within the life cycle, and through their many varied physical forms, from egg to Butterfly. Butterfly is a powerful teacher about the path and process of transformation, both within our psyches and outward in the world.

EXPLORING BUTTERFLY'S PLACE ON THE MEDICINE WHEEL

The West Direction and the Path of Self-Transformation

As we spiral around the medicine wheel of life, we cycle through seasons, elements, and life phases. The West direction is connected with the fall season and the element of Water. In the fall the season's leaves release their hold from the trees and fall to the earth. Grasses wave in the clear, cold wind—keening in gilded whispers. The creations and gatherings of the summer season are complete. The fall season encourages us to turn inward, acknowledging and honoring what is dying within us and what is ready to be reborn.

The element of Water is associated with the deep currents of feeling that run through us. Water calls us into our hearts and guides us into the poignancy of emotion. In the West direction of the Instar Medicine Wheel we have moved through the co-creative abundance of the summer months. We have manifested our first creations and built a sense of self. As the season turns toward fall, our recent creations move into the past. How we define ourselves and find meaning in life begins to change. Yesterday's soul purpose may become today's ego agenda, holding us in place.

If we steadfastly hang on to our past creations so that we may continue to define ourselves in comfortable terms, we sap these creations of their life-force energy. This season's generation of leaves gave beauty and joy, but so too must they give way into the pure void of winter. The flowers and leaves prized by Honeybee in the summer must fall to the earth so that Earthworm may compost them into the soil for next year's new soulful creations. Butterfly joins us in the descent, from tree to earth, as we prepare to transform ourselves.

The reflective Waters of the West direction aid us as we process and find perspective about the past seasons and cycles of our life path. We begin to sense that which no longer serves us, that which continues to glow as a light of inspiration to our souls, and how we have been shaped and have evolved through lived experience.

Butterfly is the opposite cardinal direction to Earthworm in the East. Opposite relationships hold a creative tension and can illuminate one another. Earthworm is a recycler and composter of that which no longer serves the psyche. Earthworm recycles the earth and creates it anew through its being. Earthworm nourishes the next season of abundant creativity through its fertile Earthen vessel. Butterfly, too, is a teacher of shamanic transformation, but from a different place on the wheel.

Butterfly spends the first phase of its life in the guise of Earthworm, as a Caterpillar. The Caterpillar's primary job is to eat and grow. This period of nourishment and growth is in alignment with the first abundant creations of sacred purpose. At a certain point, Caterpillar has grown all it can in its current physical form. In order to move on to the next phases of sacred purpose, Caterpillar must move into a new form.

The fall season and the West direction remind us that it is essential to orient our understanding of Caterpillar's transformation in terms of the willingness to let go. If we grasp and hang on to old creations—be it our role as a mother or father, a beloved job, or a past creative project—there is no room for transformation to occur. In order to undergo transformation, we must be willing to let go of this season's creations and let them fall to the earth. We must be willing to look inside ourselves, to go within, and to find the stillness of this midpoint in life.

Some people cling desperately to how they have defined themselves in the past, even if these definitions no longer work or sustain them. They may sense the growing stillness and emptiness essential to change, but instead attempt to immediately fill this void with new material possessions, relationships, or addictive behaviors. Walking into the West direction with Butterfly is not an easy path. It requires us to be fully vulnerable, processing our lived experience and identifying what no longer feeds our souls and where we are stuck. Butterfly asks us to look internally and acknowledge that our current form has reached its potential. We must metamorphose into a higher octave of being. In this way we come into greater alignment with the Divine and bring to fruition a new expression of sacred purpose.

SACRED PURPOSE

The Personal and Collective Chrysalis—Walking the Shamanic Path of the Wounded Healer

Butterfly teaches us that sacred purpose is to bring Spirit into Matter to transform oneself. Where Earthworm brings Spirit and Matter through itself, thereby transforming both of them, Butterfly embodies Spirit within its own flesh as an alchemy of the self. Earthworm is a vessel for transformation, while Butterfly is transformation itself.

Butterfly transforms itself for the highest good. On a personal level, Butterfly illuminates a process of death and rebirth, that it may emerge from the chrysalis at an evolved octave of being and soulful expression. Butterfly teaches from direct, lived experience. Only by going within, dissolving its very self, and emerging can Butterfly gain the necessary medicine to share with humanity. This is the essence of the shamanic tradition of the wounded healer. As we walk the path of our lived experience, the challenges and learning opportunities we experience are transformed into our personal medicine for healing and the evolution of our consciousness. As wounded healers we can share this medicine with others from the authentic and powerful source of lived experience.

In order to change the world, we must first change ourselves. We cannot hope to change the consciousness of the planet if our own consciousness has not yet been transformed. As Earthworm teaches, we are each vessels for the Divine and for frequencies of consciousness, such as peace, love, hope, and harmony. For transformation and evolution to occur on a collective level, it is essential that we each begin on the personal level. As individuals, we can begin to explore our own wounds, challenges, and life experiences. Through this exploration our consciousness and all levels of our being are transformed. Through our transformative work, we become divine vessels of harmonic consciousness, holding these frequencies for the planet. We are each imaginal cells in the universal body. As we transform ourselves, and embody this change as human beings, we transform the world. In addition, through this process we each develop a unique sacred medicine to share with others. The medicine of our internal wounded healer can inspire and support others as they navigate their own journeys into healing and awakened consciousness.

Butterfly teaches us how to dance with our own wounded healer and begin the journey into the heart of our own transformation—our very own chrysalis of consciousness. On the Instar Medicine Wheel, as we learn how to evolve the expression of our sacred purpose through internal transformation, we begin to embody the shamanic medicine that is ours to share with others. As teachers of the chrysalis we can inspire and support others to understand that purpose has its own life cycle. We each come to places in our lives in which the old no longer sustains us, and the creations that once energized us have outlived their purpose. We approach a place of stillness, a void. We yearn for something more, a new dimension of experience, a renewed sense of purpose. As Butterfly wounded healers, we can share the medicine of going within, entering the chrysalis of our psyche and discovering new and unknown dreams of transformation.

TRANSFORMATION

Embodying Our Imaginal Potential

Butterflies are holometabolous, which means that they undergo complete metamorphosis. *Metamorphosis* refers to a profound change in the physical body, in which the old morphs into a completely new form. This can also be understood in terms of soulful evolution and profound transformation of the self. Butterfly is an excellent teacher for helping us understand the process of personal transformation and metamorphosis.

Butterflies experience four life-cycle stages: egg (ovum), Caterpillar (larva), chrysalis (pupa), and adult (imago). Delightfully, the plural scientific term for adult Butterflies is *imagines*. When an adult female Butterfly is ready to lay an egg, she affixes it to a host plant, where it often resembles a luminous orb. Eggs can hatch within days or be held in arrested development until appropriate environmental conditions occur. Eggs, Caterpillars, and chrysalises all vary in size, shape, texture, and color.⁴

After a new Caterpillar hatches, its first meal is the remaining eggshell from which it emerged. After that, a young Caterpillar turns to its host plant as a primary food source. A Caterpillar often stays on its primary host plant, feeding, until it is ready to pupate within the chrysalis. The main goal of the Caterpillar is to nourish itself and grow. Caterpillars are often described as eating machines, made of a mouth, a stomach, and an anus. A Caterpillar's growth is almost exponential. Caterpillars can defoliate entire plants, but other animal species keep Caterpillar numbers in check. Caterpillars have developed strategies that help them avoid predators, such as impersonating other animals, grouping together, emitting defensive chemicals, and twitching in an attempt to startle prospective predators.

The Caterpillar can be understood as analogous to the first stage of human adulthood; this is similar to the Earthworm stage of apprenticeship. The Caterpillar/Worm is learning the craft of its sacred purpose, feeding and nourishing itself for future creations and preparing a foundation for future transformation. The Caterpillar feeds and grows, expanding its body. Like the Earthworm, the Caterpillar's form is the Earth element body of sacred purpose. It is dense, foundational, and physical.

As a Caterpillar feeds and grows, it experiences periodic moltings, from each of which it emerges with a dramatically different physical form. The periods between moltings are referred to as instars. Caterpillars molt between three and five times, with three to five corresponding instar periods, or forms. A Caterpillar may grow as much as 3,300 times its hatching weight before it pupates. Depending on the species and the location of its habitat, larval stages of development may take anywhere from a few weeks to a few years. High-altitude and arctic species do not have the necessary length within one growing season to complete larval development.

A Caterpillar's final molt is its formation into a chrysalis, or pupa. It is popularly assumed that when it is ready to morph into a Butterfly, a Caterpillar enters or builds a chrysalis. In reality, a Caterpillar's body *is* the chrysalis. *Pupation* refers to the stage in which the Caterpillar has changed into the chrysalis, during which even more accelerated transformation occurs. This phase is often preceded by a wandering period, when the Caterpillar wanders away from the host plant and searches for an appropriate chrysalis site.

The chrysalis is the final instar form of the Caterpillar. According to ecologist and Butterfly expert Phil Schappert, "Inside the pupal exoskeleton, the complete disassembly, or chemical dissolution, of the larval body occurs, and areas of undifferentiated cells that have persisted through all of the molts of the larvae, called 'imaginal disks,' begin to form the tissues of the adult butterfly. The complete re-creation of the body of a caterpillar into the body and wings of a butterfly is, without doubt, one of the wonders of life on Earth."[5] In other words, a Caterpillar selects an appropriate pupation site, spins a silk pad in a protected location, and suspends its body from the pad securely. In the final act of molting, a Caterpillar splits its skin, shedding it, and the chrysalis then emerges. The pupa's body is the chrysalis itself.

What is essential to understand here is that for authentic and profound transformation to occur, we need to stop looking outside ourselves. There is no spaceship that will take us away, no guru or shaman who can wave her wand to heal or transform us. We are the chrysalis; we are our own spaceship into new dimensions of self and the Divine. We each have our own inner shaman and visionary. The process of evolution and transformation begins within and is housed in the potential of our very cells. External people, situations, and ideas can inspire and support us, but we disempower ourselves when we expect others to heal us from the outside. Healer, heal thyself! Be the change you wish to see in the world. Share the wisdom of your wounded medicine with others, and support them in empowering themselves as change agents of consciousness. We do not need to look outside ourselves for the answer to metamorphosis. Butterfly teaches us that this power and wisdom resides within.

Within the chrysalis a complex process of metamorphosis continues; this is largely a mystery to science. How does a living being simultaneously dissolve and re-form its body, emerging as an entirely new creature?

Contrary to popular belief, by the time a Caterpillar takes on its chrysalis form, it has already completed much of the process of metamorphosis. Beginning in its first larval instar, a Butterfly's wings begin to form internally from imaginal disks within the thorax. This process continues through a Caterpillar's multiple larval instars, rapidly accelerating during the waiting period prior to the emergence of the pupa-chrysalis in the final larval molt (when the Caterpillar is hanging from a plant, attached to a silk pad). By the time this chrysalis form emerges, much of the metamorphosis is complete.

Let's explore this further. What we can learn here is that, throughout our life, even as we are the hungry, Earthen Caterpillar, we are simultaneously developing our own potential within. The Caterpillar spends its time consuming large quantities of energy to build a body that can house the future potential of a new form within and to provide energy for accelerated transformation in the chrysalis. The Caterpillar is the life phase in which we not only build our foundation but literally embody it. What this tells us is that we already have all we need for soulful transformation within our being.

In addition, from a shamanic standpoint, all the challenges that we face—what we "eat" through lived experience—become the energy and structure of our bodies, forming the foundation for transformation and illumination. Parallel with the sacred work of Earthworm and Honeybee, the Earthen Caterpillar form provides us with a vessel through which to experience human learning opportunities, to try our hand at our first creations, to venture out into life and experience its richness for the first time.

But, at a certain point, though we may have grown 3,300 times our original "soul vessel" size, inevitably we reach a point at which our Caterpillar body can no longer serve our continued personal growth. We have spiraled through the sacred purpose of Earthworm and Honeybee and are ready to evolve into a new phase of being. If we want to experience new levels of illumination and connection with Spirit, we must be willing to bring our latent potential to the fore. We must be willing to release all we have been, all with which we have identified.

Imagine that all you have ever known is crawling on the ground or on plant leaves. You are used to walking close to the earth, eating and expanding, getting heavier. Yet, at a certain point in your life, you sense an internal awareness that there is something more to life—something more to your soul purpose and potential—something you have not yet expressed. You have felt it growing within you for years, felt yourself preparing for something. But what? Most Caterpillars are born on their own: there is no one there to tell them what happens next or, for that matter, how or why.

As the Caterpillar, you feel a yearning, a call. This call is to leave all that is familiar to you. To leave your home host plant, to travel to a new setting, to hang yourself from a tendril of silk—and wait. Wait for what? Imagine hanging there as a Caterpillar. This is a very vulnerable time, a time of quiet and emptiness. Old patterns and roles have been left behind. You have chosen quiet, because your internal wisdom has told you to have faith. You sense that something is coming that will forever change you. Though you have never seen or experienced this before, you have taken this step into the unknown.

Suddenly, all the eating and growth you have prepared as a foundation begins to surge within you. Your Caterpillar skin splits open, and a new form of "you" emerges—a chrysalis. Your body has re-formed as a chrysalis, an interdimensional merkaba, a celestial pod whose purpose is rapid transformation and complete soulful metamorphosis.

Within the chrysalis the larval body is dissolved and recycled, while the imaginal body is created. Imaginal disks "are regions of previously undifferentiated cells that act as organizing centers for the adult tissues."[6] These imaginal cells direct the formation of the adult Butterfly body. During this time the new forms that have been growing from imaginal cells are accelerated and manifested, while the old dissolves and dies away.

Little understood by science, imaginal cells appear to be centers of potentiality within the body that incite transformation and evolution on profound levels. It is important to note that humans and other organisms also have imaginal cells within. Many scholars and writers, including Bill Plotkin and Linda Star Wolf, discuss evolution of both the self and society in terms of imaginal cells. Individually, we are capable of immense internal transformation of consciousness, emerging into new levels of being and soulful union with the divine universe. Collectively, as more of us embody our authentic selves and follow our own paths of transformation, we light up as new harmonic cells in the universal body. It has also been questioned if certain pockets of society are acting as imaginal disks, inspiring the rest of the collective into new spirals of evolution. We will address this point later on.

The chrysalis is designed to protect the process of transformation within. This occurs by adapting the chrysalis so it appears similar to its surroundings, often by mimicking leaves or taking on a reflective mirror quality. Metallic dots of color and a sense of depth within can be noted. In symbolic terms, the chrysalis becomes a shimmering portal or vehicle of transformation. But what makes the chrysalis so special is that it is the body itself. For a certain period, the organism is no longer a Caterpillar and not yet a Butterfly. Instead, its body becomes both a portal and a safe internal shelter, within which transformation takes place.

As a teacher, Butterfly reminds us of how limiting our cognitive beliefs can be. Think of the organism we are discussing. What is it? Is it only an Earthbound Caterpillar? Think of yourself prior to experiencing a profound transformation in your life. Would you have believed you could be anything else? Did it seem possible that you could change so radically that you and your former self would become unrecognizable as the same person? Would it have seemed possible that you could leave the ground to fly into new dimensions?

Most likely, what would have taken hold in the forefront of your consciousness was all the limitations and constricting beliefs of this Earth element cycle. Before we can be birthed into new forms, we must first feel the constrictions of the birth canal, the tightness of the chrysalis. This sense of constraint and discomfort often creates a breaking point, in which we say, "I don't know what to do next, but I don't want to keep doing what I've been doing. It simply doesn't work anymore." It is this encouragement that sends us into a new place within—surrender. This can often be seen when we hit bottom with addictive behaviors. We may not know how to make a change, but we open our beings to Spirit and ask for help, committing ourselves to finding a new way. And so, we hang ourselves from a silken tendril and wait.

Butterfly honors the sacred purpose stage of simultaneously dissolving and re-forming ourselves on all levels. This can be a disconcerting period. Butterfly teaches that growth and development is always a paradoxical process of embracing and releasing, death and rebirth. When you are on a chrysalis journey, in one moment you may soar with joy about the new opportunities entering your life. In the next moment you may grieve the death of outmoded relationships, projects, and self-definitions. Self-compassion and care are essential during this time. We sometimes shame ourselves for struggling while we are in the midst of profound life transformation. Society celebrates the beauty of Butterfly as a finished product—yet imagine Butterfly painting a self-portrait within the chrysalis. Butterfly doesn't look so pretty and all put together when it is half-dissolved and half-formed. Authentic transformation is often a goopy mess—critical judgment is just another blockage to be released. To truly embody our radiant potential, we must be willing to surrender and simply be suspended in a state of change for a while. During this time, ask Butterfly to infuse you with its grace and alchemical wisdom as you transform on every level. Self-love and trust in the chrysalis allow Butterfly to unfold its glorious wings in the future.

It is only through surrender—releasing the power of our old constricting beliefs—that we can move into active transformation, bringing the latent potential within our cells and beings outward into a new soulful expression of self. It is only through experiencing the wounded medicine of the chrysalis—feeling the call to enter an unknown world, surrendering oneself to something greater, and emerging at a higher octave of being—that we discover that we have become Butterflies. When asked who it is, a Caterpillar can only answer that it is a Caterpillar. A Butterfly can answer through all its lived experience: it is a dreamer and a seeker, it is an alchemical dancer of spiritual incarnation, it is a new expression of soulful authenticity.

After emerging from the chrysalis, a new Butterfly must first expand its wings and pump fluid into them before it can fly. This fluid is then withdrawn so the wings can dry. The Caterpillar has experienced a profound cycle of death and rebirth, dying to its old ego agendas and self-definitions while simultaneously activating the potential of its soul blueprint. Now weighing one-third of its original size, the Butterfly has left its denser Earthen body, the crawling Caterpillar, and emerges from its chrysalis into a new element—with new abilities and purpose. The Butterfly is now a creature of the Air. It has gained new interdimensional abilities—flight and procreation. These abilities will be discussed in greater detail in a later section.

PORTAL OF TRANSFORMATION

Entering the Chrysalis and Activating Imaginal Cells

Butterfly offers us this symbol of transformation. At the center of Butterfly's expanding new wings we see the chrysalis, a portal into new dimensions of being and soul expression. The almond shape of the chrysalis is at the center of two intersecting circles, which form a vesica pisces. The vesica pisces is a symbol of sacred union. In the image on the following page there are at least two large vesica pisces (though more can be found), symbolizing sacred union Above and Below, Within and Without.

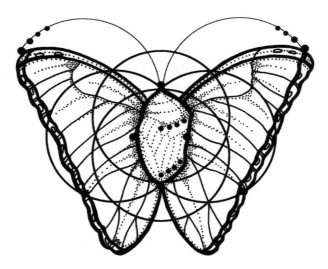

Butterfly transformational portal image,
highlighting the sacred geometry of the chrysalis,
vesica pisces formation, and sacred union

This is a unique expression of sacred union. Previously, with Honeybee, we discussed the sacred union of self and other, dark and light, human and Divine in terms of creating the sacred third—a new co-creative child or inspired idea. With Honeybee as teacher, cocreation is the paramount focus of sacred union. Butterfly's teaching of sacred union is that as we open ourselves in surrender to the Sacred moving through us, we are transformed. Butterfly's primary emphasis is on this process of self-transformation through sacred union.

Accordingly, the chrysalis is at the heart of these sacred union images. It is the portal for radical transformation and evolution of consciousness. When we experience the initiation of Butterfly, some part of our life—its forms and definitions—is dramatically changed. We evolve so much, we no longer recognize ourselves. It is as if the life phases that passed before were a previous incarnation, an old life.

This image also highlights the number four—four wings, four circles, four dots on the chrysalis and antennae. In this image the number four refers to the four life-cycle stages of the Butterfly: egg (ovum), Caterpillar (larva), chrysalis (pupa), and adult (imago). This number also refers to the four cardinal directions and life phases of the Instar Medicine Wheel. The number four reminds us that each of these phases is essential to the growth and full manifestation of the Butterfly.

Butterflies are the rarest stage of this insect's life cycle. Due to predatory, environmental, and other hazards, for many species only one in one hundred eggs will actually emerge as a Butterfly. Not every human being is ready, open, and committed to walking a spiritual path of evolving consciousness and dancing with the Divine in oneself and the universe. Many people are content to remain as Caterpillars, or are fearful of releasing their sense of security in ego attachments. Many people do not sense their own innate potential and soulful majesty. Often this sensitivity and belief in oneself has been beaten down by our cultures and families of origin.

Yet, there are those who listen to Spirit's call and follow the adventurous path of transformation and spiritual metamorphosis. They understand that their previous life stages are their wounded medicine of lived experience, which provide a foundation and nourish new dreams and the spiraling chrysalis dance of evolution. These brave souls are committed to evolving and expressing higher octaves of their soul purpose and lighting up as imaginal cells of transformation within the universal body.

You, the Butterfly shaman, are essential for our collective future. And the future begins by fully embodying your potential, now, in the present moment. Be the change you wish to see in the world!

BUTTERFLY AND THE HUMAN LIFE CYCLE

Midlife—Re-Forming Oneself at a Higher Octave of Spirit

Butterfly is the keeper of the West direction, the place of transformation and the season of autumn. Within the human life cycle, the initiation of Butterfly is anchored in the themes present at midlife. While Butterfly's teachings and initiation may be experienced many times throughout the life cycle, at midlife we have moved past the life phases of apprenticeship and the first creations of our soul purpose. We now find ourselves called to release that which no longer serves us, so that we can move into new expressions of our soul purpose, sense of self, and relationship with Spirit. As we previously noted, fall is the season of surrender, the dying of the old so that we may be reborn in a new spiraling season of creative expression. Symbolically, this is the season in which we turn within, taking on our chrysalis form. We wait in the clear stillness for the latent potential of our cells to fully activate and accelerate.

In our Honeybee life phase, many of us become parents for the first time and devote our creative energies to midwifing these children, creative projects, new relationships, or professional endeavors. As potential Butterflies, we take stock of what we have learned. We notice, acknowledge, honor, and release that which no longer serves us. We let go of our old, denser energy bodies and creations. We go within, transform, and emerge into a higher octave of our soul expression. We are capable of taking flight into new dimensions of ourselves, our creative work, and our relationship with Spirit.

This is a new phase of life, in which our first children and careers have grown and left home. We are redefining what sustains us, and what future directions we want to take. Instead of spending the rest of our lives chewing old leaves and crawling, we choose to take to the Air in search of sweet nectar. Nectar is a high-energy food, with a heavy sugar content. This fuels the Butterfly in its new stage of life.

While the primary purpose of the Caterpillar was to eat and grow, the primary purpose of a Butterfly is reproduction. Its reproductive organs are developed during the pupation stage. The difference between the two life phases is striking: Caterpillars do not reproduce and Butterflies do not grow. One spends its time connected to the Earth and its host plant, while the other takes to the Air in flight, searching for nectar and potential mates. Butterfly teaches that after metamorphosis, this new phase of life is devoted to new co-creations with Spirit at a higher octave of soul purpose.

It is also time to express new avenues of creativity that were not available to us before metamorphosis. This may take the form of a sacred purpose–focused career, in which we are paid to fulfill our soul's highest calling. Or we may begin a new creative art project, build a more beautiful and Earth-friendly home, or seek a new mate who mirrors our self-love and evolution back to us. This is a time in which we come into greater alignment with our soul's calling and live it out. Dancing round the spiral, we take our past creations and alchemize them into higher expressions of purpose and beauty.

This period just after emergence is a very vulnerable time for a new Butterfly. It is at the mercy of predators and other Butterflies interested in mating. Butterfly wings are much larger than are necessary for flight and, in fact, act as a communication system to potential mates and as a defensive system to protect Butterfly from predators.

A Butterfly's wings can give it the appearance of a much larger creature. While beautiful and showy to attract a potential mate, many Butterflies' wings are designed to warn or distract predators. Many Butterflies have wings that are cryptic on the underside (serving as a form of camouflage) and aposematic (presenting warning patterns) on the upper side. These Butterflies have developed "flash and conceal" defensive strategies. Aposematic wing designs warn potential predators that a Butterfly could be poisonous to eat, or that it may be a larger, more fearsome creature than it is. Bright colors can flash, distract, or provide false information that leads a predator to bite a nonessential area. For example, some Butterfly varieties have false eyes that mimic a larger owl. But, if bitten, the eyes have led the predator to a false head located on the wing, as opposed to the Butterfly's thorax. When closed, a Butterfly's wings conceal it from dangerous predators.

As has been previously noted, a Butterfly weighs only about one-third of its previous Caterpillar weight. After metamorphosis, the Butterfly has a new, lighter, etheric body, complete with fully articulated wings of soul expression. As Butterflies, we are lighter, finer, and multicolored—capable of new creative expressions in greater alignment with Spirit. With what we have learned above, it is evident that, symbolically, in order to fully express our new energy body and soulful purpose we must be diligent and discerning in the realistic protection of this newly expanded self.

This does not mean that we should be on the defensive or overprotective. Instead, we can be realistic about the world that surrounds our precious soul Butterfly wings, understanding its energetic and physical dysfunction. As we evolve in consciousness, we will come across many who choose to live unconsciously, in fear and denial.

In order to fully let our lights shine and have a long, rich life of soul purpose expression, we can listen to Butterfly's teachings. A shaman knows when to be visible and when to be invisible. She knows when to dance exuberantly with the Divine and other co-creative partners and when to communicate safe boundaries. This balance is very important, because shamanic Butterflies of expanded consciousness walk between two worlds. We walk between multiple dimensions. It is essential that we learn to share our shimmering wings—our soul purpose and shamanic medicine—with the world. Yet, at the same time, we must practice invisibility, humility, and healthy communication while maintaining boundaries. In this way we can fully bring Spirit into Matter on Planet Earth for the highest good and in support of our authentic soul expression.

Butterflies are able to see the widest visual color spectrum of any animal, including humans. While humans can see the red end of the color spectrum but not ultraviolet frequencies, and Honeybees can see the ultraviolet end but not red, Butterflies can see the entire visual spectrum from ultraviolet to red. As evolved shamanic beings, we have gained new abilities such as an expanded visual field, seeing all that is possible—both visible and invisible. Our senses are heightened to the beauty of the world, and we can take flight into new adventures of being and experience.

The Butterfly also represents the mature adult form of the organism's life cycle. In their lifetime only a few of the many Butterfly organisms are ready or able to fully embody their mature soul nature. This is true of Butterflies and human beings. While we all have soulful potential and divine awareness held latent within our imaginal cells, not all are ready, able, or choose to grow up into soulful adults.

As co-creative children of sacred union, we are truly the children of God. Yet, it is essential and appropriate that we grow up into the soulfully aware, mature, adult divine beings that we were meant to be. This is our potential and life path of soul expression. Butterfly provides us with an alchemical blueprint for multidimensional transformation in which we can experience and embody the evolution of our consciousness. As divine adult Butterflies we claim our citizenship, lighting up as harmonic cells within the universal body. It is time for us to step forward and spread our multicolored soul wings as the divine co-creative beings we are, express our unique soul purposes, and take flight into the universe!

LESSONS AND SHADOW
The Journey of Soulful Metamorphosis

As we journey into new expressions of sacred purpose and transformation, Butterfly has many lessons to teach us. During a Butterfly initiation the primary process we experience is the aligning of self with authentic soul. In other words, we are activating the soul blueprint held within our bodies and energetic fields. We are awakening the imaginal cells of our divine human potential. Butterfly teaches that two understandings are essential to soulful metamorphosis.

Empowerment and Surrender
First, we must empower ourselves, literally affirming that the power of transformation is in our cells. There is nothing external that can heal or change us; this process must be birthed through the self, from the inside out. Teachers and ideas can inspire and support us, but we truly have everything we need within us. The seeds of the future are within you at this very moment, listening to the resonant song of your heartbeat.

Second, for profound transformation to occur, we must be willing to surrender. We must be willing to create a space of quiet and emptiness so that we can begin to hear the quiet voice within and listen to the latent song of transformation held within our DNA. We must be willing to wander and find a new place from which to hang ourselves from a silken cord and wait.

In ancient Sumerian myth, Inanna was the queen of Heaven, and her sister Erishkigal was the queen of the Underworld. One day Inanna, full of the beauty and light of the stars, decides to visit her dark sister. On the journey into the Underworld, Inanna is stopped at seven gates. At each, in order to go forward, she must give up a vestige of her queenhood, the symbols of her self. She gives up earrings, necklaces, circlets: seven symbols corresponding to each of the seven chakra energy centers in the body. Going within, with each loss of these symbols, Inanna loses her sense of self. She cannot remember who she is, why she has come, or any of the magic that she used in the past. When she finally meets her sister, Erishkigal, the queen of the Underworld, kills Inanna and hangs her on a meat hook. There Inanna hangs, dead for all appearances.

After a time, three of Inanna's helpers fly into the Underworld. Once there, they see that Erishkigal is suffering the pangs of childbirth. She feels alone, in great pain, and believes that no one understands her. The three helpers empathize and join with Erishkigal in her birth contractions, moaning and commiserating with her. At the end of her labor, grateful to these helpers, Erishkigal grants them any wish. They request that Inanna be brought back to life.

Alive once again, Inanna passes back out through the seven gates, reclaiming the lost aspects of herself: her talents, abilities, and self-concept. But now she has gained the wisdom of journeying into the darkness, learning about herself, experiencing death, and being reborn into a new expanded nature.

Inanna's journey is mirrored by the planet Venus, which traverses through seven gates in the Heavens before emerging through them once again. Inanna's journey into the Underworld also parallels the process of the transformational chrysalis. Inanna teaches us that to embody the chrysalis of transformation and expanded consciousness, we must first be willing to surrender to a divine force greater than ourselves, to give up the old symbols and vestiges of ego attachment, and to go into the darkness—allowing the old to die so that we may metamorphose and activate our soul potential. Whether we hang from a silken cord on a leaf or from a meat hook in our own dark night of the soul, surrender is an essential act of faith that quickens the activational cells of soulful evolution.

Moth: Repressing Our Dark Soulfulness

Of the 165,000 species of the Lepidoptera order, only 11 percent are "true" Butterflies. The remaining 89 percent of this order are Moths. Most of the approximately eighteen thousand "true" Butterfly species are highly visually diverse from one another in color, pattern, and size. Butterflies are primarily diurnal, meaning they are active during the day, while Moths are nocturnal. While many Moths appear brown and dull toned (owing to their nocturnal habits) in comparison to their jewel-toned Butterfly kin, there are a large number of Lepidoptera species that do not fit easily into either category. Moths and Butterflies are organized less by appearance; rather, their differences are best explained by the adaptations of evolution for specific habitats and behavioral strategies. Recently, multiple Butterfly-Moth species have been discovered, further blurring the boundaries between the two.

Yet, human beings often have very different attitudes and viewpoints of Butterflies and Moths. Butterflies are often prized, collected, and celebrated. Meanwhile, Moths are often given negative associations and killed. To the human psyche, Butterflies can be understood in terms of the persona, the prized and accepted aspects of ourselves, symbolized by this colorful and nonthreatening creature. Meanwhile, the Moth is related to the id—our instinctive, wild nature.

Most Moths are active in the dark hours of nighttime. They are the teachers and guides of the dreamtime, of our repressed shadow aspects of self, and our often disowned wild natures. Just like Earthworms, who too have been scapegoated and ignored, Moths glory in the rich, fertile darkness of the wild psyche. They teach us that each of us has a dark side: we are both Inanna, sparkling queen of Heaven, and Erishkigal, the disowned shadow aspect of self. Earthworm teaches us that the dark earth is the fertile foundation in which our dreams take root and from which they draw sustaining nutrients. Moth teaches us that the wisdom of the dreamtime and the rich wildness of our own dark natures are essential teachers. If we do not dream, we cannot awaken, energized to dance in the sunlight with Butterfly and our gifts, talents, and abilities. It is essential for us to learn to love and acknowledge all parts of ourselves—the light, the dark, no difference. Limiting our sense of self to a sunny persona constrains the flow of life-force energy in our lives, cuts off relationship to our creative instincts, and keeps us from realizing the potential for metamorphosis that is within us. Moth and Butterfly encourage us to release a singular ego attachment and make room for the rich complexity of our authentic nature.

Butterfly and Moth teach us that there must always be death for rebirth and growth to occur. They teach us that darkness and light are an integrated co-creative force. Just as Moth revels in the night—so too is it drawn to the light. Just as Caterpillar yearns to fly with bright colors, so too it knows that its path of transformation is the dark chasm of the chrysalis. And just as scientists are discovering integrated Butterfly-Moth creatures, we too must create sacred union between the light and dark, Inanna and Erishkigal, Butterfly and Moth energies within our own natures. Only from this sacred union can co-creative miracles emerge and authentic transformation and purpose be expressed.

Dissolving into Perpetual Process

Life is an ongoing cycle of death and rebirth. We spiral through phases of transformation in soulful evolution. Every moment of life is an opportunity to learn and grow, practice opening our hearts in authentic love, and co-create and express our soul purpose. Butterfly exemplifies soulful transformation.

That said, it is important to understand that transformational process work may, in itself, become a form of addiction, holding us back. It may become comfortable to always be in process. The cocoon itself, like a mother's womb, may seem like a safe harbor from the challenges of our old lives (Caterpillar) and our fears of embodying a new future and self (Butterfly). Psychically, it may feel easier to hold ourselves back, always dissolving within the cocoon. We may say to ourselves, "I am not ready yet. I need to work on this issue before I can go out successfully into the world." Our potential and sacred purpose may seem too big and unmanageable: "Am I really capable of expressing my gifts and potential? I don't feel ready to step into the bigness of 'me.'" Transformation and sacred purpose do not ask us to be perfect. All they ask is that we listen to what is authentically in our hearts and surrender to the creative process of life.

Before it ever knows that it can fly, the Caterpillar holds the imaginal disks of its wings within its larval thorax. When Butterfly emerges for the first time from the chrysalis shell, it is wet and limp. It does not yet know how to fly. Instead, Butterfly takes its expanded new life one step at a time: it pumps fluid into its wings, expands, and then dries them. Before this, hanging limply on a leaf, it may seem desirable to go back within the chrysalis shell and stay there for a while. Just a little bit longer. There must be something else to be processed and worked on, something that could change just a little more. This limiting fear is the last barrier to stepping fully into your expanded multidimensional self and world. There will always be another chance to learn and grow, but from a new place on the spiral. And now, after all you have been through—the light and dark, death and rebirth, letting go and activation—it is time to flap your new wings, test them on the fragrant air, and fly into a new world of your creation.

EXPERIENTIAL PRACTICE

⬤ *Butterfly's Shamanic Breathwork Dance—*
Alchemical Soul Metamorphosis

Butterfly offers us the opportunity to experience the alchemical process of soul transformation through movement and dance, to fully embody change within the cells of our beings. Shamanic Breathwork utilizes the breath and powerful music to activate healing and transformation throughout all levels of being. In this experiential exercise, you are encouraged to use movement and the breath to deeply embody transformation, activation, and soulful evolution. This exercise may be completed simply as a movement/dance process, or you may add in breathing techniques in a number of forms for a deepened experience.

The first option is to consciously practice deep, slow, and even breathing as you move, further oxygenating your cells and allowing their imaginal potential to spring forth. Second, you may choose to integrate Shamanic Breathwork into your Butterfly dance. It is recommended to practice Shamanic Breathwork either individually or in a group with a trained Shamanic Breathwork and Instar Medicine practitioner who can facilitate and hold safe space for this transformational work. If you choose to do a self-led Shamanic Breathwork exercise, please read *Shamanic Breathwork: Journeying Beyond the Limits of the Self* by Linda Star Wolf before the breathwork session for safety information and breathwork recommendations.

Traditionally, Shamanic Breathwork is a powerful transformational process in which participants breathe "until they are surprised" and follow their own internal journey, set to music, on a blanket and pillow. Spontaneous movement often accompanies the breathwork, though it is limited to the breather's blanket area. Instar Medicine Wheel transformational process work integrates movement more fully into the breathwork and includes a guided process (such as Butterfly's life cycle and chrysalis) led by a trained facilitator. While instar process participants are welcome to follow their own internal compass and journey within the group process, they also have the opportunity to weave breathing, movement, and guided imagery into the dynamic energies of community circle work. Participants have personal blankets and pillows around the perimeter of the space, which they can move back to for stillness and personal space. The space within the circle is for active community dance participation. Participants are encouraged to begin on their mats with a guided meditation, and the activation of the breathwork breath. Those who choose to go more deeply within and experience active trancework are encouraged to stay on their blankets, where trained breathwork facilitators will assist them. Others may choose to breathe but keep some of their focus in the room so that they can also dance and move as they breathe in the shared ceremonial space.

Participants are encouraged to maintain a soft gaze with their eyes so that they can move safely among the other participants, weaving and increasing the dynamic group energy. This group energy is highly activational and transformational. A facilitator will lead the group through a guided instar journey, in which participants can dance, move, tone with the voice, or process emerging emotions while opening themselves to visions and transformation. Participants can return to their mat at any time to go more deeply within or to have personal space.

In essence, Instar Medicine Wheel group process work is an opportunity to co-create, bringing one's humanity and soul expression together in sacred space while integrating movement, breath, and the activational matrix of the Instar Medicine Wheel within a dynamic community of fellow journeyers. Instar transformational group journeying gives you the opportunity to light up as a harmonic cell within the universal body, among other imaginal cells. This is a life-changing and world-changing process.

After beginning and using the breathwork breath for a period of five to ten minutes, listening to an opening piece of music, participants are ready to begin actively moving and co-creating with Butterfly's life-cycle story.

Butterfly's dance begins in the Earth element. You can feel it in your bones—the dense structure that supports all life. Caterpillar moves on the Earth, crawling, climbing, and eating. Allow your movements to mirror Caterpillar's own dance. Crawl in many-legged movements among plant leaves. Feed yourself and grow; store energy for the future. Notice how your body feels in this process. Really feel into the physicality of Caterpillar's life experience.

Periodically, you may experience a tightening and a need for expansion. Molting one form for a new, more complex and expanded form is practice for the later process of metamorphosis within the chrysalis. Even now, in your Caterpillar form, you are forming and energizing the potential of your soul purpose within the imaginal disks of your body. Allow yourself to shed a skin that's too small, emerging through this serpentine sheath of old skin in personal evolution.

Eventually your active dance of eating and growth will reach a point at which you are called to go within. Feel a yearning grow within you and find a safe space for your next stage of accelerated growth. This often means leaving the host plant of your birth and wandering. You are seeking a new host plant for this next stage of your life. Notice what type of plant you are drawn to. What does it look, feel, smell, sound, and taste like? Weave your energy into this plant with all your senses. When you are called, extend a tendril of silk from your body and attach your body to your new host plant by this hanging tendril.

Your yearning has led you into a new place of stillness in your life. Hanging from this plant in your Caterpillar body you are surrounded by quiet. Your vulnerability opens into the present moment. It is time to release and let go of old ego attachments, beliefs, and self-definitions that no longer serve you. Butterfly's alchemical metamorphosis is a complete change of being and form. These old attachments would only hold you back from truly stepping in to and embodying soulful transformation. Hanging in the still air, when you are ready, release these attachments from all levels of your body, mind, heart, energy field, and soul. Ask Butterfly's divine energy matrix, perhaps in the form of Xochiquetzal, the regenerative Butterfly goddess of death and rebirth, to visit you and consume these old attachments for you. Open yourself to Butterfly's universal energetic matrix.

As you release these old attachments and beliefs, you once again feel a yearning to expand and transform. This is the deepest call to transform that you have ever felt in your Butterfly life. In the past you morphed in to progressively new stages of larval complexity. Now you are being called to change who you are on all levels of being, to move into a higher octave of soul expression. Within your old skin of Caterpillar, your internal body has taken the form of a chrysalis. When you are ready, allow your skin to split and slowly emerge as this chrysalis exoskeleton. Within it you are alive, yet externally you hang in stillness. All your focus is drawn within, as the latent potential of your soul purpose begins to be activated.

Physically, all that is not harmonic or no longer serves you is being dissolved away. All that you are, all that you know yourself to be is being dissolved into a primordial and cosmic soul broth. Allow this process to be and let go—let go even of your conscious awareness. Let go into the darkness.

As your body dissolves in this internal process, and the conscious awareness of your personality fades, the imaginal cells of your being are activating, accelerating, and directing the process of metamorphosis. These imaginal cells can be understood as your big picture oversoul, the part of you that has full cosmic awareness at all times—before you were born, now in the present moment, and after you leave your Earth body. Your imaginal cells are the keepers of your morphogenetic fields, your soul blueprint, which organizes the physical expression of your body and all levels of your being.

In this moment, call the rainbow energies of the universe into your imaginal cells. Ask the energetic matrix of Butterfly to bless, harmonize, and transform your being for the highest good. The chrysalis is a transformation vehicle within which you are journeying into new dimensions of yourself and the universe. Notice which dimensions are opening within and around you, surrounded by your chrysalis self. Allow your body to move or not move (however it is instinctively called to be), but know that internally all the cells of your being are transforming, reorganizing, and energizing in a dance of spiritual alchemy.

Your process of transformation has moved from the element of Earth to the elements of Fire and Spirit. In the process of surrender, your body has begun to move to the cosmic heartbeat of a universal presence much larger than anything you have experienced before. Allow yourself to open, receive, realign, and begin to express your soul's blueprint in new ways. You may notice your own internal heartbeat begin to change, new music flowing within, new sensations or frequencies resonating. Simply feel your body as it follows the wisdom of its imaginal cells. Through the portal of the chrysalis, you are opening into entirely new worlds of being, divine connection, and creative expression.

When this process begins to feel complete, you may notice a sense of expansion within your being. At the same time, your new body is now held within a close, small space. Once again, a new body is wrapped within an old body; the chrysalis has served its purpose. Remembering the spirit of surrender, begin to utilize your new body. Allow it to wriggle and shift. Move and encourage cracks to begin to open in the chrysalis. Move your body, almost as if you were taking off a mask that covered your being. This is your final molt—into an entirely new form and instar of life experience. You are ready to emerge as a mature, universal adult, the divine child of God, all grown up into self-awareness, wisdom, and maturity. You are now a harmonic, conscious cell within the universal body.

As a spiritual adult you have reached a new threshold. Feel your body ready to expand beyond the chrysalis. Feel the fresh air of a new world on your tender soul wings. When you are ready, begin to emerge from your chrysalis. Stretch and unfurl your wings. You are now present in the element of Air: expansive, limitless, ready for new adventures and avenues of creative expression. Your body is now one-third of its former weight. Your energy field is lighter, streamlined, and ethereal.

But first, before you can fly, you must expand and dry your wings. Bring your attention into the center of your being. Feel your heartbeat emanating from within. Call the essence of your life and imaginal cells forward. Begin to pump the essence of your vibral core out into your wings, blessing and expanding them. You are readying your wings for your first flight. Feel the warmth of the sun drying your wings. When you are ready, begin to call the essence of your vibral core back into the center of your being. Your wings are now ready to dance with a new element—Air.

Take a moment to look at your wings. Notice how beautiful and unique they are. Your wings are the essence of you—the articulation of your soul and the expression of your sacred purpose on Planet Earth. When you are ready, gather energy into the core of your being and begin to flap your wings. You are so light now the sacred Air lifts you easily and you are borne aloft on winds of new adventures and co-creation. You are ready to express a new octave of sacred purpose and taste the sweet nectar of life.

Take some time now to fly. How does it feel? Visit gorgeous and delicious flowers; cathedrals of beauty and light. Perhaps you meet a new divine consort on the wing who reflects your soulful maturity back to you. The era of the Butterfly is a time of new soulful creative expressions and the manifestation of new dreams and inspired ideas. Allow all the wisdom of your life experience to inform your being-ness. Allow the new abilities, gifts, and wisdom of your expanded soul nature to come forward. Allow new understandings to come to you. It is time to share the new expression of you with the world. Your sacred purpose is a blessing to all life. Take this time to fly, to create, and to bless the world. This is your time to fully experience all the beauty and richness that the universe holds, though it may only be fully felt by one like you: a mature, transformed, soulful Butterfly of the universe.

When you are ready, alight on a resting flower. Close your eyes and begin to bring your awareness back to the present moment. Begin to ground yourself in your human body, knowing that your etheric Butterfly body is always within and around you, in your energy field. Continue to ground the lightness of your being in the sacred arms of Mother Earth. When you are ready, open your eyes and share or journal what you experienced on the divine chrysalis journey of the Butterfly!

🦋 Butterfly Invocation

O Beautiful Imaginal Spirit of Transformation, teach us by your courageous example and from your path of direct, lived experience how to die and be reborn again. . . . Show us the way. May we learn what you already know, that only by going within, and dissolving ego's agenda again, will we be able to emerge with the essential soul medicine to illuminate the heart of humankind. . . . Show us the way. May we be inspired by your inner and outer strength to go the "distance," no matter how far or how long, to become who we truly are, and to remember as we too take flight from the remains of who we once were, that those who witness our ascent into flight may begin to awaken from their deep sleep and live their dreams now. . . . Show us the way.

6
Spider

Becoming the Ancestral Creator,
Weaver of Cosmic Dreams

The artist is a receptacle for emotions that come from all over the place: from the sky, from the earth, from a scrap of paper, from a passing shape, from a spider's web.

PABLO PICASSO

Imagine moving with the delicate speed of eight legs and looking at the world through many eyes. Imagine floating through the air on a strand of silken gossamer and weaving a home from the imaginings of your inner self. Imagine living—receptive and open to the elements—listening to the vibrations and whispers of the web of life. The intricate dance of Spider teaches us about the qualities of harmonic leadership and service, how to open into our visionary natures, and how to weave our medicine into the web of life for the highest good of future generations.

Spider has many faces and has woven itself into folktales around the world. In ancient Greek myths a mortal woman named Arachne was famous for the quality of her weavings. In her hubris, Arachne challenged the goddess Athena to a weaving contest. Both weavers created incredible tapestries. After the contest, Athena inspired Arachne to feel such shame and guilt for her hubris that she committed suicide. Athena revived her and turned her into a Spider.[1]

In Africa, Anansi the Spider is a famous folktale hero. Anansi embodied the trickster. In one of his escapades, after impressing Nyame the Sky God, he was made the owner of all stories and storytelling. In Hindu mythology Spider is the weaver of illusion and destiny, which parallels the Egyptian goddess Neith. To the Navajo/Dineh and the Pueblo peoples of the American Southwest, Spider Woman (or Spider Grandmother) was the creator of life and the original ancestor who taught the people how to weave. Spider is the Earth goddess in Hopi cosmology and has the capability to will things into being.[2] In South America the ancient Nazca people of Peru mysteriously carved a massive Spider into the Peruvian landscape, which can only be seen fully from the air.

It is said that each person is within one meter of a Spider at all times. Spiders can be found around the world and are often the first to travel into recently devastated ecosystems. It is estimated that there are more than two million Spiders per acre of land. In temperate environments at least twenty species of Spiders can be found in the average home. While Spiders have traditionally been a source of fear among people, in the vast majority of cases their danger to humans has been significantly exaggerated. In humans, Spider bites are usually less dangerous than those of Ants or the stings of Bees or Wasps. Spiders are often misunderstood. When studied, their behaviors and abilities prove to be of interest and significance to researchers and arachnophiles alike.

There are 40,000 named species of Spiders, but this number is only a fraction of the total number of unnamed species. Scientists estimate that there are 250,000 total species of Spiders. Spiders of the same species have been found to display distinctive personalities and temperaments. While there is a great variety and diversity of Spider species around the planet, Spiders are divided into one of four niche groups, based on their behaviors: those who build webs to catch prey, wandering hunters, burrowers who wait for prey that travel near the entrance to their homes, and jumping Spiders. Popular among arachnophiles for their interesting behaviors and dramatic appearances, jumping Spiders can leap up to twenty times their own length and are known for elaborate dancing and posing behaviors during courtship.[3]

Fossil evidence indicates that the first Spiders are ancient, differentiating from other arachnids by the ability to produce silk in the Devonian period 415 million to 360 million years ago. Spiders come from the class of organisms called Arachnica and the order Araneae. Spiders are then subordered into two groupings of species: primitive and modern. With large and substantial bodies, primitive Spiders, or Mygalomorphs, strongly reflect the characteristics of their ancient arachnid ancestors. In addition, their fangs point downward to pierce their prey. Most primitive Spiders live in burrows. Females can live to twenty years or more. Males mature at five years, though they often do not live much longer than that.

Modern Spiders, or Araneomorphs, tend to have more graceful and fine features; their fangs point inward horizontally to help them grab prey. Modern Spiders represent the vast majority of the arachnids we come across in our daily lives. Modern Spider species vary significantly in how long each lives, though their life spans are far shorter than those of primitive Spiders. Modern Spiders live an average of one to two years. Some male Spiders live long enough to mate again, while others do not. Some females die soon after laying their eggs, while others lay eggs multiple times and tend to their young. Wolf Spiders are noteworthy because they are the only species known to carry their young on their backs.

Most male Spiders are not killed in mating, as is popularly thought. Spider mating spans a wide range of behaviors and cannot be generalized. According to science author and teacher Lynne Kelly, "Spiders' mating behavior can only be interpreted by taking their unique arachnid biology into account. For most species, two effectively blind carnivores must meet and mate when each is almost indistinguishable from the other's last meal. As it is the male who approaches the female, he must make that distinction very, very clear to her."[4]

After a female Spider has mated, she has the ability to store her partner's sperm until she is ready to produce eggs. Spider hatchlings face high predation, so mothers often lay many eggs, potentially numbering in the thousands. When she is ready to produce her eggs, the Spider will begin weaving a silken cocoon into which the eggs will be placed until they are ready to hatch.

Because many mothers will not live to see their offspring emerge, weaving an egg sac is an act of investing in future generations outside of the self. The young hatch from their egg sac after completing one to two molts. Some species of Spiders care for their young, but most new Spiders leave home quickly. Many Spiders, whether newly hatched or as adults, use silk lines to balloon on the air to new locations. This reduces competition for food. Spiders are predators, but also prey.

Spiders are capable of deliberately self-amputating one of their legs if it becomes caught by a predator (to prevent the predator's venom from reaching the Spider's main body) or in other threatening situations. In this way they can escape and live another day. Modern Spiders molt, transforming through multiple instars, until they reach sexual maturity. Primitive Spiders molt throughout their lives. In the case of an amputated leg, a Spider can regrow a new appendage within its exoskeleton, releasing it during its next molt. Up to one-fifth of Spiders have fewer than eight legs and are able to live successfully in the wild. They are truly examples of the shamanic life path.

When molting, Spiders select safe locations; for example, going within their burrows and covering the entrance with a layer of woven silk. After the molt, in their new instar of development, Spiders are known to move ecstatically as they try out their newly advanced physical forms.

During the day Spiders are often still, but at night they become active hunters, venturing to the edge of their burrows, building webs, and hunting. The Spider web is almost synonymous with Spider itself, yet across species there exist a variety of strategies for hunting, including jumping, chasing, ambushing, stalking, fishing, mimicry (including the production of false pheromones), theft, and spitting of venomous adhesives. Spiders are limited to eating their food in a liquid form, so they inject prey with digestive enzymes to liquefy them internally.

There are many kinds of webs used to capture prey, including tube webs, tangle webs, sheet webs, lace webs, dome webs, and orb webs. Orb webs are the most iconic of web types and are also the most economical structures for catching aerial prey. Some Spider species weave patterns into their webs, such as an X pattern that points toward the center of the web, where the hunting Spider lies in wait.

Spiders can have up to eight eyes, often grouped in pairs or threes. Hunting Spiders have more and larger eyes than do those who don't rely on their sight to hunt. Most Spiders, excluding those who use eyesight for hunting, are almost blind. Instead, Spiders use the hair on their bodies to sense what's happening in their environment through vibrations. For example, a Spider's web or layers of cobweb communicate the vibrations of prey back to the waiting hunter. Spiders do not hear with ears or have a sense of smell but receive vast amounts of information that mimic these senses from the hairs on their body and through touch. Spider legs have seven segments, with very small claws at the end of these appendages. Another interesting sensory item of note is that a quarter of Spider families are capable of making sound. Though it is subauditory to human ears, the Wolf Spider is the loudest of all Spiders. We like to think of Wolf Spiders—who carry their young on their backs and call loudly to others—as wise Wolf shamanic pathfinders for humanity.

EXPLORING SPIDER'S PLACE ON THE MEDICINE WHEEL

The North Direction, Connection to the Ancestors, and the Wise Elder Phase of Life

It is said that Spider Woman is the creator of all living creatures. The Navajo/Dineh and Pueblo peoples believe that she formed us from the clay of the Earth and that, to this day, we are each connected to her by a thread of gossamer silk. Spider Woman is the original ancestor. Through her weaving we can trace the generations back to the origin of time, back to the first co-creations between Spirit and Matter. Chief Seattle affirmed this: each Being alive today is a strand within the web of life, and individual actions and consciousness affect the entire interconnected universe.

Spider Woman wove for us a living Earth web and passed on her gifts to us, her divine human descendants. She taught the Navajo/ Dineh peoples how to build a loom—a framework that holds the dance of co-creation—made from lightning, rain, sunshine, earth, and sky. Spider Woman, our ancestral creator, gave us the gift of weaving—she made us creators too. As members of Spider's ancestral lineage, we have the ability to weave our dreams into reality, creating a better world for the next seven generations to come.

Spider is the keeper of the North direction—the place of the wise, responsible elder, the ancestors, the element of Air, and the season of winter. After the leaves of autumn have fallen, we come into a place of stillness. The richness of life—our experiences, lessons, and developed abilities—is carried within our beings. Our outward energetic expressions now turn inward. Our entire life journey has prepared us for this moment: to turn our attention into the stillness, into the void, into the cosmic darkness of the galactic center.

Within each of our cells the center of the universe can be found. This central place holds the co-creative consciousness of imaginal reality, where all potential manifestations are possible. This dark center is our link to our power as co-creative weavers of reality. As we open all of our beings to the heart of this inner universe we deepen our ability to vision and bring through the new dreams that will bless and create the potentialities of tomorrow. It is in this place that we realize that we are the ones we have been waiting for.

The winter of life, our elder years, is a rich phase in which we have the ability to make meaning out of our past experiences, to find greater purpose for our long-developed gifts and abilities, to move increasingly beyond the mundane creations of physical existence into the spiritual, etheric realm. It is a rare opportunity to synthesize the meaning of our life journey with our increasing ability to pass through the veils of universal reality. We can create from this place, touching the heart of God and weaving powerful new dreams.

Spider reminds us that elderhood is a special and revered place on the Instar Medicine Wheel. We need our elders to empower themselves, to listen to the call of Spirit. We need them to share the visions they receive from the divine universe and teach us the wisdom they hear among the stars and from the call of wild birds. In the inbreath and outbreath of life, elderhood represents the moment in between—just as the winter is the quiet, still point between the disintegration of autumn and the burgeoning creations of spring. We breathe fully into our bodies, feeling the rich oxygen permeate and enliven our cells. Then we begin the outbreath, releasing into Spirit, into the veils beyond physical existence. There is a spark of possibility—the source of imaginal creativity—inherent in this moment. From this place we connect fully to the divine universe, and through our beings come the weavings, dreams, visions, and wisdom of our Spider nature. We become the ancestral creator, keeper of the North, keeper of the new dreams for humanity and all creation.

It is important to note that, while human elderhood is usually found in the latter years of the human life cycle, the wise elder can be embodied at any point of life. The developmental evolution of consciousness is a unique process for each person and is not limited to a certain decade of life or a concrete definition. In addition, many beings are coming to Earth at this time who have within them vast wisdom, heart, and cosmic awareness. They need simply to be supported and sometimes activated by life to step in to their identity as wise cosmic elders. These children are pure dreaming conduits who have much to teach those of us learning to embody our sacred purpose in this lifetime. As we have discussed, the Instar Medicine Wheel is not meant to be a linear process. Rather, we spiral round and round, integrating and experiencing new facets of the archetypes throughout our lives.

SACRED PURPOSE

Creative Visioning for the Next Seven Generations

In our elder years, Spider teaches that how we express our sacred purpose changes. Our sense of purpose is just as vital, if not more so, as other places on the medicine wheel. Earthworm, Honeybee, and Butterfly illustrate a progression of action in the world: alchemizing that which no longer serves a purpose to create a foundation for new growth, entering into sacred union and manifesting the co-creative child, and actively transforming the self into a higher octave of being. Having moved around the spiral of the Instar Medicine Wheel to the North direction, home of Spider, we learn to transform purpose itself. We release our focus on direct physical action and outward co-creation. Our purpose becomes more subtle, and we become more receptive to Spirit and the creative whispers of the universe.

Spider sits on its web, waiting. Most Spiders are almost blind; they use vibrations to sense the world. A Spider's web acts as an interconnected communication system, sending the vibrations of struggling prey to Spider. Spider waits, opening himself to the surrounding elements— the breezes, dewdrops, warm sun, and buzzing wings—instinctively knowing that the interconnected web of life will provide nourishment. Spider teaches that receptivity is an important element of purpose. We move through Butterfly's portal of surrender—through self-metamorphosis—and evolve into wise beings who understand the relationship between action and stillness. We learn how to open, listening to the wide universe around us, waiting for the telltale vibrations of Spirit sending us signals through the strands of the universal web. We merge more fully with the web of life, and in this way we practice more effective action, knowing when to wait and when to gather life's treasures to nourish ourselves and future generations. In our elder years we feel them most clearly, trembling with expectation in the web of life. We become more sensitively attuned to the subtle dance of the universe.

Yet, Spider's lesson is not to become passive and simply wait for life. Instead, Spider teaches us to build the dreaming loom, to weave our webs—to build the framework through which we can more clearly commune with Spirit and bring through creative visions. We build our dreaming loom and make it our home, living in deep connection to the imaginal possibilities streaming from the galactic center. Butterfly teaches us that imaginal evolutionary potentiality is within us. Spider asks us now to center our lives in imaginal service, visioning, dreaming, and weaving for the highest good of all life.

Not all Spiders build webs; many burrow or wander, though all can produce silk. The best-known web builders are called orb weavers. Spider silk is the strongest fiber known to humanity (surpassing the defensive might of Kevlar vests), and humans cannot reproduce it. It is light as a feather and a tenth the width of a human hair. A teaspoon of Spider silk contains enough material to build one million webs. It takes just over one pound of silk to encircle the Earth with one, long, translucent strand. It can stretch to three times its length, while resisting bacteria and fungus. Birds, after a tasty Spider snack, often repurpose Spider webbing for their own nests. Spiders produce silk through the spinnerets located at the base of the abdomen, and many species produce up to seven types of silk.

Spider teaches us that the location of potential is within. It is from this place that we can create incredible new technologies, which, in turn, can open new worlds and new possibilities. It is through our lived experience, through all the seasons of the shaman's journey, that we gather the jewels of life—our memories, lessons learned through challenges, self-awareness, the ability to open our hearts and love, learning to really listen, and the skill to communicate with clarity. Through all this we have grown and developed the soul gifts of our sacred purpose. In our elder years we have the chance to integrate and internalize our shaman's medicine. We take the truth and beauty of who we are, internalizing who we know ourselves to be and all that we have learned, and alchemize this into a miraculous ingredient that can weave the web of life for future generations.

An orb weaver begins building its web by ballooning, releasing a thread of silk and allowing itself to be carried in the wind by this strand. Attached at both ends, the Spider proceeds to complete a perimeter frame. From this point it drops down, releasing silk and attaching it, creating evenly spaced radial lines. When the web resembles a narrowly sliced pie, the Spider finishes the web by moving in an evenly spaced spiral, crossing over the radial lines. The evolutionary spiral path of life is mirrored in the framework of the dreaming web. In general, orb weavers build a new web and take it down after hunting each evening. Many insects, who have ultraviolet vision, see Spider webs shimmering with color, which attracts nourishment to Spider.

Symbolically, Spider's nourishment can be seen as attracting beneficial visions, creative projects, potential allies, synchronicities, and the ingredients that sustain life. The web reminds us that all aspects of life are interconnected, that we have the capacity to weave new realities and dreams, and that all we have to do is open our internal awareness to feel the vibrations of Spirit calling to us.

Building a web raises an interesting question: How does Spider know how to build a web? Its parents are not around to teach it. How does a Spider sense how to use the incredible capabilities of its body to build a frame on which to catch insects? DNA-bred instincts have been suggested. Symbolically, an important lesson is illuminated. To Spider, wisdom is attained when one realizes that everything essential is within and all we need to do is connect to the universe and express who we are. The magical silk of our shamanic medicine comes from within and is woven seamlessly into the web of life. We have evolved through the consciousness patterns of Earthworm, Honeybee, and Butterfly into Spiders: subtle, intricate weavers who bring the wisdom of our lifetimes through our beings, connect deeply with the entire universe, and share and receive on a more profound level than ever before.

Now that we have explored the mechanism and process of web weaving, what of its purpose? What is the big *why* of Spider? In many Native American communities, it is said that, in order for an idea or action to have value, it must "grow corn." In other words, if something does not contribute to feeding the next generations, then it has no real purpose or value. Earthworm focuses on building a fertile foundation for future creations. Honeybee focuses on creating and caring for the next generation of life—its children and community. Butterfly focuses on taking its past creations and sense of purpose to a higher octave, through self-transformation. Spider continues this evolution of purpose by placing its focus on the future, feeding the next seven generations of children with the visions and creations received through the universal web.

A Spider many of us know provides a beautiful example of this sense of purpose. Charlotte the Spider, in E. B. White's classic children's story *Charlotte's Web,* takes it upon herself to change the community of the farm on which she lives. Her friend, Wilbur, is destined to be turned into bacon. Charlotte's wise woman perception sees Wilbur's incredible heart and holds a reverence for the preservation of life.

Even though she is a minute creature, Charlotte sets out to make a contribution and change things. She begins by hanging upside down on her web, patiently waiting for inspiration to come to her. That's what Spiders do! She begins to receive messages and weaves them into her web. She weaves inspiring words of praise into her web about Wilbur. Over and over, gaining attention, she receives visions, weaves creative energies of peace, and inspires the people and animals around her to change their reality. Wilbur's life is spared, and he is uplifted by a friendship with this incredibly wise Spider.

At the end of her life, deep into her elder years, Charlotte muses and dreams.

> *The autumn days grow short and cold; It's Christmas time again.*
> *Then snows of winter slowly melt.*

The day grows short, And then . . .
He turns the seasons around, And so she changes . . .
    her gown:
Mother Earth . . . and Father Time.
How very special are we . . . For just a moment . . . to
    be . . .
Part of life's . . . eternal . . . rhyme.

Spider teaches us that we can weave the wisdom and grace of our shamanic medicine and divine inspiration into the very web of life that surrounds us, for the betterment of future generations. We can weave the inbreath of our lives as a contribution to the collective, and release into the outbreath, having become fully part of "life's eternal rhyme."

We begin to know that everything we need is within us: our imaginal potentialities have been activated in our cells and stand ready to weave the visioning loom in service to the highest good of all life. We are the ones we have been waiting for, and now is the time to gather the shamanic medicine of our lived experience and weave it into the web of life. At every moment in our lives there is an inner elder, waiting to be actualized. The more that we open ourselves to life—learning, growing, and integrating—the more magical medicine we have within us to weave into the future. We create the loom-web through which visions arrive, and we weave the future itself. We become the ancestral creator for a harmonious future.

PORTAL OF TRANSFORMATION

Weaving the Web of Life and Receiving Divine Inspiration

Spider offers us a complex and subtle portal of transformation. Having built its web, Spider waits receptively. A Spider's web is truly a dream catcher for the visions and messages of Spirit. Have you ever sat outdoors and observed a Spider web? If there is a breeze, it will ripple through the web, making it dance with an ebb and flow. Starlight falls on it while

Spider transformational portal image, integrating a dream catcher with sapphire beads, a Spider overlaid on the sacred geometry of the six-pointed star, and a silver border with ancient symbols from the stars

Spider waits, open and receptive to the vibrations of nourishing wisdom. The dew falls and clings like diamonds to the web's silken tendrils. A Spider web is made of the strongest and most miraculous material on Earth; yet, more than that, a web is a weaving of its surroundings—a flowing tapestry of the universe and the energy that moves through it.

In the image above two circles form a figure eight. Eight is the number of Ma'at (discussed in chapter 3, "Earthworm"), the Egyptian principle of divine order and balance. Eight is also the symbol of infinity, as one connects to the divine universe. One circle is made of Spider's web, spiraling out, open to the universal energies moving through it. Below, waiting and listening, is Spider. Its body is aligned with the six-pointed star. Spider and the Blue Star mysteries (which will be discussed in greater detail in chapter 7, "Cicada and Dragonfly") are intimately intertwined. Throughout this book we have moved around the Instar Medicine Wheel of sacred purpose and transformation. Moving beyond Earthworm, Honeybee, and Butterfly, Spider knows that it embodies activated imaginal cells of universal creation and dives within to the galactic center of consciousness—into the dark void through which new dreams and visions emerge. At this point in the journey of sacred purpose, Spider teaches us about activating our relationship with the Great Above star energies—the celestial frequencies—knowing that they speak from within. Spider teaches us how to integrate and express our shamanic medicine, creating the dream web and more fully connecting with the divine universe of co-creation.

In the portal image the dream catcher is a silver frame with symbols of star language carved into it. The six-pointed star and star symbolism are found throughout the Instar Medicine Wheel, because the celestial frequencies of higher love and wisdom have an intimate relationship with the insects and related creatures of this world. This will be discussed in greater depth in later chapters. What is important to understand at this point in our journey is that Spider helps us transform our shamanic medicine and through this alchemical process more fully connect to the living universe—to know ourselves as interconnected beings of life—and to step in to our new role as ancestral creators. We become the conduits to the stars, to the smallest atoms, to myriad life-forms, and we realize that our entire beings are the web itself. We embody the web of life, understanding that we are both the dreamer and the dream.

TRANSFORMATION

Embodying Leadership as the Visionary Elder

As a transformational weaver, Spider develops Earthworm's channel to its co-creative potential. It embodies the alchemy of visionary consciousness. The messages, dreams, and visions of the universe come through the portal of the web to be manifested and expressed in physical reality. It is Spider, the original storyteller and creator, who decides how to weave etheric consciousness into physical form.

Whereas Earthworm, the apprentice, learns that it is capable of bringing Spirit through its body as a sacred channel and begins practicing the craft of sacred purpose, Spider, as a wise elder, is ready to take on the Earth leadership role of the ancestral creator: receiving and weaving dreams into reality for the highest good of the next seven generations. Through Spider the celestial chords of the universe become the Earth songs of harmony, praise for life, and innovative visions for an age of peace.

Spider teaches us that leadership is not about being a prominent, hierarchical figure who oversees life from above. Instead, we are encouraged to weave ourselves into the web of life, co-creatively collaborating, imbuing the web with our wisdom, and receiving the nourishment of this interconnected universal network.

We are encouraged not to ignore or repress our vulnerabilities but to learn from them and integrate our past challenges into the personal, shamanic medicine that we can contribute to the collective. This shamanic medicine is the magical and dynamic silk that is expressed from the core of our beings, building and energizing the web of life.

We can only contribute to and enhance the web of life if we open ourselves and become receptive to the essential learning and growth of human experiences. Through this instar transformational process we molt and evolve our consciousness into new forms, many times, just like Spider. We are transformed, and so we become wise shamanic elders and leaders, capable of transforming and harmonizing the web itself. In service, we open our beings to the wisdom of the universe and weave Spirit into physical manifestation for the highest good of all life.

This is the leadership archetype that Spider teaches:

- Being open and receptive
- Integrating one's own learning and transforming it into medicine

- Learning to weave oneself deeply within the interconnected web of life
- Understanding our humanity in relation to all beings
- Building frameworks that act as a portal to new dreams and visions
- Weaving these dreams into physical form in service to future generations

Spider may appear to be solitary, but this is an illusion. It has woven itself into the very fabric of the universe, swaying with the breeze, communing with the starlight, speaking and listening to the web of life.

LESSONS AND SHADOW

Energetic Greed—Spinning a Dysfunctional Interpersonal Web

On the journey of sacred purpose, Spider teaches us a valuable lesson: the balance between direct action and receptivity within the creative visionary process. Spider's lesson on receptivity is neither to reject direct action in our lives nor to abdicate our role and ability as wise leaders in our elder years. The balance of activity is not passive receptivity. Instead, Spider teaches us to maintain a dynamic relationship between the two principles—to understand the balance of these yin and yang energies. Spider views the creative process as the ebb and flow of the ocean and the inbreath and outbreath of respiration. As a creator, how do you use receptivity in your creative process, and how do you relate it to direct action?

Receptivity and activity dance in relationship to one another throughout the creative process of Spider medicine. First, we begin to look within, integrating our life experiences and transforming them internally into our shamanic medicine of service, or silken gossamer. Then we are ready to take action, expressing this medicine and building a web that acts as a portal for visions, dreams, and divine communication. After the web is built, in our Spider form we are invited into receptivity again, sitting on the web and communing with its energies. Internally we open ourselves and weave our energies into the elements that permeate the web: rain (Water), plants (Earth), the sun (Fire), and the wind (Air). Through this elemental portal, Spirit is invited to infuse third-dimensional reality. It is then Spider's role to actively weave its visions into the stories, teachings, and fabric of Earth.

Spider teaches us how to bring the creative process home into our bodies and enhance our ability to both vision and create. Spider also orients the purpose of our creativity to that of collective service to future generations and the co-creation of a harmonic world.

The shadow side of Spider medicine is the manipulative miscreator who centers herself in the hub of a dysfunctional energetic web. The shadow web is a codependent creation whose purpose is to draw energy from external people or situations to feed the weaver. Spider is a carnivorous hunter, and while this behavior is not a part of shadow, in terms of human energetic ventures some shadow Spiders use hunting, enticement, and manipulative strategies to draw the energies of others to themselves. These strategies may include the manipulative use of sexual attraction, external validation, attention-seeking, victimhood, martyrdom, gossiping, hierarchical power, and antagonistic behaviors. The shadow Spider uses these strategies to attract energy to her web to create a sense of wholeness, completion, pleasure, self-liking, and purpose. Behaviors to gain wholeness from outside the self are inherently codependent and victimizing to self and others.

Shadow Spider behavior is victimizing to others because she asks them to play limited, reactive, and inauthentic social roles. This behavior also asks them to expend their own life-force energy and contribute it to the shadow Spider. Shadow Spider behavior has a foundation in fear-based scarcity consciousness, insecurity, low self-esteem, and disregard for others (which at its core is based in a disregard for self and life). Because the shadow Spider has a fundamental belief in the lack of the self and the lack of abundant energy in the world, she attempts to fill this inner void by using manipulative interpersonal strategies. The shadow Spider may have a sense of past hurt or being wronged by others, feel incomplete and unworthy as a person, or believe there isn't enough energy for everyone to sustain life.

These fears and beliefs prevent a person from realizing that all energy comes from within when we are healthfully connected to the web of life. A codependent, interpersonal web is only a shadow reflection of the infinite, interconnected web of life. We have the ability to weave ourselves into the fabric of the web of life, sharing the gift of who we are with this community, receiving abundance, and co-creating in sacred union. This is the lesson that shadow Spider energy teaches us.

For those who are ready to bring their Spider shadow into the light, a focus on codependency recovery is key. Melody Beattie's works on codependency, *Codependent No More* and *The Language of Letting Go,* are excellent resources for this process. In addition, Linda Star Wolf has written *30 Shamanic Questions for Humanity,* a thirty-day recovery guide to energetic codependency and connection to sacred purpose. It may be helpful to examine past wounding, victimization, and issues of self-esteem in this journey of healing and transformation.

We are all beautiful, whole, and gifted citizens within the web of life. This is your birthright. No external person or situation has the ability to make you whole; others can simply reflect your current sense of wholeness back to you. All love begins with self-love. All abundant creativity begins with an authentic connection to Spirit.

We all have inclinations to act on shadow Spider behaviors at different times in our lives. Codependent survival strategies are often a starting point on the path of human experience. As shamanic human beings we have the ability and opportunity to evolve our consciousness, transforming our beliefs and realizing a greater sense of internal wholeness. As we evolve our Spider consciousness and integrate it within our beings as wisdom, we have the ability to share this shamanic medicine of the wounded healer with others for the highest good. Our Spider shadow is transmuted into wisdom that can be expressed and shared through the web of life, inspiring others. And we become Spider elders and leaders through the shamanic path of lived experience.

EXPERIENTIAL PRACTICE

 Spider's Dance—Weaving the Vision Web

Descended from the ancestral creator, Spider Woman, you have within yourself the ability to weave the Spider's web, a portal through which visions, dreams, and medicine for the collective arrive into Earth reality. This experiential practice is intended to be a body movement and guided imagery journey, but it can also be deepened into an integrative breathwork journey (see experiential practices in chapter 5, "Butterfly," for further information on best practices).

In a sacred space appropriate to body movement, bring your attention inward. Breathe and open your intuitive awareness. Invite a life experience—one that has shaped you into the wise human being you are today—to come into your awareness. Reflect on what lessons you learned through this human dance of living and how this challenge or situation has evolved into wisdom that you are now able to share with others in service to humanity. Visualize this shamanic medicine as a jewel and place it within your belly.

Bring your focus to your belly. Invite it to fill with light, and notice that it is filled with all the jewels of your wisdom, learning, growth, and transformation—your shamanic medicine. Feel these jewels glow and pulse within you. Your life experiences have become integrated into activational energy for the collective. When you are ready, allow these jewels to unspool themselves into magical Spider silk, which shimmers with rainbow light.

It is time to weave your web. Allow your body to move as it is called; your internal wisdom knows just how to do this. You have a unique web dance. You may want to bring your hands to your belly and use them as an extension to help place the silk you release.

When you are ready, begin to release your shamanic silk out into the world. Sense it with your fingertips and notice what it feels like! A strong web begins with a perimeter. With your body, create a silken perimeter line in whatever shape you feel called to craft.

Now it is time to fasten radial lines from the perimeter into the center of the web. This is your chance to create your own medicine wheel, activating the energies of healing, visioning, and service. You can move from North to South, attaching a line to each end at the directions, and then from East to West, or however you are called. At each of these direction points (or wherever you connect one piece of silk to another) pulse your body with energy to activate this point on the web. Once you have laid the medicine wheel lines of the four cardinal directions, you can proceed to fill in radials until the web resembles a thinly sliced pie. Each slice of pie is widest at the perimeter and narrows into the infinity of the sacred center of the web.

Now it is time to connect the radial energetic lines of the web, activating them with the sacred spiral. Beginning at the perimeter of the web, begin to move slowly in an ever-narrowing spiral, round and round, toward the center of the web. The spiral touches each radial line, growing closer and closer, until you reach the very center of the web.

Within the final arc of the spiral, snip out an open circle at the very center. Do not discard this extra silk; Spider wastes nothing. This magical silk is high in protein. Take it into your body to sustain and enliven you as you vision.

You have opened a window within the web through which dreams and visions are whispered from the divine universe. Move to any place on the web to which you are called and settle in. It is now time to move from action to open receptivity. Attach yourself to the web with all eight of your legs. Begin to breathe with the web. Feel the entire web breathe in and out with you. As you breathe, call the elements of Earth, Air, Fire, and Water that surround you to dance and sing through and with the web. Breathe and dance together with the elements as you sit on this sacred portal. Then, come into stillness again, opening yourself and the web more deeply.

When you are ready, invite a vibration or sound to begin resonating in your heart. Send this vibration out into the universe. Send your heart song out to the galactic center—to the dark, creative void. And then wait, wait in the listening silence. Open yourself to receive and listen for the whispering voices of the divine universe.

Invite any messages, visions, dreams, or new creations to move through the portal of the Spider web into your consciousness. Invite them to come into your awareness, and then ask them to move into your body. Notice what they are.

When you are ready, using dance, more fully embody the visions that have come to you. As Spider, you are the ancestral creator who acts in service to future generations. Dance the vision, which has reached you through the etheric realms, into manifestation—into physical, Earthen reality. Dance Heaven into Earth, manifest Spirit into Matter. Embody your unique dance and weave new dreams into the Earth web for the highest good of all life. You are a storyteller, and your body is your voice here on Earth. Infuse your body with ecstatic joy from your heart and send that out into the web of life as you dance your dreams into reality.

After your dance feels complete, find a resting place on your web and breathe life-sustaining energies through the web from the elements of the universe into your being. Rest with gratitude, knowing you have blessed both Heaven and Earth through your co-creative sacred purpose as Spider.

Spider's Guided Meditation Journey: Connecting to the Web of Life

More than ever before, we are becoming collectively conscious of being globally interconnected. We can see examples of this in the World Wide Web of the Internet, the media, global transportation, migration of cultures . . . and Earth phenomena that connect us all: climate change, energy resource scarcity, and economic uncertainty.

In contrast to this expanding sense of interconnection, many people live with a significant sense of separation, fear, and isolation. We truly are affecting one another all the time through our actions, intentions, and consciousness. As Chief Seattle is purported to have said, "Humankind has not woven the web of life. We are but one thread within it. Whatever we do to the web, we do to ourselves. All things are bound together. All things connect."[5]

Ironically, our actions, born out of disconnection and fear, are the very things so significantly impacting our interconnected, collective future. More than ever before, now is the time to reconnect as citizens of a global web of life.

Becoming reconnected is a process sourced from within. It is born from a deep awareness in our cells that we, as human bodies, human beings, comprise a web of relationships. From our immune system and our location within an ecosystem to our families, our "being-ness" is a flowing dance of relationships with all of life. It sustains us, nurtures us on our journeys, and forms the pattern of life.

When we know ourselves as a web of relationships, we co-create a world that reflects this sense of interconnected harmony. When you know yourself as part of a web of relationships, this greater experience of connectedness and harmony allows you to embody your creative potential and fully tap in to your life-force energy.

We are also each a microcosm of the planet. As our atmosphere chokes on air pollution, our respiratory disorder rates soar. We mirror the reality of our world within our bodies and psyches, and the planet mirrors our decisions back to us. As we see nations competing with one another and promoting separation, so too do we see fragmentation and competition within our families and communities.

When we hear of nations committing genocide or attacking the integrity of Earth's natural environment, we can look within and see the mirrored reality of autoimmune disorders as body systems attack themselves. When we splinter into fragmentation and conflict our actions defy life and sustainability. Health and survival of all are intimately linked, just as our body systems, ecosystems, and social systems are intimately linked. Experiencing a profound connection to all of life is your physiological, ecological, and spiritual template as a human being.

Integration of web consciousness—into our beings and communities—teaches us that we are not alone and that all life has meaning, purpose, and value. Web consciousness gives us a template, from our primordial Source, which is highly relevant in this current time on the planet. We can transform the outdated paradigm of fear of difference and unhealthy competition and hierarchy into a life-enhancing framework of collaboration and cooperation.

In our interrelationship the gifts of our diversity create harmonious patterns of sustainability, creativity, and peace. We are each cells in the universal body. Our life journeys uphold the beauty of sacred pattern. Animals, plants, elements—we are all beautiful, essential aspects co-creating the web of life.

At this time, begin to feel yourself supported by the Earth beneath you. If you so choose, follow these words and allow them to gently open and expand different possibilities within yourself. Bring your focus to your breath. Feel it undulating from your belly to your sternum like ocean waves on the shore. Breathe in, and follow your life breath as it travels throughout your body systems, enlivening your cells. Breathe out, and let go of any energies that do not support your highest good or distract you from this moment. Nourish yourself with breath and allow each breath to bring you more and more deeply into meditative space.

Now bring your attention to your body systems. With your awareness, light up your heart center, digestive system, nervous system, glands, internal organs, circulatory system, and any other areas of your body to which your awareness is called.

At this time, deepen your body awareness and journey to your cellular level: travel into your cells. Each is a bead of dew: crystalline, primordial, glistening. Your cells contain the seeds of life. They contain the sacred pattern of the universe.

Look into one droplet. Inside it you can see shimmering waves of pattern and light. The wall of this cell becomes permeable. If you choose, enter into the primordial currents of your cell. Feel its light and ancient sea waters envelop you. Feel yourself floating in this sacred center. Relax even more deeply now. You may feel buoyant and peaceful as the Truth of Who You Are glows in every aspect of your being. Allow yourself to center in your connection to the Divine, the Source of Life. As this connection deepens, allow your heart to soften.

Using your breath as a gentle guide, allow your heart to blossom as it opens to this powerful moment. Hundreds of soft petals glowing and unfolding in the sacred light of who you are. In this cell, rest and float.

If you would like, begin to explore your surroundings. Trail your fingers through these primordial waters. Kick your feet, connect with all your senses. What colors do you see around you? What currents of energy do you feel? Floating in the sacred center of this cell, you are at the center of the universe. Feel this still point, this moment. Is there a message for you here?

As you listen, come to know that this center lives in connection to infinite cells, infinite beings, all aspects of the web of life. It is through this living relationship, this sacred pattern, that the universe is expressed. What does the web of life look like to you—this infinite pattern that connects all life-forms?

Begin to feel this center connected to its larger web: you may feel strands of a Spider web, growing vines, rainbow arcs reaching out to connect with all the other cells of your being. As it feels comfortable to you, allow these strands to go down into the Earth, intertwining with the roots of a tree.

What does this earth, these tree roots, feel like? Can you hear their voices speaking or singing? Your presence nourishes the tree. . . . You become the tree. Grounded in the earth, your body becomes a strong trunk; your arms waving branches; your hair whispering leaves. Stay with this experience for a moment.

Now feel your web soften and brush the delicate wings of a bird. Its clear, crystal birdsong dances in your cells. You become the song. You echo through the forest's instinctive melodies. Flap your wings and take flight. Feel the air currents caressing you.

Below, the opalescent ribbon of a river entices your senses. As you dive, the sparkling blue grows wider and you plunge into the river, a wriggling fish in its depths. Feel the cool, clear water coursing around you. Greet the river rocks sitting in meditation. Notice the sun glistening off your scales.

Experience the nourishment of the algae, smaller fish, elements of oxygen and hydrogen, all unifying to sustain you. You thrive in the sacred center of the web of life. You are sustainer and sustained. You are the dancer and the dance.

Feel the tendrils of your web floating out, gently touching other animals, other people, other cultures . . . all elements . . . different ways of being, different ways of knowing. Notice where the web wants to lead you.

Centered in the Truth of Who You Are, *feel* your interconnection to the entire web of life. You are precious, essential to the universal pattern, nourished and nourishing.

Balancing your sacred center and its relationship to all that is, ask yourself: Is there a particular aspect of the web of life that wants to be expressed through me today? It might be a tree, a stone, an animal, or an element. Feel it rising within you.

You are an important co-creative being, as we weave the web of life into the consciousness of the planet at this time. As you live consciously in this web of life, you manifest new awareness for our planet. Are there any energies flowing through you that want to be expressed as we weave the web together? Are there any blockages in you that keep you disconnected from the web? Simply notice and acknowledge them. They can be your guides as you become a web dancer in your day-to-day life.

Stay with your awareness of the particular energies, animals, plants, or elements that presented themselves to you during your journey. You have the opportunity to express these web energies through your body, mind, heart, and soul. As a community, through a sacred collective dance, we have the opportunity to consciously weave the web of life together.

Feel free to begin to embody these energies so that we can deepen our dance of life—a manifestation of balance, harmony, connectedness, and peace throughout the sacred pattern of the web of life. You may feel called to express these archetypal energies in your day-to-day life. The web energies with which you connected during your journey can be a source of strength and creativity as you consciously weave the web of life every day.

Stretch your claws . . . put on a panther mask . . . flap your wings . . . paint yourself the colors of these web archetypes. Be the sounds, the movements, the unique dance of each of these elements as you express your creativity in the world.

From the center of your cellular awareness you have journeyed with the web of life, exploring a wider sense of yourself as a web of relationships, connected to the unfolding universe.

While you are in deep communion with your cells and connected to your Divine Source, if you so choose, allow for spontaneous healing or balancing to occur on a cellular level. Release the need to know how . . . Simply allow the universal codes in your cells to wriggle, dance, or flow into perfect harmony. Your cells carry the Truth of Who You Are and your connection to all that is. You are a beautiful, harmonious being of universal love.

Bring your attention to the pinprick of light within each cell. Allow this point of light to grow. Notice when the light reaches the edges of your cells. Allow this light to expand out, creating a vast, interconnected web of self-love. Grow, grow, grow your light! In pure joy, release your light into a golden field around your body. You are held in safe, sacred space within the web that we are co-creating. Feel yourself glow in the bliss of who you are, in connection to all that is.

You are connected to all aspects of life. They are dancing with you—in your dreams, on your path, in every moment of your life. In this connection, feel the Truth of Who You Are bubbling from your source and flowing throughout all your body systems.

Let this light flow into the web. This truth is your life-force energy. Allow it to flow in abundant creativity, throughout all aspects of yourself, throughout all aspects of the universal web of life. Notice what you are capable of in this energetic flow. Notice your unique identity as a being of life.

Your life expression is essential to the unfolding of the universe. Your uniqueness is a blessing to the biodiversity and health of this world. Thank you for the melody of your life. Thank you for expressing the Truth of Who You Are. Feel the effects of this journey throughout all levels of your being.

Now gently leave your cells. Become grounded in your body, on the Earth, carrying with you that which is significant and letting go of that which has served its purpose. In your own timing, bring your awareness back to the present moment. Letting your breath be your guide, take a few minutes to gently integrate your meditative journey and come fully back into your own surroundings.

 ## Spider Invocation

Sacred Celestial Grandmother, grant us now the gift of becoming dream catchers through your patient persistence in weaving the magical silk web from our heart's secret longing into creation. . . . Show us the way. Ancient One, teach us as we observe in wonderment and awe the sacred manifestation of what was once within yourself now cast as a sacred net out into the world, so that we too may remember that we have everything we need deeply embedded within ourselves to attract and create our futures, while living in sacred harmony within the great web of life. . . . Show us the way. May we learn to honor the wisdom of the wise elders and awaken the spirit of truth within ourselves. . . . Show us the way.

7
Cicada and Dragonfly

Exploring Our Depths and the Stars as Visionary Shamans

I SING the Body electric;
The armies of those I love engirth me, and I engirth them;
They will not let me off till I go with them, respond to
them,
And discorrupt them, and charge them full with the charge
of the Soul.

WALT WHITMAN, *LEAVES OF GRASS*

CICADA

Cicadas have symbolized music, melody, and poetry to many cultures throughout the world. In Greek myth Cicada assists the master harpist Eunomis by replacing a broken string in the note of high C. Among Southwest Native American cultures, Cicada's human form is the sacred humpbacked flute player Kokopelli.[1]

As Cicada appears to be born from the Earth, having completed its nymph stages underground, Cicada symbolizes immortality and rebirth to Chinese, Greek, and other cultures. Cicadas were carved from jade

146

by Asian cultures and placed into the mouths of the dead to aid in res-urrection. They are related to the cycles of rebirth and reincarnation in Buddhism. Cicadas were used as funereal decorations and medicine to promote immortality.

Cicadas are from the Homopteran order of the insect class of animals. When they are recently hatched and in immature stages of development, Cicadas are known as nymphs. Like many other trans-formational animals of the Instar Medicine Wheel, Cicadas shed their skins many times and molt into new instars of development. They have two sets of transparent wings, which grow larger with each molt.[2]

EXPLORING CICADA'S DIRECTION ON THE MEDICINE WHEEL

The Great Below

The Great Below is the telluric realm of Pachamama, Mother Earth. This dimension of reality grounds, balances, and orients us to life as sentient beings. Pachamama, a name given to Mother Earth by the Quechua people of South America, is a constant nurturing and sup-portive presence in our lives. She holds us close to her heart, dances with the sun each day to bring us warmth and light, and provides us with food and beauty.

Pachamama exists in the third-dimensional reality of time and space, a space of density and form that provides humanity with the opportunity to learn and grow in a highly dynamic and evolutionary setting. Some teachers, such as Barbara Hand Clow, view the space beneath the Earth's surface as two-dimensional, a place of more height-ened density and creative fecundity, as noted in her book *The Alchemy of Nine Dimensions*. Earthworm's teachings dovetail with this idea.

Walkers of Pachamama are also Earth initiates. The Earth element holds the frequencies of structure, density, physical form, and limita-tions that inspire us to move forward into new phases of our journey. The Earth initiation is akin to gestating within the mother and readying for birth. We can feel the confines and limitations of the womb and the birth canal. For a certain phase of our development, growing and being nourished within the mother's womb is the perfect place to be. In this sacred place, much wisdom is gained that forms us into who we are as human beings. Yet, we all reach a place in our development in which the density and structure of earth have taught us their lessons and encourage us to emerge, birthing ourselves onto the surface of Planet Earth to begin a new phase of life.

Cicada is the wisdom keeper of the Great Below—the realm beneath Earth's surface and the Underworld of the psyche—because it spends most of its life cycle and many years underground.

As the Underworld of the psyche, the Great Below is an initiatory reality in which the hero and heroine's journey takes place. In the Underworld many things are not what they seem and stories of great consequence unfold. The hero's journey can be understood both shamanically and symbolically as the developmental path of lived experience that assists us in becoming who we are meant to be and fully embodying our potential. Within each of our lives we come upon intense periods of transformation and circumstances in which we feel challenged or powerless. The Underworld is this place of initiation in which we feel as if we are within a crucible. We feel great density, weight, and intensity all around us. We are transformed through this process, much like a diamond is formed from coal. Cicada honors the wisdom inherent in the Underworld—the dark night of the soul—and counsels us to perceive the grace and opportunity of this initiatory realm.

SACRED PURPOSE

Balancing Density and Expansiveness—An Earth Initiation

Cicada teaches us how to hold the balance between two realities: that of shadow and density and that of expansive light. Cicada spends much of its life cycle burrowed deeply in the ground. Cicadas are famous for spending many years—up to seventeen years—within the Earth. Underground, they build a network of tunnels that take them to the roots of different plants. Nymph Cicadas feed from the juice of these roots.

Yet, Cicadas do not begin their lives underground. Instead, living beneath the Earth's surface is a choice made after their birth. After Cicadas hatch from their eggs within the tree branches, they fall to the ground and burrow beneath the surface. And they do not emerge for many years.

Within the Earth nymph Cicadas molt and shed their exoskeleton, growing larger and more adult with each instar. As they reach sexual maturity, after many years beneath the surface, near-adult Cicadas emerge from the ground and set their red eyes on light and air once more. Their lives within the Earth dwarf the time adult Cicadas spend on the surface. Adult Cicadas live for only a few weeks before they die.

Emerging in late spring, Cicadas climb into trees and molt one last time, embodying their final adult instar. During this time the loud, piercing call of the male Cicada fills the air. As he calls to potential mates his music makes the male Cicada the loudest insect on Earth. Cicadas generate sound by expanding and contracting an abdominal muscle that vibrates and amplifies the sound of their internal membranes. After mating has occurred, fertilized eggs are laid within tree branches, the adults die, and the cycle begins once again.

Cicada experiences strong polarities in its life cycle: the density of Earth and the expansiveness of Air. Cicada lives into these extremes to learn and experience fully what the density of the Earth initiation has to teach. The pressure within this telluric crucible is immense, and through that journey Cicada learns to fully embody the Earth walk. This readies Cicada for the next plane of existence: the Air element. Through its life cycle, Cicada learns to fully embody and balance both these polarities and all the wisdom they have to offer in their synergy.

TRANSFORMATION

Gestating in the Mother and Emerging to Sing

Beneath Earth's surface, Cicada is confined by the darkness and weight of the earth that surrounds it. Eventually Cicada moves through the confines and structure of this Earth cycle and births itself into the Air. For the last part of its life Cicada flies free in the expansive atmosphere. It has attained a higher degree of fine, etheric frequencies in its being, having spent its formative years in the density of its own Earth body.

Yet during the Earth cycle Cicada is also at home within Pachamama's womb. As it waits, Cicada hears her call. Gestating and developing quietly within the Earth for many years, Cicada has a unique opportunity among creatures to commune with the deep, telluric songs of Mother Earth—to absorb her rhythms and melodies, to begin to listen to its own internal music. And so, through this shamanic portal, Cicada emerges into the Air realm with an expanded ability to make glorious sound and vibrant noise. Its high volume and piercing frequency are instantly recognizable.

Cicada does not teach us that our purpose is to transcend the darkness and inhabit only the light. Instead, its dedicated journey within the Earth and its expanded ability to sing once it emerges aboveground teach us to hold these two realities in balance. Our psyches and souls are made of both shadow and light. We combine both density and expansiveness. Cicada reminds us that it is only in the dynamic relationship between these two energies that creativity and soulful evolution can spark and come to fruition.

Cicada is also a true familiar to us when we walk in our own lands of shadow, density, and intense challenge. There are times throughout our lives when our place is within the Earth, within the density of the human learning experience. At these times we may feel heartbroken, desolate, exhausted, or confused. We may yearn for the light to break the surface of our despair. We think of Butterfly and wish we could turn our density into an entirely new creature. And then we wonder, Why? When will the good reality, the light-filled grace appear for me? Why doesn't it emerge now? Then we look beside us and find Cicada. Our friend in the darkness. A hand to hold. Clear shining eyes to look into as we walk our path. Cicada understands, because it has walked this path of lived experience and, through this, grown compassion to self and others, patience, and dedication.

In the Air, Cicada sings to us its own song of surrender. For only after surrender, waiting in the quiet stillness, could Cicada begin to hear the wisdom and the music of Mother Earth. The timing and circumstances may be inconvenient, or even heartbreaking, but this dark time of the soul is in fact a state of grace. The divine universe has placed us within the arms of Mother Earth for as long as we need to be there to truly listen and absorb the immense wisdom of Planet Earth. And, when we think we have heard her song clearly, we are told to listen some more. When we are within the Earth we begin to understand how large and dynamic her realm is. We cannot achieve, will, or pray our way out of the Cicada Earth cycle. We must simply gestate, waiting and growing in the dense suspension of the Earth, until it is our time to be born into the Air and sing. Cicada's music sings to us of the beauty of its own surrender, affirming that "this too shall pass" when our own dark time comes. Cicada's song pierces our very being, singing the praises of the joy and heartache of the human experience.

PORTAL OF TRANSFORMATION

Climbing the Multidimensional World Tree

Cicadas embody the ability to hold the balance of opposites by gaining strength through lived experience. Cicada learns the wisdom and lessons of the Earth element and the density of life beneath the Earth's surface as a young nymph. This is the Great Below Initiation of the World Tree.

The World Tree is a potent symbol found around the world, most notably in Siberian, Norse, and indigenous Central American cultures. Trees are seen by many cultures to connect life and death, to bring one into the presence of the Divine, and as a source of fertility, prayer, and wisdom. Among the Maya of Central America the giant ceiba tree is the symbol of the World Tree. Its structure illuminates the Great Above and Below of the Medicine Wheel, orientation of the directions, and multiple world realities. The World Tree includes a vast network of roots beneath the surface, symbolizing the Great Below, or Underworld. The trunk symbolizes third-dimensional reality, or the terrestrial world, and the branches above illustrate the Heavens, or higher dimensions of experience.

As we have learned, when it is new to life, the nymph Cicada leaves the higher-dimensional branches of the World Tree and travels into the Underworld, into the arms of Mother Earth. In this space it begins a developmental journey of self-evolution within the structure and density of the Earth element. The nymph draws its nourishment from the juices of tree roots. The Cicada initiate feeds on the World Tree like a baby at its mother's breast. Cicada's long period of initiation in the Underworld emphasizes the importance of this shamanic journey among shadow, mystery, and the evolving soul. Cicadas consciously choose to leave the everyday world and travel Below, gaining the wisdom of an Underworld initiation. Through this process, as it suckles on the gestational nectar of the World Tree, Cicada grows larger and gains in wisdom.

As it nears soulful maturity, Cicada leaves the Earthen Underworld dimension and travels to the Earth's surface. It climbs the trunk of the tree (the terrestrial world) and into the branches of the World Tree. In its life Cicada travels through all the dimensions of being and completes its embodied existence back where its life began. Cicada begins life in the Heavens—much like the queen of Heaven, Inanna, discussed in chapter 5, "Butterfly"—and consciously chooses to enter the density of the Underworld, learning its lessons. Having returned to the heavenly dimensions of the World Tree, Cicada sings the piercing and soulful music of its initiatory experience. It calls and beseeches us to listen and remember the importance of journeying into the dark night of the soul, into the unknown of our psyches, into the stillness and density of Earth. Cicada also blesses the next generations with its wisdom by laying her eggs within the branches of the World Tree. The next generation of Cicadas continues the pattern of initiatory wisdom as they drop from the World Tree's branches to the Earth once more.

Cicada does not glory in the extremes of life. Instead, it experiences these polarities in order to learn how to reconcile them. When opposites are held in balance, both within the self and in the world,

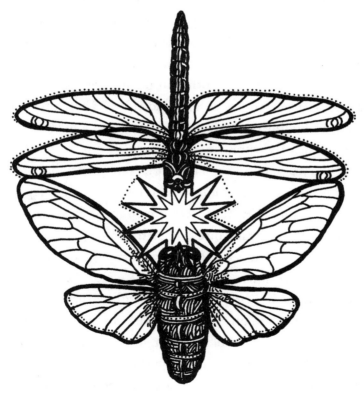

Integration of the Great Above and Below Mysteries:
Cicada, Dragonfly, and the twelve-pointed star

duality is transmuted into new creative possibilities. This is the place of magic and divine miracles. Cicada embodies the shamanic medicine of holding the balance of opposite elements, ideas, and energies as a means to create from the heart a harmonic reality for all. When we can learn to hold and balance the opposites within ourselves, we exponentially amplify our personal power and energy—just as Cicada's voice becomes the loudest insect call on Earth—increasing our ability to create positive change in our own life and bless the entire World Tree, or web of life.

Just as the cardinal direction keepers are related to one another in different ways, Cicada has a special relationship with Dragonfly. Cicada is a link of soulful evolution. Through its shamanic lived experience, Cicada has embodied the wisdom of sacred balance between the Earth and Air realms. Being able to authentically hold this balance is a key aspect of learning for the human soul experience. As you look at the linked image of Cicada and Dragonfly you can begin to see that they are mirrors of each other in many ways, especially in their eyes, wings, and legs. In its dense, round curves, Cicada represents the Earth soul embodiment. As it mirrors Cicada in a more subtle, ethereal form, Dragonfly represents the evolution from the Earth embodiment into the realm of Spirit. The short, stubby torso has grown long and links to all the dimensions of the universe, for Dragonfly is a flyer into all realms. Yet, these star dimensional frequencies are carried as seeds within Cicada into the Earth embodiment.

As we live as human beings on Planet Earth, these star seeds or imaginal cells of higher-dimensional transformation are held within us and start to unfold as we begin our own soulful journeys of transformation. The center of the universe exists within every cell of our being. As Cicada sits at the center of its Earth, in the telluric darkness, it too experiences this divine center. Through the density of human developmental experience, new stars, new awareness, and new evolutionary soul forms are born.

DRAGONFLY

Not I, nor anyone else can travel that road for you.
You must travel it by yourself.
It is not far. It is within reach.
Perhaps you have been on it since you were born, and did
*   not know.*
Perhaps it is everywhere—on water and land.

WALT WHITMAN, *LEAVES OF GRASS*

Dragonflies symbolize speed, elegance, lightness, immortality, and regeneration. Their oft-changing and darting flight patterns have also come to symbolize instability and a lack of reliability. Japan is known as the Dragonfly Island, due to its shape, and the Japanese culture views the Dragonfly as a symbol of victory. Dragonflies are known for their quick flight and activity, and a connection to whirlwinds. In Europe, Dragonflies often had negative and satanic connotations and were termed "the devil's darning needle" to warn children against dishonesty. Due to its shape, Dragonfly is often connected to the practice of sewing. Dragonfly is a sacred kachina figure to Zuni and Hopi Southwest Native American cultures.[3]

Dragonfly's presence at bodies of water assures us that the water is not polluted. Dragonflies are carnivorous and have a voracious appetite for other insects. They are part of the Odonata order of insects. Odonates lived at the same time as Jurassic Dinosaurs 200 million years ago, with insects close in form to today's Dragonflies beginning to appear 100 million years before that. Ancient Paleozoic Dragonflies had wingspans over two feet long, though smaller species were also present at the time. These Dragonflies preceded Birds and Pterodactyls by 100 million to 150 million years.[4]

There are three suborders of Odonates. Damselflies belong to the suborder Zygoptera. Damselflies are smaller than Dragonflies, have a slight body frame, and demonstrate weaker, fluttery flight. The Anisozygoptera suborder demonstrates an overlap between Dragonflies and Damselflies, sharing many traits from both these suborders. They have weak but direct flight. Dragonflies belong to the Anisoptera suborder. Dragonflies have a robust body frame and demonstrate stronger, more sustained flight.

Dragonflies have an exoskeleton body structure, and, like all insects, their body is divided into three parts: head, thorax, and abdomen. They have two large compound eyes and three simple eyes. Dragonfly's compound eyes give it the highest visual acuity of any insect. They are able to see forward, above, below, left, and right without moving their bodies. The eyes and body of a Dragonfly are often brightly colored, and display a wide variety of colors. A male Dragonfly's colors and patterns help him in competing with other males, attracting mates, and with courtship rituals. A Dragonfly's thorax evolved to assist it in eating during flight. In addition, its legs are thrust forward (unlike those of other insects), enabling it to grasp and transfer food to its mouth during flight. The Dragonfly abdomen comprises ten segments, making it long, narrow, and flexible.

Unlike almost all other insects, Dragonflies have fore and hind wings that are not connected and can beat out of phase from one another. This design provides them with unparalleled maneuverability. They can hover without moving; fly vertically, forward, and backward; and twist within a small area. Dragonflies use their high degree of maneuverability to evade predators, in addition to camouflaging themselves and playing dead.

Dragonflies have five main veins that emanate from the base of each wing. Wing vibration, or whirring, helps Dragonflies to raise their body temperature. To cool their bodies, some species move into an obelisk position, in which their tail points vertically toward the sun. This limits the amount of body area exposed to the sun's heat. The tail follows the sun's movement throughout the day. Other cooling strategies include water dipping and shade-seeking behaviors.

The strongest flyer and the most highly evolved species of the Dragonfly suborder is the *Pantala flavescens*. It is nicknamed "globe skimmer" and "wandering glider." This species breeds on either side of the Atlantic and Indian Oceans. They are capable of extraordinary flight, flying across the ocean for long time periods. Sailors have sighted them hundreds of miles out at sea. This is an example of large-scale migration in Dragonflies. More commonly, Dragonflies participate in small-scale migration as they search for egg-laying sites.

Odonata mating is almost unique in the animal kingdom. Dragonflies are known to mate while in flight, sometimes haphazardly and other times flying with grace through the air. Dragonflies form a tandem pair to mate. The male attaches his apical claspers at the base of a female's eyes. Their abdomens form a heartlike shape, leaving their legs and wings free.

EXPLORING DRAGONFLY'S PLACE ON THE MEDICINE WHEEL

The Great Above and the Great Star Nations

With your feet planted firmly on the Earth, raise your eyes to the Heavens. Above you, an infinite number of stars shimmer and bless you with their constant sustaining light. They are a presence that watches over the smallest being, from human to insect.

Some people envision the Great Star Nations to be a circle of elders, some of whom have died and passed beyond the human plane and others who are bodhisattvas of compassionate service and wisdom to humanity. The Great Star Nations and higher dimensions of the Great Above can also be seen as the subtle frequencies and patterns of sacred geometry and esoteric wisdom that permeate the universe. Above us, in the sky, is an infinitely vast field of cosmic awareness, heavenly bodies, and divine oneness and creativity at the highest levels.

Whatever our cultural or cosmological background, we are each humbled and awed when we gaze upon the Great Star Nations and the Great Above of the cosmos. They have much to teach humanity about our potential as cosmic souls who have embodied here on Earth. The Great Star Nations are always present to remind us of our hidden potential and our mandate to evolve into mature spiritual beings of the universe. We simply need to look into the Great Above and open our hearts.

Dragonfly is the messenger of the Great Star Nations and assists us in bringing this wisdom home through the dimensions to Planet Earth.

SACRED PURPOSE

Sharing Higher Love and Wisdom through Visionary Flight

As we have learned, Dragonflies are gifted with the capacity for powerful flight and highly developed vision. These characteristics are necessary for one who travels through the dimensions, to the cosmic teachers of the Great Above, and returns to share this higher wisdom with humanity in Earth reality. Dragons have long been known to be the explorers at the creative edge of the universe. Their bodies are the flaming rainbow edge that transmutes and weaves through reality. They are cosmic dancers of the highest order.

Dragonfly's body is divided into ten segments, forming a graceful and long line. Similar to the seven chakras in the human energy body, these segments symbolize the multiple dimensions and frequencies of the universe. Barbara Hand Clow's book *The Alchemy of Nine Dimensions* is a wonderful exploration of multidimensional reality.

Dragonfly has a universal key infused into the very design of its body (the ten segments), which allows it to travel through the dimensions with ease and grace. The transformation needed to gain this universal key will be discussed later in this chapter. Dragonfly has the ability to fly through each of the dimensions, to see and perceive the subtle patterns at the highest echelons of cosmic consciousness, and return with insight as a messenger to humanity.

TRANSFORMATION

Preparing to Fly within Water's Womb

Throughout their life cycle, Dragonflies experience the dynamism of opposite elements, in strong parallel to Cicada. Dragonflies spend their egg and larval stages of development below the surface of the water. At adulthood, they leave the water behind to fly in the air for the rest of their lives.

Dragonfly eggs are laid at or below the surface of the water or inserted into plants or mud in water habitats. Once they are laid, most eggs begin to develop and hatch one to three weeks later.

Beneath the surface of the water, Dragonfly larvae molt their exoskeletons between eight and fifteen times. During this transformational process they develop and grow larger. Dragonfly larvae live exclusively beneath the water's surface and are wingless. Instead, they have gills that allow for underwater breathing and movement. The larval stage typically lasts between six months and five years. This timing depends on the species, food supply, and water temperature. At the time of their final instar, all physical attributes needed to sustain life above the water have been formed.

The final molt is a metamorphosis, similar to that of Butterfly, in which the last exoskeleton is shed and aquatic respiration ceases. At this time Dragonfly breaks the surface of the water and attaches itself to a plant or a rock. The larval skin breaks, after which the Dragonfly rests and dries its body. The Dragonfly leaves its last exoskeleton behind and reveals its wings for the first time. It pumps haemolymph fluid into its new wings, expanding them, and then withdraws the fluid so the wings can harden.

The Dragonfly's first instinct is to fly away from water, where it would be easy prey for birds, fish, and other predators. After their first flight, Dragonflies spend a few days or weeks far from water while their sexual organs fully develop.

While life expectancies vary, the underwater larval stage of a

Dragonfly's development comprises the majority of its life cycle. This can last up to five years. By contrast, the average adult Dragonfly lives for only a few months.

In parallel to Cicada, Dragonfly's life cycle affirms the emphasis of a developmental initiation "below the surface." For Cicada, the element of initiation is Earth. For Dragonfly, its element of initiation is Water. Having learned the lessons of their initiatory journeys, both wisdom keepers emerge into the Air. They both spend the remaining period of their lives in this element.

Cicada's final incarnation is in the expansive Air element, sharing its shamanic soul music with others. Dragonfly harmonizes its adult life with the Air element, using its incredible powers of flight and vision to travel through the multidimensional universe and bring this wisdom back to Earth reality. Both are strengthened and informed by their initiatory journeys.

Dragonfly begins its initiatory journey in the Water element. Water is an element that suspends the journeyer in a nurturing womb-like embrace, as does Cicada's Earth element. Yet, Water is the realm of emotions, memory, mysticism, and hidden dreams. Water is the element of the Roman god Neptune, and from the more ancient Egyptian tradition, Nepthys. Nepthys is a lunar goddess, a medial channel, and keeper of veiled mysteries of the feminine, death, and rebirth.[5] Those experiencing a Dragonfly Water initiation have stepped between the veils into the unknown. Parts of the psyche may dissolve away, and one's structural sense of self may lose its orientation to reality. Yet, within the womb of Nepthys, the seeds of our soul's ability to imagine, to vision, to journey throughout all dimensions of consciousness are germinated and begin to grow.

When Dragonfly emerges beyond the surface of the water, it carries with it the ability to see between the veils and to fly, fast and sure, throughout all realms of soul and universe. Through the Water initiation, Dragonfly gains its magical wings and the eyes of clear vision. Its new body is etheric, light, and made up of ten segments that create an energetic rainbow bridge to all realities. Yet this clarity of vision and sure flight are balanced with a reverence for mystery and a willingness to journey into the darkness. It is only by dancing with the unknown darkness of the night sky that Dragonfly reveals the wisdom of the cosmos and the Great Star Nations.

When Dragonfly crosses your path, new wisdom is ready to manifest in your consciousness. Dragonfly consciousness is etheric, quick, and hard to catch. It is the also the frequency of Nepthys's deep mysteries. Surrender and allow the higher wisdom of Dragonfly to suffuse you with its own darting, graceful flight. Because Dragonfly wisdom comes from the higher dimensions of consciousness, it may not immediately translate into human words and logic. You may simply feel new frequencies, patterns, and energy moving through your being. Be fluid, open, and rejoice in the unique gifts of higher love and wisdom you are receiving. Artwork and dream journaling can be very helpful to process and understand what you are experiencing, because subtle frequencies are often best translated into symbols rather than language by the psyche.

LESSONS AND SHADOW

Balancing the Opposites and Honoring Our Journeys

Cicada and Dragonfly teach us how to journey with the human experience of initiation so that we can fully embody the ability to hold opposite elements, energetic polarities, and creative tensions in balance within our own beings. This is another form of sacred union within the self. As we each resolve our internal duality the creative child can be born as our own sacred purpose and a higher evolution of consciousness in the world.

Cicada and Dragonfly also impress on us the essential nature of surrender in the human experience. When we feel the constraints and fallow times of the Earth element, we can learn to release the illusion of control and embrace the dark gifts that surround us in the intensity of this journey. When we fear we are dissolving into the mystic dreams of Water and losing our present reality, we can open our gills and breathe in the wisdom and purpose of this phase in our lives.

The shadow of Cicada and Dragonfly is to overidentify with one phase or another. We may become overidentified with the density of the Earth initiation or the veiled fluidity of the Water initiation and come to see this element as who we are. It takes courage to dance and find ourselves in the dark womb of the Mother, yet initiation is a journey, not a destination. At some point it is appropriate for the baby to be born into the world, informed by the process of gestation. This is how we learn to embody our gifts and bring them forward to share with the world.

It is also tempting to become light polarized and disregard all we experienced in the challenging or mysterious phase of initiation. We may only want to focus on singing our Cicada song or flying with Dragonfly's visionary grace. Yet these gifts, abilities, and wisdom were alchemized in the crucible of Underworld initiation. When we deny the dark fertility of our shamanic journeys, our gifts lose their potency and our wisdom loses its connection to the higher cosmic dimensions. We can only soar and channel higher love and wisdom through our being when our feet are firmly grounded on Mother Earth, we are centered in our open hearts, and we remember the journey of becoming who we are meant to be.

EXPERIENTIAL PRACTICE

Elemental Shamanic Initiatory Journeys

Cicada and Dragonfly invite us to learn how to embody opposite elements, and create balance within our beings. For both of these wisdom keepers, the journey toward this reconciliation of opposites takes place on the initiatory path. Cicada and Dragonfly consciously choose to immerse themselves in a primary element and absorb its gifts and teachings. For Cicada, this initiatory element is Earth; for Dragonfly,

Water. These creatures then evolve their consciousness and move into a new, more expansive element: Air. They do not evolve in spite of the structure and density of Earth or the formlessness and veiled mysteries of Water. Cicada and Dragonfly are informed on a soul level by their initiatory journeys and are able to move to a different octave of being *because* of their dance with these elements. Water and Earth are the shamanic medicines of lived experience that Dragonfly and Cicada carry. These elements inform their sacred purpose gifts that can now be shared in service with others.

Human beings experience all the elements throughout our lifetimes: Water, Earth, Fire, Air, and Spirit. These elements often evolve into one another as we move forward on our spiritual paths of life experience, learning, and service. Cicada and Dragonfly teach us to embody the teachings of the elements in which we find ourselves immersed, letting our soul's potential be activated through these elemental frequencies and sharing what we have learned in service.

As we hold the Great Above and the Great Below in balance within our beings, our feet become fully grounded on Planet Earth and our intuition and consciousness open to the higher dimensions. It is only through this sacred union of opposites that we can act as conduits to bring Spirit into Matter for the highest good. It is for this reason that Cicada and Dragonfly hold a twelve-pointed star between them. As we have learned, the six-pointed star is a symbol of sacred union. Cicada and Dragonfly honor multidimensionality. Their initiatory journeys of reconciling opposite polarities merge into the vast, multidimensional sacred union formation of the twelve-pointed star. This is the sacred union of all the dimensions of the World Tree within the self. This is the sacred union encompassing all the light and dark of the Great Star Nations: the known and the unknown, the clarion call of higher love and wisdom and the depths of mystery. Cicada and Dragonfly intermarry the shamanic paths of the Great Above and Great Below into the sacred union star they carry between them.

Using the self- or group-guided model of integrative dance and

Shamanic Breathwork discussed previously, you are invited to set a scene for either Earth or Water initiatory journeys. If you feel called to this experiential practice, you most likely have a sense of which element you are currently working with. This exercise is appropriate if you want to ceremonialize and process any element and alchemize your movement into a new place of being. For the purposes of these two wisdom keepers, we will focus on Earth and Water.

If you are working with an Earth initiation, select grounded drumming music, non-English chanting, or whatever music inspires the Earth element in your consciousness. You may choose to wrap yourself tightly in blankets, to feel held by Mother Earth, as well as the structure and density of the Earth element.

If you are working with a Water initiation, select flowing, melodic music with a gentle movement. You may also want to select music that creates a sense of veiled mysteries within your psyche. Silk cloths and beaded necklaces may be used as sensory props, trailing them along your body to evoke the feeling of being touched by flowing water.

Using the breath, invite yourself to become fully immersed in these initiatory elements. Allow your body to feel the constriction and fallow quality of Earth, or to move fluidly with Water. Breathe into each of the energy centers of your body and notice what thoughts, beliefs, and emotions are brought forward. Perhaps you will be taken on a journey into the wisdom and soul-opening depths of these elements.

Begin to breathe the wisdom of your initiation into the cells of your body. Feel these jewels of shamanic medicine enliven you at a cellular level, and breathe into them. This process of embracing and integrating is the dance that allows you to bring your movement into a new element of being. With the support of a cojourneyer or facilitator, or self-led if you are comfortable breathing on your own, begin the process of moving into the element that calls you. This may be Air, or another element, such as Fire. Simply allow your soul's wisdom to guide you. Some participants move between the elements, using a rebirthing process. If this is true for you, additional support from a trained facilitator or cojourneyer is important for safety and the midwifery many of us need. You are invited to use voice toning to resonate and create cellular movement within your body. This can be very helpful in making the shift between elements and dimensions of being.

Invite your body to shed its exoskeleton, whether of Cicada or Dragon-fly. Begin to move through the Earth, or through the Water, to the surface. As you break the surface, feel the sun on your face for the first time, feel the currents of air. Listen to the sounds you hear. Bring your shamanic wings forward and pump them with fluid straight from the strength and wisdom of your heart.

Cicadans may be called to use their new body and wings by climbing through the dimensions of the World Tree. Notice what it feels like to move into third-dimensional reality, and then into the higher dimensions as you climb into the branches of the tree. Notice what new wisdom comes into your awareness. And notice what wisdom is bubbling forth from your cells to share with the world. Seek out a perch, ground your feet in the bark of the branch, and open your heart wide to share the shamanic wisdom and medicine of your Cicadan soul song. Notice how your body system responds when you share the piercing truth of your soul's journey with the world. Do you sense a feeling of expanded freedom, a movement beyond fear? Notice what you are experiencing.

Dragonfliers, too, may be called to use their wings and take flight. Your path is to leave the surface of the Water and fly with strength and graceful maneuverability into the higher dimensions of the Great Star Nations. Your Water initiation has given you the strength and ability to fly into the veiled mysteries of the Heavens, at home in the darkness, as you seek the light of higher love and wisdom. The ten segments of Dragonfly's body act as a rainbow bridge that spans all dimensions and realms, while allowing your consciousness to stay grounded with your physical body. If you choose, ask your tailbone to embody the tip of Dragonfly's tail. Ground this tail into the Earth and ask it to call you back once your journey is complete. As you begin to fly, your long Dragonfly body will stay connected to the Earth yet assist you in exploring the highest dimensions of consciousness.

As you feel the Air element start to thin, begin lighting up the sections of your Dragonfly body, one by one. Each body segment lights up with knowledge and awareness as you move through each of the higher dimensions. Notice what colors and vibrations each segment has. Notice what music is emitted from your body as you dragon-fly through a new dimension or visit a new star system. Notice which teachers come forward to greet you and share their wisdom. Allow this journey to unfold freely around you. Let it surprise you.

When you are ready, begin to move back toward Earth reality with your newly gained higher love and wisdom from the Great Star Nations. Ask your Dragonfly energy body to carry this wisdom within your cells so it is available at any time and in any dimension. As you move back through the dimensions, invite each segment of your Dragonfly body to resonate with and become grounded in the dimension of Planet Earth.

When you have returned to Earth, dance with the cosmic bodhisattva teacher you innately are, and share with the world the higher love and wisdom that runs through you. Emit these frequencies through your heart center, and invite your entire body to resonate with the love and wisdom you have gained through your journey.

Whether as Cicada or Dragonfly, as you sing your soul song, you may begin to notice that a twelve-pointed star has become encoded within your DNA and in the meridian points that surround your heart center. The twelve-pointed star is centered on the heart and also touches your crown at its top and your root chakra at its base. You have embodied opposite elements and dimensions within your being and are now an activated carrier of multidimensional higher love and wisdom in service to Planet Earth and the unfolding universe. You have awakened as a star being, whether from the Cicadan or Dragonflier path, enlivened with the sacred union energy that runs throughout all levels of your being. You are an activational blessing of harmonic balance and evolutionary consciousness that is essential for this time on the planet. Thank you for having the courage to walk your journey and show up in the wisdom of your heart as a shamanic teacher. Your time is *now*.

Cicada and Dragonfly Invocation

Great Above and Great Below, please hear our fervent prayer for the sacred union of Earth and Sky. . . . Show us the way. Great Star Nations and Beings Deep within the Telluric Realms, we are calling to you now with an urgent plea to assist us in creating the sacred union needed by all beings to discover the sacred balance within ourselves. . . . Show us the way. Plant our feet securely so that we may become fully grounded on Planet Earth and our intuition and consciousness may open to the higher dimensions. For it is only through this sacred marriage of opposites that we human beings become the sacred vessels to birth Spirit into Matter for the highest good of all concerned. . . . Show us the way. Cicada, open our voices so that our prayers may be heard from the uppermost branches of the World Tree of Life by the Great Star Nations. Dragonfly, pierce the veils between the worlds and, with a flash of your rainbow bridge body, bring down the starseed wisdom from the Ancient Ones watching over all that we do and all that we are becoming. . . . Show us the way. Sacred Multidimensional Energies of the Twelve-Pointed Star, guide us on the initiatory journeys of reconciling opposite polarities encompassing all the light and dark of the Great Star Nations—the known and the unknown, the clarion call of higher love and wisdom, and the depths of mystery. . . . Show us the way.

8
Grasshopper, Cricket, and Katydid

Integrating Unity and Diversity in the Heart

The little space within the heart is as great as this vast universe. The heavens and earth are there, and the sun, and the moon, and the stars; fire and lightning and winds are there; and all that now is and all that is not.

UPANISHADS

Crickets have caught the imagination of cultures around the world and have symbolized a variety of themes, including happiness, good luck, the heart of the home, courage, the season of summer, and resurrection. The Cricket is also said to herald the return of a lover, rain, and death. A number of cultures keep Crickets in the home as pets and view Cricket as the spirit of the home.[1]

Grasshopper is connected to fertility, nobility, and luck. Grasshopper sheds its exoskeleton and through this act has been related to resurrection and rebirth. Due to its strong impact on ecosystems in a massive population, Grasshopper, or Locust, also symbolizes disorder, plagues, and devastation, as well as irresponsibility. To ancient Egyptians,

Grasshopper symbolized beauty and the pattern of life along the Nile River. Grasshoppers adorned Egyptian tombs and furniture in ancient homes.

Grasshoppers, Crickets, and Katydids belong to the Orthoptera order of insects. Grasshoppers are part of the Caelifera suborder, while Crickets and Katydids both belong to the Enisfera suborder and are more closely related to one another than to Grasshopper. On the whole, Grasshoppers, Crickets, and Katydids are a closely related group and can be best understood in terms of their common attributes. In this chapter we will consider them as members of one archetypal family. Their unique attributes will be explored as they relate to the Instar Medicine Wheel.

Grasshoppers, Crickets, and Katydids have long legs that are crucial to their existence. Contrary to common belief, they move by walking, not hopping. Hopping is reserved for instances when they need to raise an alarm. Katydids and Crickets have long antennae, usually exceeding their body length, while Grasshoppers have short antennae. Crickets share many commonalities in appearance with Katydids, but resemble the Grasshopper less, and are smaller and flatter.

Grasshoppers, Crickets, and Katydids each begin their lives in an egg. Eggs are laid in soil or attached to plant life. The egg stage of development takes place in the cold temperatures of the winter season. After hatching they progress through nymph and adult life-cycle stages. As they develop, this family experiences a gradual change in appearance, in contrast to the dramatic metamorphosis of Butterfly.

Nymphs mature through five to six instar stages of development before the final molt that ushers them into adulthood. It is only in adulthood that wings and sexual anatomy are fully developed.

Grasshoppers, Crickets, and Katydids experience the following life cycle: eggs are hatched in spring, nymphs grow and develop in summer, and adults mate and lay eggs in late summer and early autumn. In most cases there is one generation of these animal teachers born per year.

EXPLORING GRASSHOPPER, CRICKET, AND KATYDID'S PLACE ON THE MEDICINE WHEEL

The Center and Home of the Great Within

The Center of the Instar Medicine Wheel is home to the Great Within. Just as the central axis of the body is the heart center, the central axis of the Instar Medicine Wheel is the heart path of unity consciousness. Our unity is what links us together with all of life, and this unity consciousness is centered in the heart's wisdom. This is also an expression of the Great Within: the internal knowing that guides our path. When our internal knowing loses its connection to the integrity of the heart and becomes distracted with ego or fear-based agendas, our center of balance becomes off-kilter. The center of balance of the Great Within is held in the dynamic state of sacred union between the Great Above and the Great Below. When we listen to our heart's truth, we instinctively know we are connected in unity to all life, to our own higher wisdom, and to the grounded Earth beneath our feet.

The Great Within and the Center are the home of Grasshopper, Cricket, and Katydid. As we will learn, they are the link in the chain that sustains life. Their role as wisdom keepers of the Center is the link that enlivens the entire Instar Medicine Wheel. Grasshopper, Cricket, and Katydid are linked to every other animal of the medicine wheel: Cicada directly below, Dragonfly above, Earthworm to the East, Honeybee to the South, Butterfly to the West, and Spider to the North. The Grasshopper, Cricket, and Katydid family are the unifying heart of the Instar Medicine Wheel. They teach the heart path of unity that we all must walk to live with beauty, integrity, and a sustainable vision of the future.

In paradoxical balance, diversity exists within unity. Creativity and differentiation are manifested from the void. Life articulates itself in complexity from unity, just as the big bang articulates the unfolding the universe from its origin. Within the unity of the Center exist Grasshopper, Cricket, and Katydid. They each express different frequencies of the Great Within and Center. This differentiation expresses itself chiefly in music and singing.

According to Capinera, Scott, and Walker, Katydids are a "diverse, strikingly beautiful group that is much more prone to call or 'sing' than other grasshoppers."[2] At the same time, Crickets are noted for "songs [that] are a musical delight," while Grasshopper and Katydid have a stronger, raspy quality.[3] Cricket and Katydid music are quite different from one another.

In general, males of each species are the singers of the loud "calling songs," commonly heard. These calls are used to describe a male's location, his sexual readiness, and his quality as a mate as he keens to nearby females. Females make sounds as well, though not to the same extent as males. As communication tools, sounds are often paired with visual signals, such as a flashing of colors and movement.

Sound is made through stridulation, in which body parts are rubbed together. Grasshoppers produce sound by rubbing their forewing and hind leg together. Crickets and Katydids make sound by rubbing their two forewings together. At the base of one wing is a stridulation file used for noisemaking that consists of a vein with ridges. In Crickets this file only appears on the right wing. For Katydids the file appears on the left wing. The other wing, which lacks the stridulation file, is used as a scraper against the ridges of the opposite file. Sound production is common throughout this order of insects, but Crickets and Katydids have developed it to the highest extent.

The musical differentiation of Cricket and Katydid reflect the emergence of left/feminine and right/masculine directions of the Instar Medicine Wheel. Katydids embody the left/feminine frequency as they display their stridulation file on the left wing. For human beings, left-handedness is linked to creativity, the feminine, mysticism, and nonlinear thinking. Throughout history the minority of people with left-body dominance have experienced prejudice and discrimination—as the left was associated with evil, bad luck, and the feminine. The Latin word *sinistra* was originally defined as "left" but went on to have more negative connotations as the English word *sinister*. In French the word for *left—gauche*—became a term in English to describe someone who was awkward or outside the bounds of civilized behavior. The French word *droit* is the term for the *right,* and the English term *adroit* became synonymous with capability and correctness. As instinctive creativity and the feminine were denigrated, so too was the left direction.

Cricket holds its stridulation file on the right wing and symbolizes the right/masculine direction of the Instar Medicine Wheel. Right-body dominance is associated with the masculine, taking direct action, logic, a focus on details, and linear processing. The cross-wiring of the brain's hemispheres reminds us of the inward expression of yin and yang: even in the expression of the masculine lies the seed of the feminine, and vice versa. For the human body the outward behavioral expression of the masculine is found on the right side of the body, and the outward expression of the feminine is found on the left side of the body.

Within the Instar Medicine Wheel, the left/feminine and right/masculine originate the sacred union dance that spins the entire wheel into life. The left/feminine is the bearer of receptivity, creative gestation, and weaving interconnections. The right/masculine embodies the spiritual warrior, taking right action, holding safe boundaries with linear processing, and contributing the seeds that spark the unfolding of consciousness. Together these two principles meet in the sacred union of co-creativity, forming the central connection that brings the Instar Medicine Wheel into existence and holding the frequency of unity consciousness as a reconciliation of their duality.

To human ears Cricket songs are the most musical. Katydid songs have a strong buzzing and raspy quality. This is because Crickets tend to produce a pure single tone, while Katydids often weave together multiple tones or frequencies. In addition, many of the frequencies produced by Katydids are above the hertz range detectable by humans. Cricket embodies the right/masculine in his pure, linear tones of clarity. Meanwhile Katydid weaves together multiple interconnected frequencies and emits this music into the higher realms of consciousness, which is not easily heard by earthly ears.

Katydid and Cricket are the wisdom keepers of the left/feminine and right/masculine, which meet in sacred union in the Great Within.

They balance their uniqueness and diversity with the unity of the heart. This springs forth in their divine music that supports humanity in finding our way to the heart path as we learn to balance and celebrate both our diversity and our unity as a species. An extraordinary chorus of Cricket music is included as a CD at the back of this book for experiential practices and meditation.

SACRED PURPOSE

Sustaining Life by Transforming Energy through the Self

Grasshoppers, Crickets, and Katydids are native to North America. Grasshoppers are herbivores, while Crickets and Katydids are omnivores, subsisting on both plant and animal food sources. At times these animal teachers can mass in very high numbers. Their plant feeding can decimate ecosystems, which has led to their negative characterization as a "swarm of Locusts." Grasshoppers, Crickets, and Katydids are able to eat their body weight in food daily.

However, in relation to food and food consumption, Grasshoppers, Crickets, and Katydids also play an important positive role in ecosystems. Through their digestive process they are instrumental in degrading plant cellulose and deconstructing plant matter into smaller pieces. At this point the plant matter is ready to be composted into soil by smaller animals. Without the strong eating habits and digestive process of Grasshoppers, Crickets, and Katydids, most of the nutrients in an ecosystem would be unavailable for absorption by growing plants.

In addition, Grasshoppers, Crickets, and Katydids play an important ecological role as a food source for larger animals. Grasshoppers, Crickets, and Katydids can be understood, from an archetypal standpoint, as the connecting link that nourishes and sustains life. These animals move energy through the ecosystem, both by eating and breaking down plants, so that energy can be turned in to soil nutrients to be absorbed by living plants and the animals who eat them and by acting as a direct food source themselves for larger creatures.

Grasshoppers, Crickets, and Katydids are the link that allows energy to flow and be transformed, reinforcing and sustaining the larger web of life. The sacred purpose of these wisdom keepers is to sustain all levels of life by transforming energy through the self.

PORTAL OF TRANSFORMATION
The Interlinking Spheres of Life

The symbol of Grasshopper, Cricket, and Katydid reveals their animal body form, illustrating both their sensitive antennae and their powerful music-creating legs. The insect pictured below is centered within an energetic chain of three spheres. In addition to Grasshopper, Cricket, and Katydid, these three spheres symbolize:

- The energy of Above, Below, and Center
- The feminine, masculine, and the sacred child
- The void, life, and death
- The soil level and its microorganisms, surface-level smaller creatures, and larger predators and animals

Most important, these individual spheres link into one another like a double-helix chain of vitalized DNA. Grasshopper, Cricket, and Katydid hold the Center direction, sustaining life by embodying

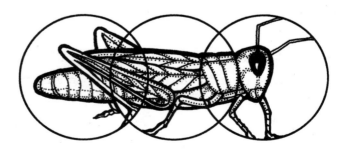

Grasshopper, Cricket, and Katydid transformational portal image,
illustrating the interconnected spheres and DNA of life

the teachings of balance. These wisdom keepers symbolize the essential link in the chain that allows the energy of life to flow through it. Grasshopper, Cricket, and Katydid transform energy through themselves and allow themselves to be transformed as food so that the dance of life can be upheld in balance and beauty.

LESSONS AND SHADOW

Learning to Walk in Beauty and Balance

Grasshopper, Cricket, and Katydid ask us: Are you living in balance? Are you a link in the chain of life through which energy flows? Are you sustainable in your actions? The shadow energy of these wisdom keepers comprises two polarities. The first polarity is the destroying swarm of Locusts, consuming everything in their path without regard to sustainability. This horde of Locusts represents consumer-driven culture, focused myopically on the self, and at odds with life-sustaining goals and the larger picture of our collective future. On the other end of the spectrum is the polarity of these animal teachers as martyrs who sacrifice themselves as energy for the collective highest good (in other words, as a food source for larger animals).

Grasshopper, Cricket, and Katydid express these opposite polarities and resolve them in the dance of their daily lives, processing and transforming energy throughout the living chain of an ecosystem and thus sustaining it. The wisdom keepers of the Center direction ask that we look at how energy flows through us in our lives. What are our patterns of consumption of material goods, the energy of the natural world, and the people/animals in our lives? What is the flow of resources in our lives? Do we live in scarcity consciousness, grasping and defending what we have, afraid to let it go? Do we consume without consciously considering the impact of our actions? Do we sacrifice ourselves as martyrs in unhealthy ways? What is our relationship with the energy that flows through our lives? Are we living in harmony with the web of life? Harmony is a relational state of right action within oneself and outward in connection with the surrounding world. We embody harmony when our relationships express balance, beauty, nonjudgment, and sustainability for future generations of life.

Grasshopper, Cricket, and Katydid also ask us how we relate to unity and diversity in our lives. What roles do duality and separation play in our thought processes, beliefs, and emotional reactions? Do we hear the call of unity through the wisdom of the heart? Are we comfortable with diversity within ourselves, our community, and the larger world? Cricket (masculine) and Katydid (feminine) teach us that it is only through the dance of unity in diversity that the music of our souls can be expressed.

The wisdom keepers of the Center direction ask us to see the School of Planet Earth as a *uni-versity.* The primary lesson that we have the opportunity to learn at this uni-versity of Earth reality is the sacred union of reconciling duality within the self: harmonizing unity and diversity. One frequency is not higher than another. Both unity and diversity must exist in order to create life in third-dimensional reality. Unity and diversity do not stand in opposition to one another, but rather have a dynamic, co-creative relationship that is centered and expressed in the heart. As we begin to understand and embody this heart path, we learn to link separate spheres of existence into a vital, living DNA chain that expresses a new harmonious collective future.

EXPERIENTIAL PRACTICE

 Activating Your Harmonic DNA Music

For this experiential practice, please listen to the CD of Cricket music at the back of this book. This very special music CD, by musician Jim Wilson, brings us the beautiful chorale music of these animals. No special effects have been added, nor has their music been synthesized. Instead, the vocalizations of Cricket have been slowed down to the timing of a human life. What we hear is an incredible, angelic choir of beings singing the sacred music of their shamanic medicine.

You are invited to create a quiet and sacred space within which to listen to this CD. As you listen, breathe deeply. Begin to visualize the energy that flows throughout your life. Visualize your human experience as an open, balanced, and harmonic flow of energy. Next, go more deeply into your being at the DNA level, and visualize the spiraling double helix of your DNA. Energy follows thought and intention. Invite your DNA to flow with the frequencies of balance and harmony. Feel these energies flow throughout all levels of your being, enhancing your health, wellness, and inner harmony in every cell.

When you are ready, link your personal DNA to the double helix of life energy that flows throughout the web of life. Allow the balance and harmony that you embody to flow into collective consciousness and the energetic network of Planet Earth.

When you feel that this linkup has been made and is flowing smoothly, bring your awareness to your vocal cords. Ask the masculine and feminine within your being to begin their co-creative dance of unity in diversity. Bring the sacred child of your voice forward and add your tone to the community of Crickets singing in the celestial choir on the CD. Acknowledge the healing and activation that is happening on all levels of your being—and throughout the entire web of life.

Grasshopper, Cricket, and Katydid Invocation

We call to you, O Ancient Sacred Singers, you who sing the songs of harmonic DNA activation. Through your harmonic choir and angelic symphonies of sound, awaken that which has been asleep within human beings for eons. . . . Show us the way. Open the portal to the pregnant void with your haunting chorus: Left, Right, and Center, the Great Mystery of Trinity, Sacred Marriage, and the Birth of our Divinity . . . Show us the way. Creature Teachers of the Heart Path, may our hearts open ever wider each time we step out into the warmth of a summer's night and are once again greeted by your chiming magnificence, inviting each of us to join in the divine dance of unity with all diversity on our sacred planet and beyond. We humbly answer your song with our own. . . . Show us the way.

9

The Instar
Energetic Matrix

*A Path to Healthy Embodiment
of Our Divine Potential*

The Instar Medicine Wheel provides us with a framework of sacred purpose and transformation as we journey throughout the human life cycle. The four cardinal direction holders of the wheel—East, South, West, and North—embody each of the phases of sacred purpose and transformation throughout the human life cycle, from apprentice to wise elder. The keepers of the Above, Below, and Center directions articulate the qualities needed to sustain and journey throughout our lives.

The Instar Medicine Wheel illuminates the personal journey of evolution and soulful development that we each have the opportunity to experience as beings of embodied soul. Yet the wheel always links the personal and the collective. The animal teachers of the Instar Medicine Wheel have stepped forward to guide humanity to a new understanding of the collective evolution of consciousness currently unfolding and how we each have the potential to be pathfinders and way-showers on this journey.

MULTIDIMENSIONAL EVOLUTION

Individual and Collective Instar Transformation to a New Energetic Matrix

Human consciousness, as part of the larger superorganism of Planet Earth and the interconnected web of life, is evolving to a higher frequency of presence and expression. Many of us sense this process of transformation within our beings and see it reflected in the world. The wisdom keepers of the Instar Medicine Wheel are teaching us that this process is not about ascending up and out of our bodies but instead is about becoming more fully centered in our physical forms on Planet Earth.

The purpose of embodiment is to create an exquisite and fully articulated vessel or instrument through which the power and creativity of our souls can be expressed and through which the wisdom of higher dimensions can infuse life on Earth with its subtle energies. As we become more fully centered in our bodies, our heart presence grows and becomes more highly articulated in space and time. This heart presence is the instrument, much like a harp or a gold horn, through which we bring Spirit into Matter for the highest good.

Our heart center is the same as Spider's web portal. Due to pain, fear, or other Earth challenges, if we step away from our heart presence and out of our bodies, our ability to be of sacred service diminishes. The instar animal teachers are encouraging us to *be here now* so that we can bring the beauty and majesty of higher wisdom and love through our souls to benefit all of creation.

As human beings, collectively and individually, we are moving through instar phases of transformation and evolution. Accordingly, this process of transformation is altering the energetic matrices of our bodies and changing who we are on a cellular level. In essence we are evolving to incorporate more dimensions of consciousness into our beings at the same time. We are transforming ourselves to hold Heaven and Earth in sacred union within our beings and allowing the wisdom and blessings of these frequencies to utilize the special opportunity our living bodies provide them. Our potential as sacred instruments is rapidly expanding, and the instar animal teachers are primarily focused on supporting us in this process. The physical forms and creations of the insects and related animals discussed in this book are focused energetically as sacred instruments of co-creation, whether it is the music of Cricket, the resonant song of Cicada, the buzzing and honeycombed chambers of Honeybee, the whispering portal of Spider, or the delicate vibrations and frequencies of other instar teachers. These animal teachers are modeling this transformational process for us and providing us with a greater understanding of what is taking place both within ourselves and in the world.

During these times of soulful and cellular transformation, as we more fully engage in a dialogue with higher frequencies of consciousness and multidimensionality, we can experience great intensity in our lives. Sometimes this intensity can be projected into different symptoms or challenges in many areas of life. Each person's journey and experience is different, yet as we transform and release energetic blockages and old wounds and call in new harmonic frequencies, we find many common themes. It is essential as we bring new frequencies of consciousness and higher dimensions of reality into our lives that we maintain nurturing balance for our human selves. As we have learned, the instar wisdom keepers are illuminating a pathway through which we can remain centered in our heart's truth and balanced in our bodies while so much swirls in transformation around us. The Instar Medicine Wheel honors the periods of shamanic initiation we experience as evolving human beings as we discover who we are meant to be and embody our potential. Instar wisdom assists us with a pathway to creating health, wellness, and harmony in our lives as we weave, transform, and pollinate a changing world.

The image on the right, and the Dragonfly/Cicada image from chapter 7 (see page 153), highlight the patterns of integration and illumination that are being woven into the fabric of our beings. Allow these images to activate and support your internal process of change

Spider, Butterfly, Honeybee,
and Earthworm co-create a new energetic form.

and discovery. We are moving into a multidimensional experience of the world. The instar animal teachers are lighting the pathway to show us how to be fully present in our bodies while simultaneously living multidimensionally as energetic beings. What does this process look like and what is happening within our physical and energetic bodies at this time? How can the Instar Medicine Wheel assist us as we engage in the process of transformation?

THE MEDICINE WHEEL AS A MULTIDIMENSIONAL DEVELOPMENTAL PATH

The Sacred Geometry of Our Divine Potential

Throughout the Instar Medicine Wheel the sacred geometry of each animal echoes and mirrors the numerals 6 and 8. The cardinal direction holders form an evolutionary developmental cycle, beginning with Earthworm in the East direction. As we experience the soul purpose initiations and teachings at each point in the wheel, we not only embody their wisdom, we are literally activating and changing our physical forms on a cellular level, increasing our potential as sacred instruments of divine co-creation and expression. The Instar Medicine Wheel guides us through the evolution of our sacred purpose—from apprentice to elder—fundamentally changing who we are and deepening our ability to bring sacred wisdom through our beings in collective service.

The instar animal teachers are offering us the essential shamanic medicine to become who we are meant to be as souls while grounding our abilities as bearers of consciousness. They assist us in being fully in our bodies as we activate our potential as divine multidimensional beings. Planet Earth needs us to be here, fully present, as we serve the collective highest good. The Instar Medicine Wheel guides us in this process of evolutionary transformation.

We begin in the East with Earthworm, who, as a creature, looks like a single line: _____ . This beginning line has progressed from a minute circle or dot, which is the cosmic egg of creation. The Earthworm moves from the circular egg, taking its first action in the world, creating a line and beginning its journey of sacred purpose discovery.

Earthworm speaks:

> *I learn to embody soulful purpose in my life by bringing divine energy through my body as the sacred channel. Through this process my experience creates a new energetic matrix in my body. My embodiment recycles and transforms old forms and structures. Through my lived experience, the new earth of our planet is created, and a fertile foundation for future creations is laid.*

From Earthworm's symbolic point of view, it moves through the earth in a line. As its journey progresses, this linear channel begins to form a hexagon shape. As we experience Earthworm's initiation, the line progresses to become a new hexagonal energetic matrix in our bodies.

The Earthworm initiate has activated and woven a new energetic matrix into her body. This is the activational matrix of the divine chan-

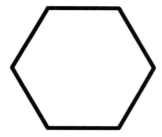

Hexagonal energetic matrix of Earthworm

nel, learning to listen and commune with the universe while opening the way for these energies to come through the cosmic channel into the time and space of the Earth dimension. In this space it becomes possible to recycle and transform old structures and forms that no longer serve the highest good. From the East direction this is the sunrise and new beginning of sacred purpose for the initiate. The sacred earth of the body has been recycled and enriched as a foundation for the next creations and evolutionary steps.

Moving to the South, domain of Honeybee, the initiate has already embodied the hexagon matrix, or divine channel. The Honeybee initiate now carries the cellular codes and information of the Earthworm within his being.

Honeybee speaks:

I learn to manifest and nurture my co-creations through sacred union. Through this dance, unifying my will with the Divine, I experience the sweetness of life and bring the sacred co-creative child through the honeycomb portal. Through this process of learning to embody sacred union, a new energetic matrix is created in my body—the six-pointed star.

The initiate has evolved in his relationship with the Divine, first learning that he can connect with and bring the Divine through the self. Now he co-creates and synthesizes will and manifestation through sacred union internally and externally. The hexagon has flowered into the six-pointed star.

Six-pointed star of Honeybee

At this instar phase the initiate has now gained the ability to experience the sweet bliss of union with the Divine and manifest new forms and creations through the self. On a cellular level our energetic matrices have journeyed from egg to line to hexagon and now hold the form of the six-pointed star: joining Heaven and Earth, Above and Below, masculine and feminine, familiar and opposite into harmonic co-creation. New and vital creations now flower through the self out into the world.

It is important to note that the six-pointed star symbolizes the union of the seven chakras. Meeting in the central fourth chakra, the triangle of the three lower chakras merges with the triangle of the three upper chakras. Noting that union takes place in the heart, or fourth, chakra, all other chakras are represented as points on the star. Interestingly, as they merge, each of these points add up to 8 (1 and 7, 2 and 6, 3 and 5). From the cosmic egg the cylindrical Earthworm has evolved through the dimensions of sacred purpose into the six-legged Honeybee, keeper of the six-sided honeycomb (a third-dimensional form of Earthworm's transformational channel) and embodiment of the six-pointed star. Yet in sacred union we find 8 (the number of divine order and balance) to be inherent in this soul purpose progression.

Moving to the West, home of Butterfly, the initiate has already embodied the six-pointed star matrix and readies herself for new levels of soulful transformation.

Butterfly speaks:

I learn to release attachment to past creations, going within and dissolving
so that I may alchemize my soul body into greater alignment with the
Divine. This activates my imaginal cells of universal potential. Through this,
my six-pointed star matrix is transmuted, evolving into new dimensions as
a star tetrahedron matrix, or merkaba, of multidimensional travel.

Now, through the alchemical portal of the chrysalis, the initiate has
embodied a merkaba energetic matrix, allowing her to fully experience
and travel within multidimensionality.

Star tetrahedron of Butterfly

The star tetrahedron is formed through the union of two triangular
pyramids. Bringing new dimensions to the six-pointed star form, the
star tetrahedron has eight total points. Again, as we progress through
the transformation of our sacred soul purpose into new avenues of
experience and expression, the potential for creativity is exponentially
magnified. Within our bodies, as we come into greater alignment with
cosmic awareness of our soul purpose, our energetic form blossoms into
new dimensions of expression (the star tetrahedron). Our awakened
imaginal cells of infinite possibilities are the merkabas for interdimensional journeying. We now have the ability to fully experience multidimensional awareness. And, running throughout our metamorphosed
energetic being is the golden cord of divine order and harmony (eight).

The initiate has moved through the soul purpose phases of the
apprentice, the co-creative parent/midwife, and the midlife journeyer
who releases past definitions to make way for profound soul alignment
and wisdom—embodying the star tetrahedron matrix. The advanced

soul purpose initiate is now ready to move into elderhood, direction of the North, home of Spider.

Spider speaks:

> *I learn how to receive new visions, weaving them creatively into physical reality, to sustain and support the next seven generations. I am the ancestral creator and visionary, and through this I embody the cosmic web—as a being fully connected to the entire universe, and all dimensions.*

This is the matrix of the multidimensional web (which can be expressed as the flower of life or a Spider web with a merkaba at its center).

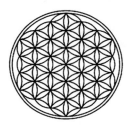

Multidimensional web of Spider

We have moved from the Honeybee (six legs, six-pointed star matrix), activating the imaginal cells of multidimensionality through the chrysalis Butterfly portal (eight-pointed star tetrahedron), to the eight-legged Spider who embodies the cosmic web, interconnected with the entire universe in every cell of its being. Divine co-creation and sacred union have merged with divine order and harmony into a human experience of limitlessness, of infinity.

Through the Instar Medicine Wheel, our physical and energetic bodies evolve into greater complexity and exquisitely beautiful articulation of the soul in the human body. This process allows us to step in to our potential as divinely harmonic co-creators, centered in our bodies on Planet Earth and capable of extraordinary soul expression and sacred service.

The energies of this process of soul evolution come to us from higher dimensions of consciousness; namely, the Great Star Nations and the Blue Star/Sirius, keeper of the frequencies of sacred geometry. (Barbara Hand Clow's excellent work on multidimensionality, *The Alchemy of Nine Dimensions,* is a wonderful resource for exploring these alternate dimensions of consciousness.)

As we have learned, Dragonfly is the keeper of the Great Above and the messenger of the Great Star Nations. The star beings, who surround us with their loving gaze as we walk on Planet Earth, have sent us this wisdom to be experienced in physical reality. Dragonfly and the other wisdom keepers of the Instar Medicine Wheel allow us to access these subtle frequencies while embodied on Planet Earth, creating the opportunity for sacred union of Heaven and Earth through our physical beings. Through the unique opportunity of lived experience we can evolve our consciousness and develop our shamanic medicine of purpose. Through this process of soulful evolution, we can truly be of service to the collective highest good, bringing Heaven to Earth through ourselves while simultaneously experiencing interconnection with all dimensions and the entire universe.

This is no small task, yet the Instar Medicine Wheel teaches us that the more we embrace life and unite the opposites within our beings, the more capable we become of realizing our Divine potential. This potential is to live harmonically on Planet Earth and express the authentic creativity of our souls in service. We are each capable of this. We are each waking up to the Truth of Who We Are. It is time to *be here now.* It is time to bring All of Who We Are to the present moment. Through our actions we recycle that which no longer serves us and lay the fertile foundation for future growth. We reconcile the opposites within ourselves and within our world, merging into the bliss of sacred union and bringing forth new creative possibilities. We awaken new multidimensional avenues of communication, experience, and connection. We become the wise elders we were born to be and weave harmonic new realities in service to the next seven generations.

You are the one you have been waiting for, and the time is now.

10
Grace in Daily Life

Creating Community with Insects and Related Animals

In general, human beings have not worked to live in community with insects and related animals. We have viewed their buzzing, swarms, and near-constant presence in our lives as a source of irritation and fear. We have equated insects with bites, stings, and occasional infestations. We have swatted them, sprayed poisons on them, and sought to eradicate them from our lives.

As this book has taught, insects and related animals play a special role in the life of Mother Earth and in the lives of her inhabitants. Many animals, such as the Earthworm, work directly with our planet, creating the soil and providing us with a foundation for our homes and a place to grow our food. Others, like Spider, help maintain the balance of creatures on the planet. Butterfly and Honeybee help to pollinate the plants and create sweet and healing essences. These animals deserve a place of honor in our lives, for not only do they better our world, but, as we have learned, they are profound teachers about what it means to live a soulful and purposeful life on Planet Earth.

Accordingly, it is essential that we find new ways to live cooperatively with these creatures. For, as we come into respectful and compassionate community with our animal teachers, new opportunities for healing and wisdom emerge.

SACRED SPACE

Creating Habitat in Our Own Backyards

Many of us visit sacred spaces regularly. We garden and see the link between the sacred and growing beauty and nourishment in our lives. Now that you are familiar with the Instar Medicine Wheel, it may become clear that building habitat for insects and related creatures is not only essential for the protection and sustainability of their species, but it also creates sacred space in our own lives.

Consider building a garden. It could be small or large. Let it be a natural space in which you can feel and rejoice in the elements of Earth, Air, Fire, Water, and Spirit. In your garden place a spot to sit so that you can be with the animals and plants. Add plants that are native or related to your region. Seek out plants that attract pollinators. You will find that many of these plants are hardy, tough, and drought tolerant, creating a self-sustaining landscape for years to come. The elements will weave themselves together into a sacred space, and soon you will begin to hear the vibrations of wingbeats in the air. Honeybees and Butterflies arrive to pollinate the plants and fill the garden with their jewel-toned wings and gentle buzzing. Earthworms proliferate between the roots of your plants and create new soil for future plantings. Among the fronds and leaves, Spiders build their webs and wait patiently for their meal. Cicada and Cricket offer you their music, while Dragonfly flashes in the sunlight with graceful flight.

Consider also placing Mason Bee housing near your garden (non-honeycomb-forming) as habitat, or starting your own beehives to cultivate honey using harmonic practices. Seek out flowers and fruiting plants that bloom throughout the year, in a variety of colors that sustain steady pollination and food sources. Include host plants on which Butterflies prefer to lay their eggs. Insects also appreciate shallow bowls of water with places to land (such as a stone above the surface of the water), so that they can drink. Do not use pesticides or herbicides on your property, and educate others about the importance of doing the same. The book *Attracting Native Pollinators: The Xerces Society Guide to Conserving North American Bees and Butterflies and Their Habitat* is an excellent resource for planning your garden.

You may also decide that you want to honor the Instar Medicine Wheel in your garden. You can do this by placing special stones for each of the directions and planting special flowers or habitat plants beloved by the direction keeper near the stone. For example, you may choose to place a crystal in the South for Honeybee and surround it with bee balm and cat mint. Meanwhile, butterfly bush, milkweed, and coneflower may be placed in the West for Butterfly. Honor Spider with native grasses, sticks, and bushes on which to build webs or burrow nearby. Consider a special stone that honors the Earth element in the East for Earthworm, and perhaps put a compost pile or a fallow area nearby. Create a sacred center in your garden, which integrates and celebrates all the diverse energies of the animal teachers, the elements, and your own presence in the garden. In this way you will encourage the blossoming of new harmonic connections and loving wisdom with these animal teachers.

As you sit in the sacred chapel of your instar garden, you will be gently surrounded by the creatures of this medicine wheel. You will begin to hear their songs and watch the beauty of their diminutive lives. They may alight on your skin and visit with you for a time. They will bless your plants and weave their blessings into the air, into the earth, into the sunlight, and into the waters of your garden. Their presence can become a sacred energy that offers wisdom and meaning to your life.

COMMUNICATION AND BOUNDARIES IN THE NATURAL WORLD

Because some people are fearful of insects and do not know how to communicate with them, poisons and swatting are often used to establish boundaries of personal space. These heavy-handed and violent strategies are rarely necessary to maintain balance and respectful boundaries in community with the natural world.

Because insects and related animals are sensitive to subtle frequencies, patterns, and vibrations in their environment, it is possible to communicate using your energy field and intentional thought to establish boundaries or live in cooperative community. If an insect or related creature, such as a Honeybee, has traveled too close to your body for comfort, practice using the following steps.

1. Set the personal intention to maintain calm energy in your field. Feel your energy as a calm, serene lake that surrounds you. Feel your own buoyancy and sense of claiming your own safe space. If any fear or negative reactions arise for you, bring your attention back to an intentional sense of calm, and release all other energies.

2. Explore the possibility of surrendering to the present moment and interaction with this sacred animal teacher. Do you feel safe to do so? What are your first instincts for action? What could you do to promote co-creative community? What does it feel like to surrender and allow the instar animal teachers to be in your energy field? If an animal lands on you, provide yourself with a moment to assess its behavior. Oftentimes animals simply want to commune and co-create with us. Explore what it is like to hike along a path with a Spider on your shirt or rest with a Honeybee on your arm in the golden sunlight. New friendships and connections with these wise teachers will begin to open to you.

3. Honor this animal teacher and send it your respect and reverence for its place and sacred medicine within the web of life.

4. Allow your energy field to soften and merge with the consciousness of this animal teacher. Ask your animal teacher why it has come into your field of awareness. Open yourself up to any healing or learning that may reveal itself. Practice observation, quiet, and stillness.

5. If an animal teacher (or group of animals, such as an Ant swarm)

has gotten too close to your energy field for comfort, or is imbalanced in some way, continue to open your third eye and heart center to awareness of why this situation has appeared in your field. At the same time send a strong, direct vibration of energy into your field (nonaggressive and nonreactive) that feels like the following statement: I respect and honor you and ask you to leave my energy field and find a place of balance in this environment. You can envision how much distance or what type of behavior you deem appropriate for your sense of safety and personal space.

Insect and related animal teachers sometimes communicate in very subtle ways, though sometimes their medicine appears as a sting or a bite. Remember to trust your own sense of safety, and consult a health professional as needed. These techniques can be quite effective, though sometimes it is necessary for us to enforce needed boundaries in a more forceful manner. The Dalai Lama is said to have communicated with a Mosquito that pestered him, asking it to leave his space multiple times. When it still persisted, as is its nature, the Dalai Lama told the Mosquito that he would now send it to a higher plane of consciousness, and swatted it. While we hope aggressive strategies can often be avoided, the Dalai Lama's example reminds us that respect, compassion, and indeed direct communication are always possible. In this way new wisdom, ethical treatment, and cooperative community open as new doors into healing and transformation.

It should be noted that these energetic and communication strategies work well with other animals, such as unfamiliar dogs, as well as people. The frequency that permeates our energetic field is a strong, co-creative contributor to our experience of the world and its inhabitants. As we become conscious and choose respect and compassion in our thoughts, energy, and actions, we promote harmonic interaction with the web of life.

11
Vibrational Healing Medicine and Stories of the Instar Medicine Wheel

As we have explored, this planet is populated with a teeming community of insect and related animal teachers. We are far outnumbered, and our daily experience is permeated with their quiet lives. Why? For what reasons do we find ourselves in near-constant interaction and community with them? Do they present an opportunity for human beings to heal in new ways? Because insects and related animals are, by their very essence, creatures of vibration, pattern, and sound, they are special healers and activators of consciousness, flying in our midst. In this chapter we will discuss the opportunities that instar animal teachers present to us for healing and share how we (the authors) have been touched by instar magic in our lives.

As you go about your daily life, begin to notice the animal presence around you. Insects are as omnipresent as the elements of Earth, Air, Fire, and Water. In fact, these animals make up their lives in active co-creation with the elements and represent the weaving of Spirit into all things. Breathe, smile, and relax into a world in which you are surrounded by angels, teachers, and guides.

The teachers of the Instar Medicine Wheel each offer distinctive perspectives and facets of vibrational healing. When we connect to an

194 Vibrational Healing Medicine

animal as individuals, our authentic and unique experience is what is most important. In addition, there are commonalities in the experience of these animal archetypes. Let us explore each of these animals individually.

EARTHWORM

Earthworm offers a vibration that is much slower and more subtle than its other medicine wheel counterparts. Earthworm vibrates with the pulse of Mother Earth. Its sinuous body moves and dances with an intentional focus on the rhythms of the Earth element and the planet as a whole. If you seek balance in your physical body or life experience—particularly in terms of digestion, elimination, menstruation, or detoxification issues—working with the vibrations of Earthworm may promote transformative healing.

Earthworm brings Earth through its body, transforming and metabolizing what is necessary, and releasing the rest to be of future service. If you are experiencing imbalance in how you bring nutrients into your body, the process of transforming them into nourishment, or how you release waste in your life, Earthworm's vibration may help you create harmony in your relationship with these Earth energies.

Bring your awareness to your physical body and ask the vibration of Earthworm to assist you in healing and transformation. Feel the steady, grounded, and rhythmic pulse of the Earth permeate your entire physical being. Surrender any need to control to the all-consuming call of Mother Earth's physical presence. Feel this heartbeat of the Mother swell within your body. Let its vibrations clear and harmonize any past discordant vibrations in your field. Allow the pulse of Mother Earth to harmonize the blood cycles and hormones in your body.

Envision your body as a channel between the Divine and Earth reality. Know that you are held in the sacred center of these dimensions and that through your being Matter is harmonically transformed for the highest good. Know yourself as the rhythm of Planet Earth.

HONEYBEE

Honeybee emits a beautiful, velvety buzzing sound as it flies through the air and visits the flowers that surround you. You may notice a Bee nearby, one may choose to land on you, or you may wish to call Honeybee's energy into your field with conscious intention. However Honeybee comes into your life, it is often an affirmation to claim your own divinity as a co-creative being of the universe, to enjoy the sweet and blissful moments of life, and to explore how you experience sacred union.

Honeybee has a much lighter and more delicate vibration than the grounded pulsing of Earthworm. It is a creature of the elements Air and Fire primarily, and it can best be felt thrumming in the Air, absorbing the liquid golden Fire of the sun, or stopping for a moment to rest on your body. Allow its light intensity to fill your field and act as an affirmation of self-love and self-knowing as the divine, gifted being you are.

Honeybee also acts to bless the new or potential creations in our lives. Are you in the midst of bringing something new into being? Do you have wounds connected to sacred union or important exploration that is needed in this area? Honeybee's vibrational energy can help—like a gentle vitamin or homeopathic remedy—to boost and enhance your co-creative and sacred union journeying with light, love, and grace.

If Bees are not in your immediate environment, use your conscious intention to vision and imagine their presence and vibration in your field. Honeybee's energy has an insistent, yet gentle, loving warmth that can permeate your entire being, even in the depths of winter.

When a Honeybee stings, its stinger and thorax are torn apart. It will only sting to defend itself or the interests of the hive, for in doing so it gives up its life. Bee stings are actually quite rare in Honeybee behavior, while gentle companionship is more commonly experienced. If you are stung by a Bee, consult a health professional and apply appropriate first aid to ensure your health and well-being. A Bee sting can be an intense form of energetic activation, which, while it has some health risks (appropriate caution should be used), it is interesting to note that venom therapy is being researched for its efficacy in treating a number of chronic diseases. If you have experienced a Bee sting, pay attention to the energies moving in your life.

Neesa's Story

During the week of the 2012 Venus Transit (in which the Planet Venus traversed across the face of the sun), the transformations unfolding in my life accelerated rapidly. I had come to a choice point about sacred purpose in my life and its future directions. The timing of this choice point came as a surprise to me. In the morning, as I walked to my car, I came across a rare and precious sight. I had found a queen Bumblebee and her male consort in midunion laying upon the ground. They were in the midst of their nuptial flight but had come to Earth in front of me. I watched the male consort quiver with his queen for a period of time, transmitting his seed to her, and then fly off. The queen lay trembling in front of me for a time and then took to the air, her nuptial flight complete. Her creations had been fertilized, and it was time to share them with the world.

I felt incredibly honored to have witnessed this sacred instar ceremony. Within the window of the Venus Transit, Bee, who has been linked to the energies of Planet Venus, activated my consciousness and opened my eyes to the pivotal point I had reached on the path of sacred purpose. Later that day I participated in a meeting in which it became abundantly clear that it was time to leave my current place of employment and focus my energy fully on sharing my soulful creativity with the world. As I drove home, I realized a Spider was walking across my windshield, right in front of my eyes. The instar teachers were clearly telling me to pay attention and wake up to the pivotal moment of transformation I had reached in my life.

BUTTERFLY

Those who have had the pleasure of experiencing a Butterfly land lightly on their skin know it is a special magic. When Butterfly connects with you, it is often a reminder to be gentle with yourself in the midst of soulful transformation. Butterfly's vibration is that of gentleness, grace, and gratitude for the opportunity to evolve and metamorphose from one state to another. This process can be challenging for those of us in the chrysalis of change. Butterfly reminds us of our ability to float and dance softly through the air, appreciating the expansive universe, having emerged through the spiral journey of transformation. Butterfly counsels us to nurture our souls and bodies and reminds us to remember the big picture of our soul's journey. Butterfly brings this grand perspective into the present moment, and finds joy in the light of the sun and the sweetness of flowers.

The beauty of Butterfly arriving in our lives can also inspire cathartic emotional release and opening to the next stage of our journey. As Psyche, Butterfly symbolizes both the fragility and the infinite strength and wisdom of the soul. When you need nurture and healing, visualize the bejeweled wings of Butterfly gently brushing your face and your heart. Know that, when invited, Butterfly whispers quiet words of strength and love into the core of your being. It is only from caring for and honoring the center of strength in our beings that we can spread and hold our own great wings aloft.

SPIDER

The vibrational medicine of Spider has touched both our lives on a profound level. Spider has the capacity for both gentle delicacy in its weavings and penetrating insight into the heart of how we live in relationship with our creations, divine inspiration, and the world around us. We will explore Spider's transformational energy medicine through our personal journeys with this instar teacher.

Neesa's Story
Spider has been a special teacher in my life. It has helped me to access and bring forth my soul purpose as a teacher, writer, and medicine woman.

This purpose has culminated in my Spirit name, Blue Spider Woman. To read more about my personal journey with Spider, please refer to the preface of this book.

Recently I stepped out my back door and came face-to-face with a giant orb web. I first noticed a Spider making a hasty retreat to a leaf on a bush that anchored the web. The Spider had made its web between the step railings and the eaves, so that the orb web shimmered in the air less than two feet from the doorway. I carefully stepped out and stood face-to-face with the two-foot-wide web.

I watched as the breeze gently buffeted the web, coursing through it, thrumming it like a harp. Because I knew that orb weavers rebuild their webs daily and the night's hunting was complete, I gently put a fingertip to the satin web strands. They attached and followed me with elastic strength as I gently pulled my hand away.

As you might remember, Spiders use the vibrations of their web to sense and hunt prey. In fact, most Spiders' entire world is illuminated through vibrations brought to them by their sense of touch. They smell, hear, and largely see the world through the sensations brought to them by hair filaments on their body and through the changing vibrations of the web.

I am much more attuned to the subtle and exquisite music I sense from the movement of a Spider's web or from the buzzing of a Bee than I am to much of the human world. I experience motorcycles and trucks as harsh and overpowering to my senses. Many who read this book may be highly sensitive to environmental stimuli. While much of the human-made world is at odds with spiritual sensitivity, Spider teaches us that our sensitivity to the patterns and phenomena of the natural world are a source of strength. As we interact with the subtle vibrations that surround us (for what are light, color, sound, and physical objects if not different frequencies of vibratory energy?), we open ourselves to the wisdom of the universe. We enhance our ability to listen to the messages of our body, to what is authentic beneath the layers of social convention. Spider counsels us that we have the ability to listen and perceive with profound depth, and in this way heal ourselves and our world.

If you seek the ability to remember or enhance your practice of deep listening, bring Spider's giant orb web to the center of your awareness. Lie down in a quiet place and visualize the shimmering spiral pattern of the woven strands. Feel the incredibly strong and yet delicate threads with a brush of your fingers. Perceive all the elements with every aspect of your being: sunshine (Fire), the breeze (Air), Water drops of dew, the grounded Earth that anchors the web. Finally, attune your senses to the faint, yet wholly sacred music that gently weaves its way through the web from the greater universe. You have entered the realm of Spirit. Let your wise sensitivity be your guide to healing, activation, and sacred service to life.

Star Wolf's Story

Among the creatures in the garden of my grandmother Mammy Jones were the Spiders. There was one type of Spider in particular, called the Writing Spider, that captured my imagination. These very large, very brightly colored black and yellow Spiders (sometimes called Garden Spiders) would weave massive, sprawling webs throughout her garden. These webs and these Spiders were no ordinary encounter, however. Within the regular concentric circles one is used to seeing in a Spider's web were thick bundles of silk arranged in a zigzag pattern that looked as if the Spider were practicing some rudimentary form of handwriting; thus, Writing Spider. I would sit and "read" the zipperlike writing in the webs. In addition, the Spider's behavior is unique in that, when it senses the presence of another living thing, it rocks back and forth from the center of the web. Helped by its weight and gaining momentum as it rocks, it quickly becomes a lunging, pumping mass of Spider and web—truly mesmerizing to watch.

One morning Mammy and I walked through the garden en route to gather the chicken eggs—the large webs were especially beautiful adorned with tiny pearls of dew in the mornings—and read the word *God* in one of the webs. Mammy said that there were all sorts of messages in the webs if we just had the "eyes" to see them. It became a ritual for me to go and sit in the warmth of the morning sun and read my daily message from the Spiders in the garden, and often I would find a word or a symbol that would mean something significant to me at that time.

These creatures became very sacred and mystical to me. After my grandmother's death I developed an inexplicable phobia of the Spiders who had been my allies for many years. Whenever I would see a Spider it was only a matter of time before it made its way to me and eventually on me. I would notice a Spider on the ceiling in the corner of my room, and, the next time I saw it, it would be crawling on my sheets toward me. Without understanding what was happening, I became very frightened of them. It wasn't until many years later, at a time when I was doing ceremonies with Native teachers, that I learned what these encounters truly meant.

I was with a teacher in Louisville, Kentucky, at a very traditional sweat lodge that had been unused for some time. Unbeknownst to me, the layers of hides and blankets that formed the roof of the lodge had become home to many, many Spiders. During the ceremony, as the steam filled the lodge, numerous large Spiders began to drop from the ceiling. At first I simply thought it was drops of water that often condense and fall from lodge ceilings. In addition, one often finds it difficult to separate experiences from the various dimensions while in the altered state of the lodge ritual. However, I began to realize that the other lodge participants were restless and could hear them brushing the Spiders off their bodies as well. I began to panic, and the person next to me said, "Don't worry, it's only Spider medicine." This wasn't something I was particularly happy to hear in the dark, enclosed space of the lodge, but there was some part of me that knew that it was a kind of initiation for me at that time. I closed my eyes and trusted the experience. This became a powerful experience for me, and my relationship with Spider medicine changed forever. I remembered that Spiders had been sacred to me in my younger years and once again accepted them as an important part of God's creation.

A few years ago at the Wise Wolf Women's Council—an annual gathering of women cofounded by me and my shamanic sister Amai Clarice Munchus, that is held at Isis Cove—a Spider bit me.[1] When I was getting into our hot tub after a full day, I noticed a sting on my hip. I thought I had somehow pinched my skin on the side of the tub. It's probably a good thing that I then got into the water because it was so hot that no doubt it pulled out a lot of the Spider's venom.

My colleague Laura Wolf joined me in the tub, and we spent the next hour or two talking, until we were wizened and looked like a couple of prunes. When I got out I went straight to bed and right to sleep. I hadn't realized that I had been bitten by a Spider, but oddly enough that night I dreamed of Grandmother Neith, an Egyptian deity who has appeared in my shamanic visions in many different forms. In my dream that night she appeared to me as a huge Brown Widow Spider. At that point I didn't even know that Brown Widow Spiders existed. Grandmother Neith showed up as the crone of legend, that archetype of the wise old woman, but in Spider form.

I had seen her in a vision before, as a black Spider at night who cast her web across the sky, catching and upholding all the starry constellations. In *Vermeer's Hat,* a history book written by Timothy Brook, the author employs a similar metaphor to make this point: "Buddhism uses a similar image to describe the interconnectedness of all phenomena. It is called Indra's Net. When Indra fashioned the world, he made it as a web, and at every knot in the web is tied a pearl. Everything that exists, or has ever existed, every idea that can be thought about, every datum that is true—every dharma, in the language of Indian philosophy—is a pearl in Indra's net. Not only is every pearl tied to every other pearl by virtue of the web on which they hang, but on the surface of every pearl is reflected every other jewel on the net. Everything that exists in Indra's web implies all else that exists."[2]

In the *The Shamanic Mysteries of Egypt,* the Spider that is Grandmother Neith holds the web of energies of the Great Star Nations in her legs. When I saw the Spider in my dream—even though she appeared as a huge crone, a form unlike any I had seen before—I knew she was Grandmother Neith. She was busy weaving her web and walking around doing various things when she caught me looking at her. She glared at me with very red eyes. "What?!" she demanded indignantly. Her eyes pierced into me and I felt intimidated, so much so that I didn't know if what I was experiencing was a dream or a nightmare.

It was a lucid dream, though, so I knew it was important, and I asked if she had something to tell me. She replied, "I'm here to tell you information that everyone on the planet needs to know—that everything people need is within them. They have every single thing they need to create their life any way they want to." She conveyed this to me through mental telepathy.

And I said, "Well, I don't know if that's possible because so many have a little and so few have a lot." She replied, "That's a misperception." Then she added, "You're not getting this . . . Watch!" And she proceeded to spin her beautiful, gigantic web, which spanned the whole universe. "This is the web of life, and everything is in this web," she told me. "You already have everything that you need: the Water, the Earth, the Air, and the Fire belong equally to everyone. And no one can buy it because it's not for sale."

"But people are overusing the resources," I informed her.

"You're still not getting it," she replied. "They belong to everyone, and people have forgotten and become victims because of what's happened on the planet. Watch this." She pulled a long string of stuff out of her old body to show me. She had used this string to create the web.

"See, it comes from within you. You have it inside you all the time. Now watch what it can do. Are you hungry?" At that very moment a big fat June bug flew into her web. Nodding her head at the bug, she asked me, "Would you like some?" I tried not to recoil and simply said, "No, thanks. Not right now. Maybe later."

After she finished catching many different things, I was in awe of her ability to attract to her web just what she needed.

"That's amazing," I told her.

"Yeah," she said. "But I didn't really want all this stuff." So she took some things out of the web and kept the things she wanted. All of a sudden, a big wind came up. Looking into the sky, she murmured, "Uh-oh, a storm is brewing," and she tucked away a few things to eat later. She kicked out all the other stuff and kind of shook the web, and then she took the long sticky strands back into her body.

She crawled off toward some thick bushes and trees that would protect her from the rain and re-created her web again. She turned and told me, "See, wherever I go, I have my home and everything I need to create my life. I put up my web, and I attract a lot of things, and what I don't want I shake out. No big deal."

She conveyed all this to me, and it was very powerful. And then she said, "All of you human beings are my grandchildren, and you all have the ability to do this." At that moment I remembered the Hopi myths of the Spider Grandmother, who was said to have created the world and even language. I realized that the creator Spider of many spiritual traditions was an aspect of the Great Mother, just in another form, represented by a different archetype.

The next morning, lying in bed, I thought, Oh my God, what a powerful dream. It must be from all the energy of the men and women who are at the Wise Wolf Women's Council. I got up and felt a little hot, a little feverish, but I didn't think too much of it. I got dressed and went about my morning. That afternoon, when I had a chance to relax, I told my friend Judy Red Hawk about my powerful dream.

Just then I felt a hot spot on my hip, which I began to scratch. When I looked down, I saw a large red welt and simultaneously had a flash of insight: I knew I had not been bitten by just any old Spider—I had been bitten by Grandmother Neith herself.

My dream had been about a Brown Widow Spider, which resembled a Black Widow Spider, so I went to my computer and googled that phrase. As it turns out, although Brown Widow Spiders are mainly found in the Deep South, in states like Alabama, they also are known to exist in North Carolina, where I live.

Although I didn't see the Spider who bit me, I intuitively knew that it was a Brown Widow. The website showed a picture of a Brown Widow Spider's bite. It resembled a bull's eye, which my bite was like, except that mine, oddly enough, was in the shape of a heart.

Obviously, I survived the encounter with the Spider, but the synchronicity of my dream with the actual bite forced me to pay attention to the dream's message: everything that we need to heal and regenerate is within us. When I remember that, I remember something else: because I have a shamanic spirit, I don't need to look outside myself for someone else to be the shaman and fix me. That's not to say that I might not want to have someone give me a lovely massage or an acupuncture treatment, or that I might not get confused for a little while and need someone to hold space for me while I get back on track.

CICADA

As a shamanic healer, Cicada honors the human experience, from the intensity of the Earth initiation, through emergence into the expansive Air element and higher dimensions of the World Tree. Cicada lives the Above–Below polarity within its own life, and anchors this on Earth in connection with the celestial frequencies of Dragonfly.

Cicada brings two vibrations to our attention. The first is the absence of vibration. This is the still emptiness found in the void of all manifestation. In all the busyness, activity, and distortion of life Cicada reminds that there is always a time and place for stillness. Earth's fallow times are the boon for future creations. We commonly think of the East as the direction of morning and new beginnings, the place of Earthworm. Cicada quietly reminds us that the void, the Great Below, comes before all creations. It is from this fallow field that Earthworm begins its work of recycling and transformation.

If you find yourself exhausted or overstimulated, meditate on Cicada's void vibration of stillness and silence. Build these periods into regular intervals in your life. You will spend much of your life in the mental activity of Air and human experience. Creating space for stillness, silence, and fallow times balances this polarity and sets the creative stage for new beginnings.

The second vibration of Cicada is its piercing cry. Having emerged from the Earth, Cicada sings of life and pierces us to our very core. Nothing can be denied the piercing frequency of Cicada's call. Cicada's vibration of song calls to those parts of us that would prefer not to listen, that find it painful to be conscious. Cicada vibrates a shamanic melody of its life experience.

Cicada sings to us:

> *Yes, there are painful times. Yes, it can feel easier to shut down. And, when you are ready, there is support and love around you to live fully into your human journey. Challenges and loss will pass, and you will move around the spiral into a new dimension of experience. It takes courage, but is necessary, to face the parts of yourself you would rather not—to acknowledge what holds you in this current cycle. This is the only way to move forward.*

Cicada's shamanic vibration has the ability to cleave us to our very core, open us, and remind us of what we need to hear. Keen with Cicada and, when you are ready, begin again.

DRAGONFLY

Dragonfly is a cosmic messenger. When Dragonfly visits us, we are receiving a message from our higher selves and higher dimensions of consciousness. The whirring thrum of Dragonfly's wings and its lighter-than-air body communicate frequencies from the Great Star Nations, sacred geometry, and esoteric mysteries that are beginning to unfold from the Heavens into our lives.

Dragonfly's vibration is often a move beyond healing, activating consciousness and opening the psychic pathway to multidimensional exploration. If Dragonfly's vibration appears in your field, it is likely that an aspect of your sacred purpose is to be of collective service and to assist others by activating their consciousness—as your awareness has been awakened by Dragonfly.

Because the frequencies of Dragonfly have their origin beyond time and space, they can be difficult and mysterious to analyze with human understanding. Often their purpose is best served less by attempting to organize them according to the human intellect and more by opening yourself with faith to the activational energies you are receiving. Know that they assist you in unfolding into more of who you are meant to be as a soul. Our DNA, consciousness, and energy fields—especially those of the intuition and the heart—blossom into fullness when visited by the star carrier, Dragonfly.

Neesa's Story

Through the writing of this book, Dragonfly opened a portal of unexpected and profound initiation in my life. Up until that point, my experience with Dragonfly had been limited to lazy summer days at the lake, watching and catching them in my hands. Early in the fall of 2011, Star Wolf and I had a phone conversation to catch up with one another. As often occurs, our discussion turned to dreams. I had experienced a powerful dream vision earlier that summer, which I believe was sent to me from Grandmother Twylah. In one part of the dream blue and red symbolism emerged. When I shared this symbolism with Star Wolf, she exclaimed that similar red and blue symbolism had appeared to her in a past dream.

Talking on the phone, I walked around outside near my grandparents' lake home, and we discussed what these energies meant. Standing still, as I listened to Star Wolf share her red and blue dream experience, a small red-amber Damselfly landed on my stomach and stopped to enjoy the sun with me. I noted this with pleasure and continued listening. A couple of minutes later, while the Damselfly rested on me, a giant bright blue Dragonfly landed on my nose! It buzzed my face with its frequencies for a number of seconds and flew away, only to return thirty seconds later and land on my nose and third eye again! I can still feel the energy of Dragonfly in my face and intuitive center to this day. At that point, awestruck, I stopped Star Wolf and told her what had just happened.

We both laughed in amazement at the Blue Star magic that Grandmother Twylah was sharing with us (the Blue Dragonfly is keeper of the Blue Star mysteries in our lineage). The Dragonflies' visit was, in itself, amazing. Yet, at the very time we were discussing red and blue symbols, red and blue Dragonflies showed up and shared their multidimensional frequencies with me. I knew to pay attention to the energies coming through from the higher dimensions of the Great Star Nations.

As I examined the Dragonfly visit further, I began to understand it as a blessing of understanding and new consciousness entering my field of awareness. I was in the midst of writing and giving birth to this book, which was a huge creative endeavor. At the same time my professional career was expanding, my husband and I were ready to conceive a baby. I began to see that the small, red-amber Damselfly was an affirmation of upcoming fullness, creativity, and motherhood. The giant blue Dragonfly was an affirmation that I was on the right track with the energies moving through me in service to humanity as a Blue Star medicine woman. More energy was ready to come into my awareness so that I could step fully into my soul's shamanic medicine and purpose. Having yet to write anything about Dragonflies, my Blue Star medicine and understanding of these beings as multidimensional carriers of consciousness was activated. That these two Dragonflies appeared together on my body was a clear blessing, indicating that all my sacred purpose paths, coming to fruition at the same time, could coexist in harmony, and mutually enhance and inform one another. I became pregnant ten days later!

As the fall progressed, my pregnancy grew. Through many synchronicities I came to understand that, on a soul level, the baby in my womb was most likely a very wise spiritual teacher connected with the energy of the Andes Mountains. In August, I had hiked the Inca Trail with my husband and opened myself to allow higher dimensions of consciousness to move through me and out into the world through ceremony. I was an open portal to the Great Mysteries of the stars and mountain Apus at high elevations. In October, I participated in a Blue Star sacred union ceremony and laid a Peruvian Quechua mesa cloth as a portal for this ceremony. My baby became my teacher, participating in the sacred energies of Planet Earth in physical form, and activating me on many levels of consciousness and experience during the autumn season.

At the time of the full moon on 11/11/11, I had a powerful dream vision.

I was in Egypt with my mother and a white Lion as companions. At one point in the dream I went outside. The desert sand glowed with a pearlescence from the starlight and moonlight above. I saw two full moons in the sky. Suddenly, a shooting star arced between them. Then, the full moon on the left spread the wings of a Dragon and flew away into the Heavens. When I looked down, the white Lion stood by my side. I understood that the full moon on the left was not a moon at all, but a hidden Dragon.

In the waking world, a few days later I began to miscarry. That morning a huge antlered male deer had run across my path in the city as I was driving. He was magnificent. My miscarriage was painful and challenging on both physical and emotional levels, but also very meaningful. I saw the blessings and lessons that were unfolding, even as I grieved for the baby and the hopes I had lost. I began to understand what my vision had foretold: while my baby would always be a part of our family, he was actually a teacher who needed to return home after his purpose was fulfilled. He was not a moon-egg, but a Dragon-Flier who traveled through all the dimensions—from the Spirit world, to my womb, and back again—as a teacher and messenger. When I shared what had happened with Star Wolf, she told me that the women of Egypt often pray to Sekhmet the Lion goddess when they are on a journey of fertility, miscarriage, or pregnancy. I was grateful to have this fiercely compassionate guide after the miscarriage. Later I learned that the white Lion is revered as a bearer of cosmic consciousness, just like Dragonfly. I began to understand that both white Lion and Dragonfly consciousness are carried within me as shamanic medicine.

When the Dragonflies landed on my belly and brow earlier that fall, they were a message that a great Blue Star teacher was coming to work with me. I have experienced a profound initiation into the Dragonfly mysteries that I am only beginning to understand. Dragonfly's energy has activated, changed, and opened me on the deepest levels of human experience and sacred purpose. I will always love my Little and Great Dragonfly. He has been a teacher from the stars within my own womb and heart. For this, I am immensely grateful.

My journey with Dragonfly continues to unfold in mystery and magic. Exactly one year later, on Labor Day weekend of 2012, I stood at the edge of a lake. Suddenly, a blue Dragonfly and a red Dragonfly flew into my field of vision. They were mating in midair, blue and red in sacred union. They came to rest together on my left hip. I felt their frequencies move through me, remembering the transformative initiation of the past year. Once again, I opened my heart into new dimensions of my soul's journey.

Star Wolf's Story

During my childhood I developed many significant connections with the creatures I encountered at my Grandmother Mammy Jones's house. Her large yard with grand mature trees and a flourishing garden was home to all manner of life, including myriad bugs and insects. Among the most prevalent of these were the Dragonflies. Of all sizes and colors, they thrived because of the pond just over the hill and made their way into Mammy's garden in droves. They were interesting characters and seemed to have a prehistoric, ancient energy and look to them. Their translucent wings reminded me of a stained-glass window and were mesmerizing to look at. With my child's imagination I always viewed them as magical creatures.

Especially rare and always a special find were the ones that shone with an almost neon cobalt blue. Mammy called them "snake doctors." Indeed, that is what I called them as a child. When I asked about this name, Mammy would say that they had a special relationship with the snakes and that they could even help heal the snake when it was injured. Many of the superstitions and old wives' tales that Mammy told me are actually myths passed down through ancestral oral tradition. She didn't explain the specifics of these roots but simply told these treasured stories to me, and I wholeheartedly accepted her stories as the gospel truth. Undiluted by scientific explanation, my childhood as experienced with Mammy was full of magic and wonder—a tradition I now joyfully share with my grandchildren and adopted grandchildren.

My adopted Seneca grandmother, Twylah Nitsch, once told me a story of how, in ancient times, Dragons existed but were so misunderstood and persecuted by humans that they had to become invisible to human beings. On the brink of extinction, the Dragons found a way to morph into Dragonflies so that they could still fly around in the natural world without being feared and totally destroyed. However, when nobody was looking and when all was safe, they could still gather as Dragons in their true forms. I once heard a Cherokee teacher tell a story of how the Dragons still reside in the Great Smoky Mountains. Their smoky breath is so well camouflaged by the mountains' mist that they come out of the hidden caves and dance and fly beneath cloud cover in the rain. Because the Dragon could shape-shift between these forms, it became a powerful medicine keeper for certain mysteries.

I have always felt that the Dragonfly is one of my animal allies, and its medicine has shown up for me in many different ways. On the day that Gram Twylah passed, I received from her a huge energetic download concerning the Blue Star mysteries and specific instructions on creating the Blue Star Medicine Wheel of Transformation. At that time I was teaching a workshop at the Still Meadows Retreat Center in Oregon. Our group followed the directions laid out to me through the vision I had received and we built the first Blue Star wheel several days later. Just as we finished the wheel we gathered around in a circle and a Blue Dragonfly landed on the center stone that had already been named the Grandmother Stone—the stone that represents the originator and protector of the wheel from which all the other stones and energies emanate.

Dragonflies continue to show up in my life in amazing ways and at synchronistic moments. Oftentimes when I walk in nature to center myself and regain my vision and connection to the spirit world, the Dragonfly will appear to me. Many times it is the Blue Dragonfly, but often I will see the Blue and the Red Dragonflies flying in tandem. Recently, while teaching the Blue Star mysteries, I noticed a Dragonfly in my window as I sat writing. It seemed to appear from nowhere, as I had been indoors with the room closed up, writing for some time, and it seemed determined to gain my attention flying around the room in a spiral-like manner until it finally flew out the door I held open for its release back to freedom. A few weeks later I was teaching a training program with my husband at a retreat center called the Sanctuary at Sedona and was awakened earlier in the morning than I usually arise. I felt that familiar tugging that always signals me to pay attention or take a specific action. I felt called to go sit in the beautiful medicine wheel located on this very special sacred land and meditate. Upon returning to the room, once again I was startled by the sound of buzzing and the rustling of wings. There was a Dragonfly in my window. It gave me a sense of wonder as I captured it and held it in my hands very carefully and once again released it into the Arizona sky.

What some would push aside as coincidence I recognize as synchronicity, and I knew that Dragonfly was coming to me as a keeper of some mystery concerning the teachings of the Great Star Nations. Dragonfly has been with me since I was a child, myself a nymph—part of my spiritual lineage—and is also appearing now, demanding attention to the teachings of the Great Above mysteries.

GRASSHOPPER, CRICKET, AND KATYDID

At the Center of the medicine wheel, or sacred drum, Grasshopper, Cricket, and Katydid embody the drumbeat of life. Just as Cicada and Dragonfly hold the polarities of Above and Below, forming a drum mallet in sacred union, the Center of the wheel is the place upon which the drum is struck and music emanates. This drumbeat holds the vibration of unity and the differentiating frequencies of music that radiate from this central core. This is the drumbeat of the heart path. The heart path teaches us to walk in harmony and beauty, as we learn the lessons of balancing unity and diversity, masculine and feminine, inward and outward.

These animal teachers offer vibrational healing through the heartbeat at the center of our body. Our blood runs through the heart to the farthest extremities of our physical form. Our blood expresses the diversity of paths inherent in the unity of life. When we feel polarized or reactive in our lives, we can turn to the resonant songs of Grasshopper, Cricket, and Katydid. We can turn to the center of our own hearts, practicing the way of harmony between unity and diversity. This practice can be supported through drumming, meditative breathing that focuses on the heartbeat, and by listening to the *Cricket Chorus Meditation* CD enclosed with this book. Cricket song is the angelic whirring of our blood as it courses out from the unified heart of creation, enlivening the cosmic/human body and returning in greater wisdom to the heart once more. With every heartbeat the cycle begins anew, sustaining life now and for the future.

Star Wolf's Story: Grasshopper

When I was very young, my grandparents lived in an area that was quite rural. It was the late 1950s, and down the road was a small country store— the kind that doesn't exist anymore. The sights and smells of its rough-hewn wooden floors, old-fashioned meat counter, produce crates, and fresh-baked pies and cakes will stay with me always. The owners also ran the local lumber company. I would go to the country store with Grandmother to pick up some of the items that we couldn't get from our own garden.

One day, sitting outside on one of the benches on the front porch of the store, I encountered Mr. Hawkins, who owned a mule that he would ride to the store and tie to one of the porch's posts. I especially loved seeing the mule, whose name was Pete, and Mr. Hawkins would sit me up on him. In my mind Pete was my trusty steed, and I was a cowgirl or a Native princess. Often I would sit outside talking to Mr. Hawkins as he chewed his tobacco and as Mammy shopped inside. He was known as a kind of healer who helped people with various ailments. One day as we sat chewing the fat I showed him a wart on the ring finger of my right hand. It was an especially persistent and bothersome wart that had been with me for some time. Mr. Hawkins began chewing vigorously and worked up a concoction of tobacco juice and saliva that he spat out and rubbed on the wart. A couple days later the wart was gone, the finger completely healed, and his legend solidly affirmed. Perhaps it was the tobacco juice, but more likely it was his healing energy and the quiet prayer he said over me that thwarted the wart.

Like the medicine men of indigenous tribes, many rural areas had characters such as Mr. Hawkins who were known for their healing abilities. That same summer I had a pet Grasshopper—the kind of very large brown and yellow Grasshopper that is common in the fields of western Kentucky. As anyone who has ever had a pet Grasshopper like this knows, they have a reputation for secreting a black or dark brown juice from their mouths. Inevitably, this "tobacco juice" ends up on the fingers of Grasshopper-loving children everywhere. Now I know that the Grasshopper spit is, in fact, a chemical defense mechanism designed to keep me from eating him, or at least make me spit him out once I had tried.

I often brought my animal friends to the store with me to show them off to Mr. Hawkins, and he was especially impressed with my Grasshopper, whom I had taught to sip sugar water from the tip of a tiny bottle that had come with one of my baby dolls. He told me that I was also a healer and full of magic and then told Mammy, "Mrs. Jones, that child could charm the Bees out of the trees."

Mr. Hawkins's healing energy and Grasshopper medicine have stayed with me to this day. The characters and friends of my childhood proved to be wonderful teachers in my life!

Star Wolf's Story: Cricket

When recounting these happy times at Mammy's house I am struck by the contrast between the way I grew up and our modern attitudes toward nature, as if it were something to be feared or controlled—as if it would overtake us if we allowed even the smallest bit of it to infiltrate our hermetically sealed homes. The final story I will share is of the Cricket.

Growing up I had always heard stories of the Cricket as an omen of good luck. Perhaps those stories are rooted in a combination of ancestral folklore and literary references to Crickets bringing good fortune, such as in Charles Dickens's *A Cricket on the Hearth* and in Disney's *Pinocchio*. Regardless of the origins of these stories, to me Crickets were childhood symbols of abundance and peace. Mammy taught me to be gentle with

Crickets, even after feeling the surprising prick of their little barbed legs when catching and putting them back outside. To this day, when I hear the Cricket, I smile and think of Mammy, Jiminy Cricket, the first days of summer, becoming "real" in the spirit of Pinocchio, abundance, and other happy childhood memories.

The sound of a summer Cricket symphony in the country can be deafening. However, if you find yourself sitting outside when the waves of their song ebb and flow through the air, you'll notice that it causes your heartbeat and your breathing to slow, and a feeling of relaxation and calm sets in.

Mammy and Pappy Jones and I would go out onto the back porch as the sun began to set and the dew would fall in anticipation of the orchestra of the Crickets. We were protected from the Mosquitoes by a screened-in porch that acted as a sanctuary, but we could still watch the Lightning Bugs as they began their own nightly ritual in the air and trees and on the ground and bushes. Darkness would fall and the only other sight was the glow of my Pappy's cigar. The sweet smell of the smoke was pleasing to me, and he would blow the smoke onto our arms and legs to ward off the few Mosquitoes that had breached our screen barrier—a technique that was surprisingly effective. "Listen to the Cricket chorus," Mammy would say. I always wondered what message was hidden in this song that was at once mysterious, beautiful, overwhelming, and relaxing.

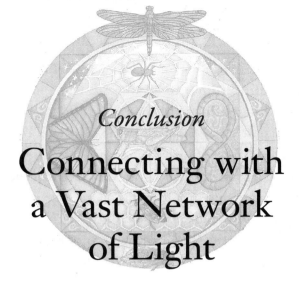

Connecting with a Vast Network of Light

As we have learned, 425 million insects (arthropods and related organisms) can be found in one acre of forest soil, or 9,759 per square foot. A cubic mile of air contains 25 million insects and other arthropods. For each human being, there are 1 million insects. These statistics illuminate the truth that our Earth reality of lived experience is intimately connected with, surrounded by, and tended by a vast multitude of insects and related creatures. Beyond their obvious achievements, much discussed in this book, their sheer presence in an intentional universe begs the question: Why? Why are our lives so intertwined with those of insects, perhaps more so than with those of any other creature? Is there a wisdom in our shared citizenship of Planet Earth?

The superorganism, or living being, of Mother Earth (made up of all her creatures and ecological patterns—see James Lovelock's *Gaia* for more information on this) can be seen as a parallel of the human body. On many levels the Earth is your body and your body is the Earth. Your body is made up of cells and DNA that co-create to form who you are. As we have already discussed, your consciousness can be understood as one cell in the body of the universe. In this way, in addition to our actions in physical reality, we all have the capacity to be of service through the expansion and development of our consciousness. We each have the opportunity to light up as a harmonic cell of authentic consciousness and divine co-creation.

Just as our consciousness is a cell in the great multitude of the universe, the vast population of insects and related creatures can be understand as minute members of a network that is woven together into a dynamic whole. The impact of this is that, in our physical reality, we human beings are surrounded by a divine network of grace that permeates our every moment. These creatures mirror our own smallness, and yet also our own potential to co-create for the highest good and profoundly evolve our reality.

As teachers and vibrational messengers, these creatures, with their omnipresence, also offer us the opportunity to connect with grace, wisdom, and Spirit in each moment. This vast network of insects and related creatures mirrors our own tiny cells, but also the vast network of stars that light up our Heavens. In their delicate vibrational exoskeletons and sinuous forms, insects hold the higher dimensional frequencies of Divinity, cosmic love, sacred union, co-creativity, and universal wisdom here in physical reality for us to experience.

Insects and related animals teach and guide us, not only as individual archetypes but also as a network of grace that surrounds us in everything we do. Throughout your day take the opportunity to tune in to the subtle music of insects surrounding you. Listen to the beautiful melodies and vibrations of wisdom that permeate the landscape of your life. We are not alone in our yearning for unity and harmony within the web of life. For hundreds of millions of years these animal teachers have been present with us, their life patterns energizing the matrix and unfolding story of Planet Earth.

As you journey around the evolutionary spiral of the Instar Medicine Wheel, transforming into who you are meant to be and embodying your potential, know that you are guided by the higher love and wisdom of these teachers. Your life is a blessing to this interconnected web, joined in a harmonious dance of creation and discovery.

As you center your life in sacred purpose, you many notice a growing energetic partnership with the web of life and its creatures. When you need assistance in your journey, or wish to synergize a ceremony or action to effect positive change, weave your awareness into this vast network of insects. Your actions will be amplified by the constellation of creatures found within and beyond the Instar Medicine Wheel. In shared community, our sacred service, actions, and consciousness are synergized for the highest good.

Notes

INTRODUCTION. ILLUMINATING
THE INSTAR MEDICINE WHEEL

1. O. Orkin Insect Zoo, http://insectzoo.msstate.edu/Students/basic.numbers.html
2. Buxton, *Shamanic Way of the Bee.*

CHAPTER 1. THE MEDICINE WHEEL

1. Sun Bear and Wabun Wind, *Medicine Wheel.*
2. Ibid.
3. Sams, Carson, and Werneke, *Medicine Cards.*

CHAPTER 2. THE SHAMAN'S PATH

1. Readicker-Henderson and McCarty, *Short History of the Honeybee.*
2. Ibid.; Siegel and Betz, *Queen of the Sun.*
3. Waldbauer, *What Good Are Bugs?*

CHAPTER 3. EARTHWORM

1. Stewart, *The Earth Moved,* 10.
2. Ibid., 11.
3. Ibid.
4. Lorde, *The Cancer Journals,* 13.
5. Williamson, *A Return to Love*
6. Jung, *Mysterium Coniunctionis,* paragraph 513.

CHAPTER 4. HONEYBEE

1. Ellis, *Sweetness & Light;* Readicker-Henderson and McCarty, *Short History of the Honeybee;* Kritsky and Cherry, *Insect Mythology.*
2. Ellis, *Sweetness and Light,* 32.
3. Melchizedek, *Ancient Secret of the Flower of Life.*
4. American Apitherapy Society, www.apitherapy.org/what-is-apitherapy/products-of-the-hive/beeswax (accessed June 30, 2011).
5. American Apitherapy Society, www.apitherapy.org/what-is-apitherapy/products-of-the-hive/royal-jelly (accessed June 30, 2011).
6. American Apitherapy Society, www.apitherapy.org/what-is-apitherapy/products-of-the-hive/bee-pollen (accessed June 30, 2011).
7. American Apitherapy Society, www.apitherapy.org/what-is-apitherapy/products-of-the-hive/propolis (accessed June 30, 2011).

CHAPTER 5. BUTTERFLY

1. Kritsky and Cherry, *Insect Mythology;* Russell, *Obsession with Butterflies.*
2. Schappert, *World for Butterflies.*
3. Russell, *Obsession with Butterflies;* Schappert, *World for Butterflies.*
4. Schappert, *World for Butterflies.*
5. Ibid., 35.
6. Ibid., 143.

CHAPTER 6. SPIDER

1. Kritsky and Cherry, *Insect Mythology.*
2. Ibid.; Kelly, *Spiders.*
3. Kelly, *Spiders;* Hillyard, *Private Lives of Spiders.*
4. Kelly, *Spiders,* 171.
5. Perry, attributed to Chief Seattle, 1971.

CHAPTER 7. CICADA AND DRAGONFLY

1. Kritsky and Cherry, *Insect Mythology.*
2. Miller, *Cicadas and Aphids.*
3. Kritsky and Cherry, *Insect Mythology.*

4. Silsby, *Dragonflies of the World.*

5. Star Wolf and Falconer, *Shamanic Egyptian Astrology.*

CHAPTER 8. GRASSHOPPER, CRICKET, AND KATYDID

1. Kritsky and Cherry, *Insect Mythology.*

2. Capinera, Scott, and Walker, *Field Guide to Grasshoppers, Katydids, and Crickets,* 6.

3. Ibid.

CHAPTER 11. VIBRATIONAL HEALING MEDICINE AND STORIES OF THE INSTAR MEDICINE WHEEL

1. Wolf and Dillon, *Visionary Shamanism,* 136–40.

2. Brook, *Vermeer's Hat.*

Bibliography

Abrams, David. *Becoming Animal: An Earthly Cosmology.* New York: Random House, 2010.

———. *The Spell of the Sensuous.* New York: Random House, 1996.

American Apitherapy Society, www.apitherrapy.org.

Beattie, Melody. *Codependent No More: How to Stop Controlling Others and Start Caring for Yourself.* Center City, Minn.: Hazelden Publishing, 1986.

———. *The Language of Letting Go.* Center City, Minn.: Hazelden Publishing, 1990.

Brook, Timothy. *Vermeer's Hat: The Seventeenth Century and the Dawn of the Global World.* New York: Bloomsbury Press, 2008.

Buxton, Simon. *The Shamanic Way of the Bee: Ancient Wisdom and Healing Practices of the Bee Masters.* Rochester, Vt.: Destiny Books, 2006.

Capinera, John, Ralph Scott, and Thomas Walker. *Field Guide to Grasshoppers, Katydids, and Crickets of the United States.* Ithaca, N.Y.: Cornell University Press, 2004.

Carson, Rachel. *The Sense of Wonder.* New York: Harper, 1998.

Clow, Barbara Hand. *The Alchemy of Nine Dimensions: The 2011/2012 Prophecies and Nine Dimensions of Consciousness.* San Francisco: Hampton Roads Publishing, 2010.

Ellis, Hattie. *Sweetness & Light: The Mysterious History of the Honeybee.* New York: Harmony Books, 2004.

Hillyard, Paul. *The Private Lives of Spiders.* Princeton, N.J.: Princeton University Press, 2008.

Jung, Carl. *Mysterium Coniunctionis: An Inquiry into the Separation and Synthesis of Psychic Opposites in Alchemy, The Collected Works of C. G. Jung,* vol. 14. Princeton, N.J.: Princeton University Press, 1970.

Kelly, Lynne. *Spiders: Learning to Love Them.* Sydney, Australia: Allen & Unwin, 2009.

Kritsky, Gene, and Ron Cherry. *Insect Mythology.* Lincoln, Neb.: Writers Club Press, 2000.

Lorde, Audre. *The Cancer Journals.* San Francisco: Aunt Lute Books, 1997.

Lovelock, James. *Gaia: A New Look at Life on Earth.* New York: Oxford University Press, 2000.

Melchizedek, Drunvalo. *The Ancient Secret of the Flower of Life,* vols. 1 and 2. Flagstaff, Ariz.: Light Technology, 1999.

Miller, Sara Swan. *Cicadas and Aphids: What They Have in Common.* New York: Franklin Watts, 1999.

Mascaró, Juan, trans. *The Upanishads.* New York: Penguin Classics, 1965.

O. Orkin Insect Zoo. *Basic Facts, Insect Numbers.* Starkville: Mississippi State University, 1997. http://insectzoo.msstate.edu.

Pinkola-Estes, Clarissa. *Women Who Run with the Wolves.* New York: Random House, 1992.

Plotkin, Bill. *Soul Craft: Crossing into the Mysteries of Nature and Psyche.* Novato, Calif.: New World Publishing, 2003.

Readicker-Henderson, Edward, and Ilona McCarty. *A Short History of the Honeybee: Humans, Flowers, and Bees in the Eternal Chase for Honey.* Portland, Ore.: Timber Press, 2009.

Russell, Sharman Apt. *An Obsession with Butterflies, Our Long Love Affair with a Singular Insect.* Cambridge, Mass.: Perseus Publishing, 2003.

Sams, Jamie, David Carson, and Angela Werneke. *Medicine Cards: The Discovery of Power through the Ways of Animals.* New York: St. Martin's Press, 1999.

Schappert, Phil. *A World for Butterflies: Their Lives, Behavior and Future.* Buffalo, N.Y.: Firefly Books, 2005.

Scully, Nicki, and Linda Star Wolf. *Shamanic Mysteries of Egypt.* Rochester, Vt.: Bear & Co., 2007.

Scully, Nicki, Linda Star Wolf, and Kris Waldherr. *The Anubis Oracle: A Journey into the Shamanic Mysteries of Egypt.* Rochester, Vt.: Bear & Co., 2008.

Siegel, Taggart, and Jon Betz. *Queen of the Sun.* Film: 2011.

Silsby, Jill. *Dragonflies of the World.* Victoria, Australia: CSIRO Publishing, 2001.

Star Wolf, Linda. *Shamanic Breathwork: Journeying Beyond the Limits of the Self.* Rochester, Vt.: Bear & Company, 2009.

————. *30 Shamanic Questions for Humanity.* N.C.: Self Published, 2010.

Star Wolf, Linda, and Anne Dillon. *Visionary Shamanism: Activating the Imaginal Cells of the Human Energy Field.* Rochester, Vt.: Bear & Company, 2011.

Star Wolf, Linda, Casey Piscitelli, and Antonia Neshev. *Spirit of the Wolf: Channeling the Tranformative Power of Lupine Energy.* New York: Sterling Ethos, 2012.

Star Wolf, Linda, and Ruby Falconer. *Shamanic Egyptian Astrology: Your Planetary Relationship to the Gods.* Rochester, Vt.: Bear & Company, 2010.

Stewart, Amy. *The Earth Moved: On the Remarkable Achievements of Earthworms.* New York: Workman Publishing, 2004.

Sun Bear and Wabun Wind. *The Medicine Wheel: Earth Astrology.* New York: Touchstone, 1980.

Waldbauer, Gilbert. *What Good Are Bugs? Insects in the Web of Life.* Cambridge, Mass.: Harvard University Press, 2004.

White, E. B. *Charlotte's Web.* New York: HarperCollins, 2001.

Whitman, Walt. *Leaves of Grass.* New York: Simon & Brown, 2011.

Williamson, Marianne. *A Return to Love: Reflections on the Principles of "A Course in Miracles."* New York: Harper Paperbacks, 1996.

Xerces Society. *Attracting Native Pollinators: The Xerces Society Guide to Conserving North American Bees and Butterflies and Their Habitat.* North Adams, Mass.: Storey Publishing, 2011.

Index

About the CD

The *Cricket Chorus Meditation* CD, created by musical artist and producer Jim Wilson, will surprise you! This meditation journey does not include a synthesizer, human vocal choir, or any special effects. Instead, a harmonic chorus of Cricket song will fill your ears, activating the energy matrix of your body and connecting you more deeply to the vast network of light created by insects around the planet. Jim Wilson created the *Cricket Chorus Meditation* CD by first recording Crickets in nature and then slowing down their vocalizations to parallel the timing of the human life span.

Crickets are part of the trinity of wisdom keepers that sustain the center direction of the Instar Medicine Wheel. Their angelic voices will truly inspire and illuminate your instar journey, transmit gentle healing energy, and connect you with higher universal frequencies as you listen. Please refer to chapter 8 of this book, "Grasshopper, Cricket, and Katydid," to learn more about how to journey with this CD. Blessings on your journey!

Visionary musician and producer Jim Wilson (1946–2012) dedicated a lifetime to bringing the sacred music of Mother Earth, her native peoples, and animals to life. Wilson was known among his fellow musicians as an alchemist of sound. He was dedicated to making music that touched the heart and soul. Wilson was a three-time Grammy nominee and a 2005 Grammy Award winner as writer and producer for *Sacred Ground*. He collaborated with many acclaimed artists and luminaries, including Walela, Krishna Das, Robbie Robertson, Timothy Leary, Allen Ginsburg, Mayan elder Don Allejandro, and James Twyman, in addition to his own musical groups, Little Wolf and Tulku. Wilson explored Siberian and Native American shamanism, the New Native genre, Sephardic prayer, kirtan, and country rock in his music. Born in Oklahoma of Choctow and Irish descent, Wilson lived with his family in New Mexico and France for many years. As you listen to the *Cricket Chorus Meditation* CD, please join us in celebrating the life and music of this creative soul. You can learn more about Jim Wilson and his music at www.tulkumusic.com.